THE COMMONWEALTH AN

Joint Chairmen of the Honorary

SIR ROBERT ROBINSON, O.M., F.R.S.

DEAN ATHELSTAN SPILHAUS, MINNE

ESSENTIALS OF MARKETIN

General Editors: D. W. SMALLBON

THE DYNAMICS OF PLANNING

THE DYNAMICS OF PLANNING

BY

E. PETER WARD

MANAGING DIRECTOR OF PETER WARD ASSOCIATES (INTERPLAN) LTD.
CHAIRMAN—INTERPLAN RESEARCH LTD.

PERGAMON PRESS
Oxford · New York · Toronto
Sydney · Braunschweig

PERGAMON PRESS LTD.,
Headington Hill Hall, Oxford

PERGAMON PRESS INC.,
Maxwell House, Fairview Park, Elmsford, New York 10523

PERGAMON OF CANADA LTD.,
207 Queen's Quay West, Toronto 1

PERGAMON PRESS (AUST.) PTY. LTD.,
19a Boundary Street, Rushcutters Bay, N.S.W. 2011, Australia

VIEWEG & SOHN GMBH,
Burgplatz 1, Braunschweig

First edition 1970

Library of Congress Catalog Card No. 73–103593

Printed in Great Britain b   A. Wheaton & Co. ,Exeter

08 015513 8 (flexicover)
08 015512 X (hard cover

CONTENTS

EDITOR'S INTRODUCTION

The Dynamics of Planning is a new contribution to the theory and practice of planning. This original and authoritative book represents the results of 8 years' work by one of Britain's leading planning and marketing consultants.

In addition to his experience in marketing, Peter Ward is an engineer and a Fellow of the Institution of Mechanical Engineers. In 1958 he produced a 30,000 word report on diversification in the British Aircraft Industry and since then he has taken part in countless planning studies for government departments and almost every kind of company. The present book is a distillation or synthesis of that experience.

The book contains nearly a hundred illustrations and a wealth of valuable practical information; lists of sources, check-lists for every phase of planning, critical path diagrams, and reports taken from actual planning studies.

The author has attempted to define a comprehensive view of planning based on planning work in several hundred companies. He has sought to produce a theory and a system of procedures for planning which will apply to all kinds of companies.

Finding some existing planning methods limited in application he has developed his own approach to corporate planning which he calls "Dynamic Planning". He questions both production-oriented planning and market-oriented planning as being partial and biased in their approach, and suggests instead an integrated framework which aims "to exploit the company's existing and potential assets in the context of present and emerging markets with profit and survival in view".

In contrast to other writers on marketing, he suggests that planning should start not by defining market needs but by identifying those "differentiated assets" which give an organization its competitive advantage. He suggests that Theodore Levitt's inspired question "What business are you really in?", though a landmark in the development of marketing philosophy has to be used with caution and the kind of answer being sought defined precisely. He proposes instead that a company's overall identity should be subdivided into a number of continuing areas of interest or "dynamic product areas".

The book covers the whole field of strategic planning and product planning including: defining the corporate identity; establishing corporate objectives; identifying market opportunities; developing a corporate strategy; diversification studies; acquisition studies; forecasting and the use of econometric models; risk analysis and the assessment of investments; proposals, the management of R & D and, finally, the organization and implementation of plans.

The author has produced a system of planning which has been thought through from first principles and tested in practice. This is a remarkable book and I recommend it to all who are interested in marketing and corporate planning.

BERNARD TAYLOR

PREFACE

THE original paper on which this book is based was prepared in October 1962 while I was employed by Martech Consultants Limited, and since then has been progressively expanded and elaborated. Certain sections are reproduced from *The Chartered Mechanical Engineer*, January 1965, by permission of the Council of the Institution of Mechanical Engineers; from *Metra*, the journal of Metra International; the *Revue Française du Marketing*; the *Journal of Marketing* (USA); *Achievement*; *FCI Viewpoint*; the November 1967 issue of *Marketing Forum*, the journal of the College of Marketing; *Synopsis* (Belgian Productivity Agency); and *Technological Forecasting* (Edinburgh University Press). Additional material has been taken from talks and papers presented for the following bodies:

Ashridge Management College
Asociacion para el Progreso de la Direccion (Spain)
Association of British Launderers and Cleaners
Belfast Junior Chamber of Commerce
British Institute of Management
Centre for Industrial Innovation (Glasgow)
College of Marketing
ESOMAR (Eire and Yugoslavia)
Industrial Marketing Research Association
Institution of Electrical Engineers
Institution of Mechanical Engineers
Institution of Production Engineers
International Marketing Programme (Oxford)
Intersearch (at Australian Institute of Management)
Management Centre (Birmingham)
Management Centre/Europe
Management Research Groups
Minister of Technology and colleagues

Ministry of Commerce (Northern Ireland)
National Development and Management Foundation of
    South Africa
New Product Centre
Regent Street Polytechnic
Ship & Boat Builders National Federation
SOBEMAP (Brussels)
Universities of Aston and Birmingham
University of Bradford
University of Strathclyde
University of Sussex

and a number of industrial companies in Britain and abroad, including the Avon Rubber Company, Davy-Ashmore, General Refractories, Gevaert-Agfa (Belgium), the Hawker Siddeley Group and SKF (Sweden). Much of the thinking was developed in the course of consulting work with Proplan, a member of the European Metra Group, and more recently with Peter Ward Associates (Interplan) Limited and Interplan Research Limited. None of the bodies named is in any way responsible for the content of this book; and, except where otherwise indicated, cases used for illustration are fictional, constructed from a variety of instances.

Where I have drawn on other people's work I have tried to name them. But it is not always possible to know where checklists and other standard data originate or when ideas have sprung independently from several sources. To cover these contingencies I have included a substantial bibliography.

I should like to acknowledge with gratitude the help of former colleagues, naming only Fred Roberts, editor of *Engineering*, whose imaginative approach to publishing laid the foundations for much I have done since; Henry Novy of Martech and Metra International, who first gave me the opportunity to practise in the planning field and generously supported me; and Denis Lindon of SEMA (France) and Metra, who showed confidence and interest in what I was setting out to do.

Most of all I should like to thank my present colleagues who have developed working methods in the field and contributed so much by discussion, and in particular Balint Bodroghy for his interesting concept of hot and cold money in the financing of risk and for most of the material contained in the section on analysis of information in company planning.

Again, I very much appreciate the help provided, directly and indirectly, by Joan Pick, who has formulated and applied a new practical approach to technical market research; Chris Logan for his work on regional and economic planning; David Cecil, who has organized some of the text for me and developed the accounting aspect; and Barry Weedon, whose capacity for lucid argument has forced me to resolve a number of outstanding problems in the application of my thinking. Eric Harris, a former Proplan colleague, has also contributed ideas and kindly read the manuscript; and Bernard Robinson has amusingly redrawn the illustrations in Figs. 1.3, 7.17, and 7.18. I am also greatly indebted to Marjorie Tasker who has typed and retyped the text so many times.

My purpose has been to write a book for reading rather than for reference, but I hope the reader will also find it useful as a practical guide to planning and in particular to product planning.

South Godstone,   E. PETER WARD
Surrey, England

CHAPTER 1

PREAMBLE AND SOURCES

IT WAS at the beginning of this decade that I first became practically involved in what we then called product planning. I had been invited to join a consulting company and build up a forward planning activity. Between jobs I had intended to take a short holiday, but 2 days before I was due to start, my new colleagues insisted that I accompany them on an urgent visit to Scotland, where a major company was seeking to diversify.

We had not been in the managing director's office more than 5 minutes when I was dismayed to hear myself described as "our specialist in product planning". During that interview (and for the next 6 months) I had to think furiously and fast.

Fortunately the managing director was a sympathetic man, recognizing that few people at the time knew much about industrial product planning and that, at least, I was trying very hard. Indeed, this first encounter with top management taught me that authority, business sense and generosity were sometimes found together.

Before working on this project my only knowledge of the subject came from editing weekly notes on management and marketing for an engineering journal and writing a 30,000 word report on the diversification of the aircraft industry in the light of reduced defence requirements. I remember a key conclusion of this study. Referring to aircraft companies entering new fields of manufacture, I noted that few problems facing the industry were "more intractable than those arising from the high level of its skill and the high quality of its normal products." There was "only one real solution: that the aircraft industry should continue making aircraft."

1

Even in 1958, when this article was written, aircraft companies had tackled many new areas of business, as will be seen from the table reproduced as Fig. 1.1.

My next consulting venture into product planning was with another northern company, which went into liquidation 3 months later, half-way through the study. When I started, their only chance seemed to lie in concentrating their resources into a single factory, introducing compatible new products and hoping that the principal creditors would rather see a small and longer-term return on their investment than no return at all. Some were institutions who might have had an interest, too, in not creating further unemployment in the area. In the event, after liquidation, certain of the assets were taken over and development, broadly on the lines proposed, took place.

The third episode in the forced growth of my experience in product planning occurred when I was invited to participate in the deliberations of a planning committee at Imperial Metal Industries Limited, meeting once a week. The committee consisted of some very talented and knowledgeable people whom I was expected to guide in the mysteries of my speciality. By feverish application I managed to keep, often but not always, one step ahead, and the result was an accumulation of ideas, generated and refined in the practical and questioning context of industrial reality.

Since then I have taken part in countless planning studies for government departments and almost every kind of company. The present book is a distillation or synthesis of that experience. What I have attempted to define is a comprehensive view of planning, based on actual planning work in several hundred companies, not the least our own. I have sought to discover what all approaches to planning, in small and large companies, short-term and long-term, have in common.

The next chapter considers the nature of planning itself and the context in which it is conducted. I shall then develop what I call "organic planning" and mention the contribution of marketing to planning philosophy, before embarking on a detailed account of "dynamic planning", which forms the central subject of this book. I shall also attempt to show how dynamic planning can be used in practice, with pertinent techniques, and will introduce the concept of "catalytic planning".

In the last analysis, problems in industry can only be solved empirically: we must observe and record what actually happens when certain steps are taken, use our good sense and apply whatever methods and techniques seem suitable. What I am setting out to do, with considerable diffidence, is to provide a flexible framework within which the planner can think usefully about his work and about his company's future. It is an approach based largely on experience in the engineering industries, but will, I trust, have wider application.

Dynamic planning is concerned with the changing relationship between a company and its environment, and how this relationship may be exploited to the company's advantage. In other words, it is the means by which a company maintains its competitive position in a changing world, and its purpose is profit, survival and growth, through progressive and selective innovation.

Commercial benefit springs not just from innovation but from relevant and timely innovation. Like any other creative process, innovation is a consequence of interaction, and in business the basic interaction is between a company and its commercial context. Using this dialogue to focus corporate imagination, dynamic planning also serves to foster the right kind of innovative thinking, in particular by matching capability with present or emerging needs.

A company is in effect an organism which adapts to its environment in order to survive. Also like an organism, it attempts to alter its environment. Products (or services) play a central part in the adaptive process, since it is through them that change is communicated to the company—and conversely. As the market changes, so must the product portfolio; but the portfolio can only change in step with existing or accessible resources. A product (or service) is thus the consequence of interaction or tension between company and market, as represented figuratively in

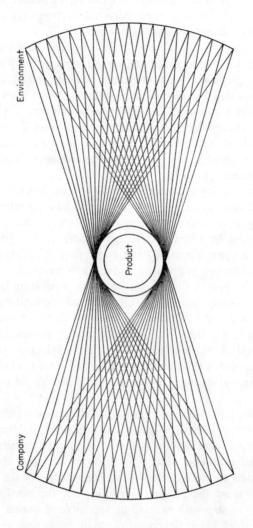

Fig. 1.2.

Fig. 1.2. The ideal innovative product is one which establishes a new harmony between them.

The function of dynamic planning is to promote the continuous realignment of a company in the light of changing markets and does so through an evolving product policy, taking available assets as the first premise.

It is a view of business that strikes a satisfactory balance between immediate profit and longer-term survival.

Since present or potential assets are the starting point, the first step is to identify those differentiated assets—special facilities, a favourable location, experience and market outlets—which in combination make the company unique. The company which plans solely in terms of its undifferentiated assets, particularly capital resources, will tend to innovate in competition with every other business, from steelmakers to supermarkets.

At the same time, management proceeds by a series of decisions, each a discrete step or change in direction. The purpose of this book, therefore, is to suggest an approach to corporate planning that will assist in decision making, while maintaining continuity, and to introduce the basic concept of dynamic corporate identity. Consciousness of its identity in relation to external change helps a company to recognize those innovative opportunities best suited to its own nature and potential.

A company is surely most competitive when it does something it is well equipped to do. But "do what you are able to do well" is not the same as "do what you do now" or "do what you have always done". Assets may be redeployed in many different combinations to exploit new market situations and technical discoveries.

Before I can elaborate this theme, it is necessary to examine the nature of planning itself and the field of space and time in which we plan. The belief that he is already intuitively conscious of its nature has led the planner in many curious directions.

Aware, for example, that objectives have played a useful part in certain areas of management, the planner has sometimes become excessively preoccupied with target setting, forgetting that

FIG. 1.3. "The whole business is economically unsound, gentlemen. With a train of this length and 40 miles of track, we find that only 0·0568 per cent of the track will be in use at any given time, representing a constant idle investment of 99·9432 per cent." (Idea and text taken with permission from *Dilemma: People in Motion*, published by United States Steel Corporation.)

forecasting is an imperfect art and that events can destroy a target overnight.

Also we are inclined to believe anything that is sufficiently sophisticated. I am conscious that the time scale for many industrial projects is increasing and that companies take more and more decisions affecting the remoter future; but long-range planning, as now conceived, is often unrealistic, as are technological and econometric forecasting. It is dangerous to take for granted, or dismiss, what we have scarcely grasped. The emperor's new clothes were equally substantial. Fortunately the argument stated with such authority in Fig. 1.3 was forestalled by the facts. Much, too, has been written on the incidence of product failure, but, conversely, we can never know how many first-class opportunities have been rejected for superficially sophisticated reasons, incompletely understood.

I also wonder whether asking the question "What business are we in?" is a complete approach to the definition of corporate identity, and feel that over-emphasis on marketing (derived from practice in the consumer industries) has made us blind to the importance of corporate resources, masking the essentially inclusive and integrated character of planning.

I have also been disturbed to see the use of detailed organizational charts as the foundation for company development, particularly where a structure devised for one company is imposed upon another. Though structural complexity may be unavoidable in practice, I have put forward a simple basic organization (Chapter 11), for subsequent elaboration, designed to promote the dynamic or adaptive development of companies in a continuous and self-sustaining way.

Perhaps I could summarize my purpose. Noting the degree to which forecasting is unreliable, I have questioned the value of longer-term objectives in planning and whether the illuminating concept of marketing has not to some extent been overplayed. In their place, I have proposed adaptive or dynamic planning, whereby a company is geared to take advantage of its changing situation. The approach is neither technology nor market oriented, but embraces all aspects of business, through the projection of differentiated assets on the market panorama, using a procedure which I have called successive focusing.

Change is seen in terms of interacting commercial, economic, and innovative forces, particularly those which operate between a company and its environment. Hence my title, *The Dynamics of Planning*.

CHAPTER 2

THE FORESEEABLE FUTURE

IF PLANNING is to be realistic it is necessary to understand the nature of the world in which we plan. I shall try to dramatize this aspect of the problem by illustration and by reference to familiar events. In other words I want to suggest the structure of the future (if anything so fluid, so complex and in such infinite variety could be said to have a structure) as it really is and not, as for comfort and assurance, most of us instinctively consider it to be. My aim is to question the extent to which forecasting is possible and to assert that in so uncertain and disorderly a world, the only practical approach to planning is through purposeful adaptation.

Planning is often seen as an attempt to plot a route across the future to a predetermined destination. All we need is a satisfactory map. But, sadly, we cannot chart the future. There may be one or two uncertain points of reference, some lines of credible continuing development, branching in various directions, but mostly areas of doubt and emptiness.

We are like Columbus facing the Atlantic; we do not even know that America is there. For part of our voyage we may hopefully depend on a number of recorded soundings and legendary channels, fix our position by observation of the stars, calculate wind force and direction, anticipate a hazard or advantage, but that is all. Worse, in forecasting the future, uncertainty is absolute and only probabilities have meaning.

The future is inevitably abstract (we cannot see it, touch it, measure it or test it, only think about it) and we therefore tend to simplify its structure and its content in our minds. The predictables are all too clear: we know that we shall take our holiday as planned and that the Hanover Fair will still be held next year. Such confidence wrongly leads us to assume that a substantial sector of the future is foreseeable. Why should the future be any less complex than, say, the geographical world with which we are so much more familiar?

We may impose a reference grid on time but cannot say to what the grid refers.

Planning in such a world is clearly not as simple as we might suppose. But planning is a part of life and, without it, no industrial operation could survive for long. Can a suitable planning frame-work be devised, a framework for thinking usefully about the future, embracing, directing and reconciling the many methods and techniques that have been applied to planning problems?

In later chapters I shall endeavour to build such a framework, but first I feel it is important to consider what is meant by plan-ning. As an initial working guide I would define planning as the purposeful programming of action, with reference to available resources and the predictive context in which the proposed action is likely to be taken. By "predictive" I mean uncertainly and partially predictable; and by "predictive context" an indicated or anticipated future subject to continuous reformulation.

Although I believe that purpose, intention and determination are much more critical in planning than many planners seem to realize, it is the predictive aspect that presents the greater problem. I shall therefore begin by examining in depth the con-ditions of uncertainty in which we plan. I shall consider the processes of change; the nature of cause and effect; the projection of a probable future by tracing in detail the patterns of the past, sometimes without interpreting or understanding them; and, in a later chapter, the construction of a predictive view on known or highly probable datum points or intersections.

In the second chapter I shall also introduce two complementary planning concepts—dynamic and catalytic planning, from which all else will follow. Fortunately, planning, as a subject of study, is at such an early stage and of such a nature that no laboratory is

needed to test hypotheses. It is sufficient to recall a great variety
of real experience and use it as a measure of validity.

Future Without Maps

Already I have tried to convey the indeterminate nature of the
future by comparing it with a virtually uncharted sea, full of
unknown or only half-anticipated currents. The comparison
is only intended as a metaphor, and in fact the future, unlike an
unknown ocean, becomes continuously more indeterminate as
the time scale is extended. We can be reasonably sure that a
certain exhibition will be held next week. But will it be held again
next year? And will it still be taking place in 10 years' time?
Probabilities vary even for the same event. The 3 o'clock at Ling-
field racecourse will almost certainly be run (weather permitting)
but we are able to select the winning horse with much less confidence.

Neither is it a question of scale. The main sweep of events runs
no more true to form. Perhaps in Britain and America we have
been relatively sheltered, but what central European family,
corporation, government or nation has not been shaken by some
cataclysm every 10 or 30 years? History cannot be conceived
as built from countless tiny elements, smoothing the curves
statistically as they become more numerous. Violent transitions
occur throughout society and not predominantly at any level of
supposed importance.

The long-term plan that will survive its period, faced as it will
be with social change, radical innovation, upheaval and disaster,
is very rare indeed. We are always surprised in the event and
wisdom only teaches us that surprise is an immature emotion.
Always? No, that is too certain a prediction. "Forecasting", a
Danish economist is reported to have said, "is very difficult.
Especially about the future."

Certainly, the planner has no map. Should he then despair?
In looking for a map, a complete and comprehensive forecast,
it may be that the planner is approaching his problem in a hopeless

way. "If I were going to Killimore", replied an Irishman in answer to a motorist's inquiry, "I wouldn't start from here."

No doubt we have a partial and imperfect chart, and that can help to some extent. But it may be the most important features that are missing, like the outbreak of a war or the liquidation of a key supplier. What is the use of a roadmap that does not show a motorway or shows a motorway that does not yet exist?

The Pattern of Change

Perhaps it would be better to examine change. Change is more accessible to study than the world in 10 years' time since it is occurring here and now and has been taking place for all recorded history. We can therefore observe it and possibly discern its nature.

The determinist sees change as a fully interlocking system of cause and effect. Neglecting Heisenberg's uncertainty (which Einstein was unwilling to accept) and supernatural intervention, the world is reduced to primary units of energy or matter such that their action in one moment determines their situation in the next, applying equally to brains and battles as to billiard balls.

Were we able to ascertain the precise condition of the world today we could calculate its state tomorrow and for a thousand years. But only a sublime computer could handle the necessary data: to build it we should need to duplicate the universe and stagger it in time.

Although we can conceive no analogue to represent the total pattern of experience, cause and effect remain fundamental to our thinking. Can they illuminate the processes of change at any other level than the nuclear? Certainly, if we wish to understand some situation, say an accident or a delinquent child, we try to identify the causes. But often it is only in retrospect that we are able to select and highlight the factors that are most significant.

Chain Reaction

Cause and effect can be regarded as a chain reaction, constantly branching and recombining, with consequences multiplied at every junction. Often it proceeds so rapidly that we cannot follow or control it, as with the complex of events, including the intermeshing timetables of military trains, that led to the European war in 1914. A man speaks harshly to his wife at breakfast and, depending on her state of mind and the pressures of her day, may return at night to find her gone—or at her most affectionate.

It is not only women who are unpredictable but the world itself. In *Breaking Strain* the science fiction writer Arthur Clarke observes that "A single neutron begins the chain reaction that in an instant can destroy a million lives and the toil of generations. Equally insignificant and unimportant are the trigger events which may sometimes change a man's course of action and so alter the whole pattern of his future."

If we consider cause and effect as a branching or generative sequence, it may be shown as a series of nodes linked by lines and increasing in number over time. Take, perhaps, the simplest example of cause and effect: the fission reaction in nuclear physics, illustrated diagrammatically in Fig. 2.1.

A neutron collides with the nucleus of a uranium 235 atom. Given that the neutron is travelling at the right velocity, the nucleus undergoes fission, producing heat (the fast-moving fragments) plus on average rather more than two emitted neutrons. Each of these neutrons enters the nuclei of two further uranium atoms, with the same result. If the number of emitted neutrons were exactly two and each neutron always found a target nucleus, there would clearly be a doubling effect.

Any physicist, biologist or mathematician knows that a doubling process develops very rapidly indeed: take a sheet of paper, say one-hundredth of an inch thick, fold it once, then fold the double sheet, repeat the operation altogether fifty times, and the total thickness, if such an exercise were practical, would be more than 60 million miles—greater than the distance to the sun.

With a critical mass of fissile uranium, we have a devastating explosion—with virulent bacteria an epidemic.

Sometimes we find a doubling process moving backwards through time, making it more susceptible, one would suppose, to observation and interpretation. Every man has two parents, each of whom likewise has two. Go back twenty generations and his ancestry far exceeds the population of the earth. There

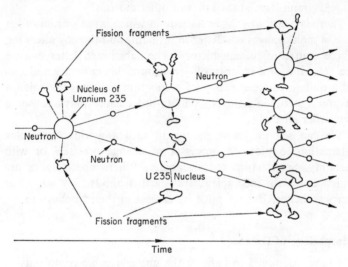

FIG. 2.1. Simplified representation of chain reaction in nuclear fission to illustrate process of cause and effect.

must be duplication and a complex interweaving of inheritance that records cannot disentangle. The European monarch who has no Arab or Negro in his lineage is very rare indeed. When numbers are great the unexpected becomes commonplace and the apparently impossible occurs, as monkeys randomly typing out the works of Shakespeare and the existence somewhere among the many myriad planets in the universe of another species speaking English.

Causes have seldom one or even two effects, but many. Each

cause is a node from which a dozen or a million consequences spring, each consequence in part conditioned by other causes too. The route becomes more complex and very soon untraceable.

It may be said that great causes are responsible for great events, that little incidents arise from petty circumstances; so we need only watch the paths of glory, the intercourse of kings and queens. Yet kings in origin are very small and their conception no less circumstantial than that of other mortals.

There is a story by Isaac Asimov in which, at the whim of his wife, a man changes one letter in his name and thereby alters the whole course of human history. The substituted letter catches the attention of a security officer, arouses his curiosity and sets off a quite credible sequence of events that redresses the balance of power between nations. A tenth-order cause may sponsor a first-order effect.

We can seldom know enough in such a world of complex interaction to plot the processes of change precisely or with certainty. So we turn to probability. Where uncertainties are legion and data incomplete, statistical methods may serve our purpose better. But we must be careful in their application.

Morphology of Data

I have attempted to indicate the unmanageable complexity of nature at the most fundamental level of cause and effect. But there are other levels of interpretation.

If we set out to understand the mind at an atomic or molecular level, human behaviour would remain a mystery. The social scientist concerns himself simply with the way that people act, being rather more humble than the physicist. He would not presume to fabricate an all-embracing and everlasting law about his subject matter. He simply watches and records: What happens if? What happens when?

Again, weather forecasting on a direct causal basis is unreliable and short term. In long-range weather forecasting we seek to discover the sequential pattern of seasonal conditions over many years, and the successful forecaster is one who, perhaps with the aid of a computer, is quick to see a pattern in events. If we find on a substantial number of occasions that a certain sequence of weather conditions over several days (or months) is followed by persistent rain, then re-occurrence of the initial sequence may enable us to forecast rain again, though we may not know the reason. More simply, the shepherd learns from experience to welcome a "red sky at night", though he may be ignorant of meteorology.

The approach is unrelated to the billiard-ball logic of classical mechanics: we do not need to understand the underlying mechanism—indeed, we never really do, and scientific laws are at best an inspired and superbly concise, but impermanent and incomplete description of reality; at worst a transient mnemonic. Newton's view was, and remains, useful in a mundane context; Einstein's picture is more helpful on a cosmic and sub-atomic scale. I have an elastic band and pegs theory of scientific theory which I once elaborated in *Engineering* when the editor was away on holiday.

The patterns we endeavour to discover in the predictive context for purposes of planning are again several planes above the fundamental level, as psychology is above the electroneural. Useful observations can be made, with practical results, but still the map can never be complete.

But patterns should be recognized with caution. On the one hand, they may be implicit in what we observe, as in the mathematical expression for a trajectory; or, on the other, purely subjective, as when a constellation is remembered as a plough or bear. There may thus be an underlying reason for a pattern or it may simply be imposed as a mnemonic. Some five classes of pattern are considered in a later chapter on forecasting.

Modelling

Sometimes an artificial pattern can be contrived to correspond quite closely to a real situation or dynamic system, such as a guided missile or a process of economic change. Econometric models, often calling for the handling of data by computers, have had a measure of success in forecasting requirements for consumer products in the shorter term. Numbers are large and, hopefully, the period not long enough for unconsidered factors to emerge. If the time scale is extended, the hazard grows at an accumulating rate, and extrapolation becomes a particularly vulnerable technique.

Power consumption, being basic to our economy and widely distributed, would seem susceptible to mathematical treatment, but predictions made within the last two decades have proved grievously mistaken. It is not the superficial trends we should extrapolate, but their underlying causes, which in practice are seldom easy to discern.

Econometric methods can only be successful if we constantly relate our data to realities and endeavour to anticipate the impact of intermediate events. Both are very difficult. Where mathematics goes underground for any length of time, it frequently emerges blind—and pointing in the wrong direction. When using mathematics or data-processing techniques, it is essential that the input data be properly interpreted and understood. Otherwise, as F. L. Pitt of Honeywell Controls predicted at the Third Control Convention: "The computerized management system will be processing rubbish quicker than ever before. Garbage in—garbage out."

Few would feel anything but sympathy for the retired mathematician or economist who, to supplement his pension, spent his savings on an isolated country pub, dependent on the carriage trade—6 months before the introduction of breathalyser tests. The house might well have yielded a comfortable income for the past 500 years, but may not last another 10—though the motorist, no doubt, will find a way.

Never can we insulate ourselves, or our affairs, from the external world. I raise my hand and, through gravity, disturb Arcturus—as, to a more perceptible degree, movement of our moon disturbs the ocean. One factor or a thousand in combination may reverse a trend that has seemed set for centuries.

Such factors may be quite unconnected with our present interests: if I am a successful manufacturer of razor blades, familiar with developments in steel and cutting edges, I may not know that, somewhere, a chemist has at last developed a comfortable, effective, quick-acting, odourless and cheap depilatory, without unhappy secondary effects. Yet I may be out of business overnight.

Although I am unqualified to write with authority about econometric models, there are some questions I feel obliged to ask. Perhaps the operational research scientist will feel that I have described his work to suit my argument and then discredited his methods. That is not my intention.

A model, I understand, is a conceptual or working analogue of a real situation such that, however the model's individual parameters are altered to accord with changes in the real situation, correspondence of other significant parameters is maintained. Generally, the model performs in time, and parameters deemed to be irrelevant are excluded. A working model is conceivable, where, for example, turning one wheel in a mechanism will produce movement of other parts in keeping with developments in the system which it represents.

It might, for example, be possible to build a hydraulic model of a national economy in which water levels represent economic parameters. The consequences of raising the bank rate and simultaneously devaluing the pound (represented by readings on graduated glass tubes) could then be predicted. More practical analogues include electrohydromechanical systems depicting the movement of guided missiles in real time, and simulation devices.

Sometimes a system in nature is found to behave like the system being studied. A colony of fruit-flies, say, might be seen to grow and decline consonant with the same mathematical rule as a particular consumer market.

In practice, working models are either unnecessary or too costly, and natural analogues are only helpful in that they may provide the clue to a suitable mathematical expression. Models are therefore almost always mathematical, with the advantage that computers can be used for calculation.

Operational research scientists no doubt distinguish between models and metaphors by emphasizing that a model exhibits one-to-one correspondence with all significant parameters in the real system, and between models and maps by noting that a map is a static and includes too many details. But what is significant? The significance of an event may only be clear in retrospect.

The experienced modeller will not make the error of over-simplification and will be suspicious of any coincidental likeness he may discover in the natural world. If he spots a similarity between a market and a colony of fruit-flies he will be sensible enough only to use this resemblance in conceiving and formulating the appropriate mathematical expression. He does not say that the market will behave like the colony.

Even if he takes an equation developed by a fruit-fly ecologist as a starting point, he will modify the terms until they correspond more closely with the known behaviour of the market, adjusting them also in the light of any other relevant experience. The colony itself is not a model of the market, but both have elements or tendencies in common.

A model could be a four-dimensional analogue in space and time, expressed as a set of mathematical relationships, corresponding in all significant respects with the system being studied. Correspondence is established in the three spatial dimensions and in the past tense of the fourth, but inevitably the one-to-one relationship is abandoned when dealing with the future.

But what leads us to suppose that the future is a single unknown in an equation where all the other variables are known? It is almost as if we are now using the terminology of mathematics as a metaphor. Why should we assume that in modelling reality in three and a half dimensions, mechanics will permit us to describe the remaining half-dimension with any genuine success?

This may not be the way that the operational research scientist sees his task. But take Sheet 158 of the United Kingdom Ordnance Survey and tear it in equal halves. Examine the real terrain corresponding to the left-hand half of the map in as much or little detail as may seem desirable. It will be seen from Fig. 2.2 that the River Thames is flowing roughly west to east.

Given only the information that may be gathered in this area, on the ground itself, however scientifically, could anyone construct a model which would permit us to predict the river's course in the right-hand half of Sheet 158 without knowing the contours and features of the countryside through which it passes? Even the position of a single tree could change the whole direction.

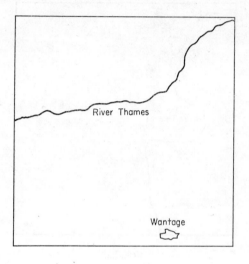

FIG. 2.2.

In fact, as will be noted from Fig. 2.3, the river flows virtually due south.

Are we any better able to determine the configuration of the future? Because it is unknown and hence less detailed in our minds, can we assume it is less complex and irregular than the surface of the earth? In the case of the two adjacent sections of the map, all we can say with confidence is that the direction of flow at the right-hand edge of the first half will be the same as that at the left-hand edge of the second half.

The next minute of the future is equally predictable. No doubt a trend in time differs from a trend in space, but who can say in what manner it is different?

The analogy is fairer if we are allowed to use any information we can gather while standing in the left-hand half, including such ground in the right-hand half that we can see from vantage points. Various hills will be visible and also other evidence,

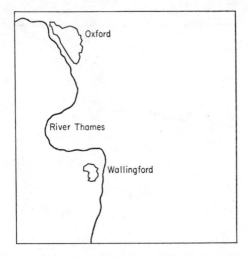

FIG. 2.3.

distorted by perspective. The course will still be difficult to calculate, if not impossible. We are reduced to a statement beginning "All things being equal . . ."—but all things never are.

The conclusion to be drawn is not that forecasting is useless but simply that it cannot help us to plot a comprehensive future map. I am not saying that we should avoid imperfect forecasting techniques, but simply that we should be aware of their shortcomings.

Controlling Disorder

Change is a manifestation of cause and effect, but causes may not always be perceived or recognized. Predictability is largely a function of our ability to discern, and sometimes to control, these processes of change—the network of causes and effects. But there are some systems which behave, for practical purposes, as though they were relatively isolated. *sensibly*

Mechanistic predictability, where causes and effects are seen to be closely correlated, is not confined to nuclear physics. Eclipses of the moon can be foreseen with considerable confidence and accuracy, as can the motion of the planets, the equinoxes and the extremes of temperature that we on earth are likely to experience. Again, an aero-engine, carefully designed and built, will develop a certain thrust at given speeds and altitudes and will continue to perform reliably for many years. But even suns have been known to become novae and jet engines to fail.

In engineering design it is as if, by careful selection and location of component elements (containing many particles but neatly oriented), we stroke causes and effects into alignment, like passing a magnet over iron filings. For a moment in the endless sequences of time we are able to reverse entropy and impose an alien order on the natural pattern of the universe by gathering together lines of force and redirecting them.

Mixing metaphors can be misleading and thermodynamics, where entropy provides a useful concept, is concerned with heat and the motion of molecules, not with philosophy. On the other hand, in trying to explore the planning context, we are considering reality, and thermodynamics has some useful things to say about the natural world, particularly the second law.

This law states: "It is impossible to make a device that, operating in a cycle, will produce no effect other than the transfer of heat from a cooler to a hotter body." Like other scientific laws, it is not a statement of absolute truth but a statement to which no exceptions have so far been discovered.

From the second law it is possible to deduce that all natural processes are irreversible and that the molecular disorder of an isolated system increases (like our living room when the children are around). Work involves order or orderly motion. Entropy is a measure of molecular disorder and therefore defines the extent to which the thermal energy of a system is unavailable for conversion into mechanical work. In other words in an isolated system, energy tends to be continuously degraded.

Only the universe is truly an isolated system, but many systems can for practical purposes be treated as sensibly isolated, particularly since the law is more correctly stated in statistical terms.

A tendency for disorder to increase seems contrary to our experience if we consider world history from nomadic times to the highly organized present day. But the law relates to energy and we produce mechanical order by burning coal, oil or gas, or by consuming nuclear fuels. We also draw on energy from outside our local system, notably the sun. From energy, which is a universal currency, all else can be created.

Since supplies of energy, now and potentially accessible, are inexhaustible in human terms, we can continue to establish order for a very long time, but the method by which we do so is interesting and relevant to the planning or predictive context.

In planning we seek to bring order into the indeterminate chaos of the future. We are acting against the statistical nature of the universe, where overall molecular, and hence actual, disorder tends to increase over time. We achieve our purpose by pinching the available but randomly distributed "order" into local concentrations—by mining coal and putting it in boilers, for example.

In other words, intellect operates on energy and matter to produce a purposefully ordered world, within the limits of its scope. Scientific method is one tool we use, which is curiously akin to magic. To test a hypothesis we create conditions that do not, or rarely, exist in nature and thereby conjure up a wonder.

Take pure fissile uranium equivalent in volume to a large crystal ball; construct such a ball in two halves, keeping the halves separate; put them in a cauldron with some explosive so that on ignition the two halves are blown together; surround the cauldron with a carefully selected isotope of hydrogen, and, hey presto! you produce a fireball and a mushroom cloud many leagues in height.

Or for the drawing room, take a strip of paper, twist it once, muttering the incantation of Möbius, join the ends together, and using a pair of scissors, cut along the centre of the strip: now we have, not two small paper rings, but one of twice the size.

A Measure of Predictability

A principle is beginning to emerge. In any system, the level of predictability is related, inversely, to the number, proximity and magnitude of interacting elements, their randomness of orientation and the time scale, and, directly, with the degree of insulation from external factors and the scope for control. Number, proximity, control and insulation are clearly interrelated, since no system is truly isolated. The relationship may be shown algebraically as follows:

$$\text{Predictability } (Y) = f_1\ (S, C)/f_2\ (N, P, M, R, T)$$

Planning, unfortunately, is conducted in a context where all the inverse variables are at a maximum, while insulation and control are at a minimum. The significance of the formula is that it shows why in some areas predictability may be of a high order, whereas in business forecasting is virtually impossible over any considerable period of time. I am almost ready to admit that planning, likewise, is impossible. As an Indonesian was heard to observe at an international gathering: "They say they understand our economy. Then they have been gravely misinformed."

Perhaps chess (a very simple game compared with business), with its almost infinite variety of contingent moves, depending on the activities of only one opponent, underlines the problem. I have developed the argument towards the end of Chapter 9 on forecasting and risk.

Forecasting, or even anticipation, is extremely difficult in a planning situation, and it may be necessary to devise an approach to planning with minimum dependence on forecasting, a form of planning confined to the more intelligible present. Here it seems we have a paradox, since planning is essentially directed at the future.

CHAPTER 3

ORGANIC PLANNING

GIVEN the changing complexity of nature, how can it best be governed to achieve our purposes? Perhaps a clue lies in the story by Isaac Asimov mentioned in the preceding chapter. Could we determine a principle in nature that will enable us to generate by modest effort major desirable results? If such a principle exists, then it is likely to possess many of the features that we associate with the word organic.

An organism is an entity (whether tightly knit and contained within a single envelope, like an animal or human being, or diffuse and loosely interrelated, like a society or Fred Hoyle's Black Cloud) in which the elements of a control system are present but incompletely understood or understandable. In other words, an organic situation is one in which there is a complex of inter-acting and perhaps conflicting parts. It is also a situation, to change the metaphor, in which the best way to reach a given destination may not be to drive straight for it but to tack against the wind and use the currents as we discover them.

When a situation, a company, a region or a nation is very complex, it is more useful to study it as an organism, rather than a mechanism. We may not be able to foresee precisely what a woman will do, unlike a machine, but after living with her for a few years one comes to know her ways. Even then, it is still possible to be surprised.

Perhaps I can illustrate my meaning by reference to the task of management. As I see it, the work of management is to create a context in which the desired things happen.

It is an aspect of responsibility. If, while I am head of a national undertaking, a disaster occurs within the province of that undertaking in which many lives are lost, I may not be to blame, but I am responsible. It is essential that consciousness of this responsibility be underlined (perhaps by the tradition of offering resignation) so as to maintain the necessary vigilance. Whether resignation is accepted would naturally depend, not on this or any other failure in the past, but the considered future value of that individual to the undertaking. Conversely, I am an effective managing director if my company is successful, however inefficient I may seem.

The experienced manager knows that to give an instruction is not always to achieve the intended outcome, as in a control system cumulative feedback may lead to undesirable conditions. Where many different interests are involved and direct communication is precluded by the size of an organization, management does not lie in telling people what to do, which is seldom effective even in the smallest company. It is better to establish a framework within which individuals, in seeking their own ends or pursuing paths that interest them, also serve the common purpose.

The problem is to recognize that framework or to release the self-refreshing source of energy that can generate, through doubling or multiplication, the maximum benefit from the least stimulus.

Catalytic Stimuli

Retrospectively it is possible to detect some examples of critical stimuli or catalysts in history. We are told by historians, for example, that the breeding of the war horse and the invention of chain mail gave the Normans and the Franks that supreme self-confidence, with its concomitant energy, which sent them to conquer and administer the greater part of Europe, even to the Middle East and Antioch.

But a still more important factor was the feudal system itself, in which land held in fief was the only security and second sons must needs go far afield to find it. Here, three elements in combination gave birth to a new vitality and way of life.

Nearer our own day, and possibly more significant since the consequences were at least in part intended, were the Companies Acts pertaining to limited liability. These measures created a situation in which a man might risk enough on a new venture to ensure responsibility, but not so much as to deter his enterprise, leading to a proliferation of business and to an enormous growth in wealth.

Patent legislation may at one time have had a similar effect on innovation; and increased disclosure of company information may likewise help to catalyse the further development of business. Limited liability is perhaps the best example of what we may conveniently call "catalytic planning".

It would be optimistic, however, to suppose that we could achieve every desirable aim in so dramatic and definite a way, but by giving the concept a name we increase the probability of doing so. In other words, catalytic planning provides a context in which we are more likely to experience the shock of recognition when a similar device or mechanism (like limited liability) comes to our attention, thereby raising the effective strike rate of ideas.

The human faculty for recognition is a curiosity. At the cinema, immediately before the projectionist is required to change a reel, a black or coloured spot appears in the top right-hand corner of the screen. Until someone told me of this practice I had never seen the spot. Since then I have never been able to ignore it.

Facts come to light by chance and not to order. Creative inspiration can seldom be commanded. New markets emerge, new technical discoveries are made. The effective planner is one who is predisposed to recognize an opportunity when it arises. But it is only a real opportunity when it is suited to his own peculiar talents or local situation.

I have defined catalytic planning as the introduction (and where necessary the subsequent withdrawal) of self-sustaining active or effective agents into a complex economy in order to induce desired changes or results. It is complementary to what I have called "dynamic planning".

Dynamic Relationship

Dynamic planning, which is the subject of this book, is planning from the viewpoint of the individual, company or other self-organizing entity. It is concerned with the changing relationship between a corporate body and its environment and how this interaction may be usefully exploited.

In a situation where the future springs on us as if from ambush and change is indeterminable, there is one well-proven planning method. It is the way in which a human being plans his own career, indeed his life.

When I was a child I wanted to be a pilot, at one stage an interpreter, later a novelist. I am none of these, but they have all contributed.

I entered planning consultancy indirectly as the result of an article I wrote as a technical journalist in 1958 on the diversification of the British aircraft industry in the light of reduced defence requirements. The editor gave me this assignment, partly because of my interest in aircraft and partly as a *quid pro quo* for a visit to the United States on which I was anxious to embark. That journey came about because I had visited the Soviet Union the year before and it seemed good journalism to straddle the launching of the first sputnik with a complementary series of articles on how the Americans were reacting to the new Russian challenge. I won my trip to Russia on the strength of speaking Russian, which I had learned in the Army. Looking back now, I can see that the threads of my various ambitions have all played a part in producing the current weave.

My identity has evolved, in response to opportunity and circumstances, but has retained an essential continuity throughout. I am now unlikely to direct a hose through my neighbour's upstairs bedroom window, but have still a predilection for experiment and possibly for mischief. I adapt to my environment, changing it occasionally to increase my comfort, but in some basic sense remain unchanged myself. In the same way a company evolves, conditioned by its history, faculties and aspirations.

As the comedian Kenneth Williams remarked in an interview: "Let's face it ducky, you don't plan your career, you get a job"; but there is usually some constant theme.

It is perhaps a poor substitute for absolute planning where firm objectives are inflexibly pursued within a perfectly predicted world. But it is rather more practical. "Between grief and nothing," declares a defiantly human character in William Faulkner's *Wild Palms*, "I will take grief".

We can act upon our world to achieve our purposes, but never completely or with certainty. But this is precisely the situation in which any organism finds itself, whether natural or contrived, including companies. How should we seek to understand the ecological relationship of a corporate organism with its environment? It is a matter essentially of adaptation and from the viewpoint of the organism itself, the ideal solution may be the habit of optimum adaptability, taking into account, not only the present and immediate environment, but also the predictive future. Dynamic is in fact adaptive planning and provides a framework within which companies can foresee their own emerging character.

Such a framework could be based on the idea of dynamic corporate identity, which will be developed in later chapters. It is a concept that accepts the continuity of planning. A plan may be subdivided into the short, medium and long term, but only artificially.

Release of Energy

Dynamic and catalytic planning are such as to encourage concentration of effort, while at the same time generating energy. When energy is focused or forces are concentrated, purpose is more easily achieved, whereas the over-extended company, or nation, tends to be vulnerable. Conversely, contraction (or condensation) can be taken too far, leading to a state of relaxation as in the white dwarf or dead star. The forms of planning described here are designed to keep these tendencies in proper balance.

Such planning is particularly important in a declining company

or country where energy has been sapped by a succession of set-
backs and consequent lowering of morale. In such a situation it is
essential to collapse or reduce one's aspirations to a level somewhat below the current equilibrium, wind up the spring, and
proceed from strength. The successive surges and recessions of
the Roman Empire demonstrate the principle, as did the recovery
of GEC. After each disaster, Cannae, Carrhae and the Teuto-
burger Wald, Rome recovered its power with incredible vitality,
and only the company or country that accepts decline is finished.
The Romans, like the ancient Egyptians, Britons and modern
Americans, did, of course, constantly refresh themselves by
assimilating other races.

Maybe the Americans, who after all speak English, could be
persuaded, through skilful public relations, to call their country
England.

Both dynamic and catalytic planning are instances of "organic
planning", which recognizes the limitations of extrapolation,
forecasting and target setting, and provides a framework within
which a company or country may work out its purpose progressively, by taking advantage of opportunities as they arise. I
suppose it is a kind of pre-planned opportunism.

It is also active rather than passive. Indicative planning, on
the other hand, is a form of passive planning in that a set of
interrelated targets is prepared but no steps are taken to see that
they are met. In fact, according to David Nixon's fox, Basil, the
reverse is true: "A planned economy is when there aren't any
eggs, the government make sure you can't get any bacon."

Again, organic planning is planning without permanent and
detailed maps. We can alter the environment by catalytic planning
and keep on a profitable course within it through dynamic planning. There is also less dependence on the definition of remote
objectives.

Organizing the Future

George Schwarz in one of his weekly columns in *The Sunday
Times* noted (with the full weight of his articulate and individual

attitude) that all his colleagues and masters believed profoundly
in planning, but they had not planned a single item in the next
week's issue. They did not plan the newspaper; they were organized to produce it. A newspaper is a reflection of the changing
world, and we can no more predict the context in which a company
will be operating next year than we can foresee the content of next
Friday's *Daily Mirror*. We can be fairly sure that somewhere,
even in a favoured position, there will be a picture of a pretty girl.
More thoughtfully, we may be able to foresee an account of
drug addiction in San Francisco to coincide with the date fixed
for a leading pop star's trial; or a feature article on trends in
kitchen design to appear shortly before the Ideal Home Exhibition. But front-page news presents a greater problem. A paper
must be organized, not simply to produce next week's issue, but
for constant adaptation, as when a new lead story emerges half
an hour before the paper goes to press.

Similarly, when we are walking hungry through a forest, we
do not foresee precisely where berries may be found, but when
we spot them we are quick to gather those within our reach.

In other words, we should be organized to take advantage of
change, bearing in mind the occasional tracks and landmarks in
the future we are able to distinguish. But how we see the future
and where we choose to go depends on who and what we are.

Objectives and Identity

In planning, identity necessarily comes before objectives.
Intention not associated with any individual has very little meaning. Also, for reasons I have tried to indicate, long-term objectives
are inevitably vague and hence not very useful. Make them more
specific and their achievement becomes increasingly improbable.
Reduce the time scale and they are no longer relevant to long-
term planning.

The chairman arrives one morning, notes that he is not satisfied
with recent performance and declares that the company should
have a long-term plan. Everyone agrees.

"I devised one in my bath this morning," he continues, "by

1975 we shall double our turnover, at the same time increasing by 10 percentage points our return on capital employed." And then he slips away.

It is certainly his function to encourage, to suggest we do a little better than before; but such a proposal does not constitute a plan. As a plan, it is too arbitrary: why not treble the turnover and double the return on capital employed? At the same time it is not unique to any company or individual. "We are in business to make money" is a familiar statement of intention. But so is everybody else. No one will remain in business very long if he fails to make a profit.

Only rarely can objectives be defined with clarity for the remoter future, as when we have a pacemaker or are pursuing some other more advanced individual, company or nation. For many years the Soviet Union was able to set industrial targets based on material production in the United States. But where does the greyhound go if it overtakes the hare? How does a company plan when it is abreast or ahead of its competitors?

There can be no genuine objectives unless there is first an individual or corporate identity to have objectives. Rather it is necessary to gear ourselves to take advantage of appropriate opportunities in accordance with predilections and potential. That is why I have defined planning as the purposeful programming of action.

One aim in formulating this new definition is to collapse planning as far as possible into the present, as discounted cash flow analysis makes it possible to compare rival future projects in present terms. By drawing back planning to the present, we may in some degree defeat the indeterminable nature of the future.

To avoid the weaknesses of planning by objectives it is better to speak of purpose, which is uniquely associated with a single company or individual. In this context I would define purpose as the fusion of identity and motivation, as planning is described as the fusion of purpose and anticipation, where motivation corresponds to unformulated ambition in a man. Put as two equations, therefore,

$$Planning = Purpose + Anticipation,$$
$$where\ Purpose = Identity + Motivation.$$

In this way we have placed planning, as far as we are able, in the knowable, intelligible present.

Again, purpose suggests adaptability and continuing initiative, whereas objectives tend to be determinate and rigid, mechanistic rather than organic. It is as if we were setting the rudder of an unmanned vessel and launching it from Liverpool in the hope that it will reach New York. It is more realistic to think of a manned vessel, the course of which can be adjusted in the light of circumstances: the captain of a ship bound for New York, which loses its rudder in a storm, will seek to make landfall anywhere. His objective has changed, but his purpose remains steadfast.

Anticipation, a more modest word than forecasting, is our capacity to visualize the predictive context, in particular to imagine and forestall the contingent alternatives that may be presented to us. It is not enough to extend a trend along a single line, but to anticipate the many different paths into which it may conceivably divide. I always suspect the statement that there are only two alternatives. That is the virtue of science fiction—it possesses the psychedelic or mind-expanding property of revealing the incredible variety of credible futures, the scope of possibility.

Again I would emphasize that we must always endeavour to anticipate the outcome of our action. But purpose is the greater part of planning.

Purpose in a man may be to live a full and fruitful life and is unique to him in that it will depend on that man's own potential and constraints and what he considers to be full and fruitful. A talent for mathematics, for example, might lead a boy to enter accountancy, computer programming or operational research.

The same is true of companies. Purpose in companies can only be meaningful in terms of present and potential assets and in the light of opportunity. Dynamic planning could therefore be defined as continuously programming the exploitation of accessible resources in the context of a changing world with future needs or benefits in mind through an understanding of corporate identity.

It is concerned with the dynamic relationship between a company and its environment, both of which are in a constant state of change. In particular, it suggests how business assets may be profitably redeployed so a company may maintain a competitive position in changing markets through adaptive innovation and product succession. In later chapters I propose to discuss its practical application, but before doing so would like to examine certain of its implications.

In particular it suggests that we should organize for adaptation to a greater degree than we have ever done before. Perhaps there is a need for more mobile commando units and fewer massive, ponderous and inflexible armies. (It would not be necessary to sacrifice the undoubted advantages of large concerns, but care should be taken to define the optimum distribution of initiative and internal freedom, say in terms of cost and profit centres.) Likewise we might usefully redress the balance of our funding policies between long-term and liquid investment.

It may be better, for example, to have one power station, commissioned and operating following a single year of intensive construction, than ten one-tenth complete, all of which will be out of date when they are finished. The application of this principle to the planning of research is discussed briefly in the chapter on organizing for innovation.

Following my earlier reference to pre-planned opportunism, I find that if my wife and I deliberately go shopping for a dress we spend a whole afternoon wandering around the shops and finish at best with nothing at all, at worst with something that neither of us likes. We do better (I keep my wife's parameters in my diary) if either one of us spots a really attractive dress when we are not positively looking and buys it there and then.

Now to shop in this way it is necessary to have some ready cash, which will not be available if we have already committed the bulk of our resources to next year's holiday in Zanzibar or mass bookings for Glyndebourne a season in advance.

Dominating Purpose

I am not dismissing long-term projects such as Concorde or the proposed chemical complex at Invergordon, they are essential to any industrial society. Likewise we commit ourselves to long periods of study when we decide to become surgeons, accountants, engineers or craftsmen.

But in cases of this kind, purpose must heavily dominate the planning equation. The further off the consequences of our planning, the more weight we have to give to purpose and the less to anticipation. Anticipation has a place, but drive will be critical. Naturally in planning Concorde the best possible attempts were made to foresee future requirements for communication.

When I asked a friend what was the alternative to building Concorde he said "not building Concorde", no doubt deliberately misunderstanding what I meant. But the alternatives to Concorde are not just other aircraft but the development of multi-channel visual radio or cable communication links, reducing the need for high-speed human travel; the advent of highly intensive utilization of resources that may lead individual countries to becoming more self-sufficient and less dependent on international trade and personal negotiation; changes in the social order having the same effect (I note that following the appeals for self-government in Wales and Scotland a militant group in East Anglia have joined the queue); the outbreak of a major war; and so on.

Having decided that these alternatives are either impracticable, improbable, irrelevant or, if relevant, so disastrous as to be ignored, made such calculations as we can, and demonstrated that we have the necessary resources, we should pursue the project with all the force at our disposal, only reviewing it at, say, monthly or yearly intervals to see if accumulated evidence, analysed objectively, should legitimately change our view. Purpose, again, is the greater part of planning, as when we decide to build a swimming pool or climb a mountain.

Determination should not be confused with inflexibility. In this world of accelerating change, a company must necessarily equip itself for optimum (not maximum) adaptability, bearing other needs in mind. It can then plan without being forced into a straitjacket.

Dynamic, adaptive or creative planning provides an adequately flexible framework and permits the use of many methods, just as a man trying to cope with or develop his environment will draw on any tool, technique or formula that may help him. What is important about dynamic planning is that it gives conscious direction to planning, just as awareness of his true situation enables an ambitious man to act more forcefully. Formulation is the key to understanding and understanding to successful action.

Planning in a shifting environment calls for constant adjustments to the course. The tracks of certain missiles are computed and determined before they leave the launchers; others continue to correct their direction during flight. A company whose course has been irrevocably set is unlikely to be going anywhere important. It follows that the more practical approach to business planning is in terms of vectors rather than objectives—not where the company would like to be in 10 years' time but in which direction it should currently be pointing and the force it should employ.

CHAPTER 4

TECHNOLOGY AND MARKETING

A SATISFACTORY approach to planning should therefore serve to reconcile a company with its environment and its present with its future in a continuously profitable way. It is also clear that products form the fundamental link between the unique company and the universal market.

All living organisms adapt to their environment in order to survive. A company is no exception. But owing to the time lag from concept to marketable product, a company must be ready to adapt in advance of its environment. In other words it should take the pill half-an-hour before it feels the pain coming on, though with certain pills and pains half-an-hour is hardly long enough.

As already indicated, my purpose is to suggest how that adaptation can be accomplished most effectively and suggest a framework which may bring together the most important elements in business planning. The framework is designed to guide immediate action in the context of a longer-term perspective.

Adaptive Process

Considered in these terms, product and business planning are not easily distinguished. Every company is in business to supply, at competitive prices (and with competitive returns), marketable products and services. It may develop a product to meet a market need or create a market need for products never before conceived. It is thus the product that forms the fundamental link between a unique company and the universal market.

36

Quite rightly the exponents of marketing have directed companies away from introspective preoccupation with manufacturing facilities to extrovert consideration of the market. But perhaps the pendulum has swung too far. Planning is essentially an all-round activity and must keep every side of business in proper balance.

Market-Oriented Planning

Marketing made the last substantial and consolidated contribution to the study of company planning. It opened the eyes of management to a necessary change in emphasis. As Commander Edward Whitehead observed in 1966:

> Modern marketing means looking at goods and all problems associated with them from the customer's point of view, seeing that the right goods and services reach the right market, at the right time, and in the right way. The old concept was that marketing was the task of selling what the company makes. The new concept demands that the company should make what it can sell.

Perhaps the clearest and most comprehensive explanation of the transition was made in 1965 by Leslie W. Rodger of McCann-Erickson Advertising Limited in his book *Marketing in a Competitive Economy* (Hutchinson), where he drew distinctions between production-oriented and marketing-oriented companies in the table reproduced in Fig. 4.1. I also found usefully descriptive the phrase Henry Novy adopted as a slogan for his consulting company, Martech, namely: "What to make and how to sell it."

This sensible view of business has, however, led some enthusiasts to overlook entirely company resources and potential. I have occasionally been asked to recommend the ideal product, exclusively in market terms, with no reference whatsoever to the assets of the company concerned: "We can make anything. If necessary, we are prepared to buy the appropriate facilities, experience and skills." Unfortunately, by the time these assets are acquired, some other company is already selling a similar product and no doubt at a price which an uninstructed newcomer could hardly hope to equal.

FIG. 4.1. Table showing distinctions between production-oriented and market-oriented companies. Reproduced with permission from *Marketing in a Competitive Economy* by Leslie W. Rodger, Hutchinson 1965)

Function or activity	Production-oriented	Marketing-oriented
TOP MANAGEMENT	Technological considerations predominate Production and engineering personnel in highest level executive positions	Customer considerations paramount Marketing personnel in highest level executive positions
OBJECTIVES	Internal influences predominate Business objective is to match total company resources against production requirements. More emphasis on technical efficiency and method. Want to be known for technical or production know-how	External market influences predominate Business objective is to match total company resources against market opportunities. More emphasis on market strategy and planning. Want to be regarded as style and market leaders
MANUFACTURING	Production less flexible The company sells what can be made	Flexibility in production so as to match product sales opportunities. The company manufactures what can be profitably sold
MARKETING	Aims to fulfil existing needs and develop workable products to meet these needs. Company's future bound up with markets already supplied and products already in existence Marketing function not considered to be as valuable as manufacturing, engineering or finance	Seeks to create markets and develop saleable products Company's future bound up with markets yet to be identified and developed and with products not yet in existence Marketing considered to be co-ordinate with manufacturing, finance and other major business functions
FINANCIAL	Emphasis on cost rather than selling price; greater	Greater attention to what the customer will pay, to

Fig. 4.1 (cont.)

Function or activity	Production-oriented	Marketing-oriented
	concern on how to do things cheaply and well Budgets based on financial or production require- ments rather than mar- keting considerations	how pricing can be used as a marketing weapon and to how competitors will react Budgets based on marketing requirements and funds are allocated on the basis of marketing tasks to be accomplished
RESEARCH	Leads in technical and scientific research Market intelligence system relatively undeveloped	Leads in analytical and marketing research Market intelligence system well developed
PRODUCT PLANNING	Based on technical research suggestions for new or improved products stem from functional perform- ance and cost improve- ments. Performance and applica- tions are prime considera- tions Engineering considerations tend to predominate Laboratory testing more predominant than sales or market testing. Pack- aging viewed as a ship- ping and protective de- vice. Chief concern is engineering, materials handling and packaging machinery	Based on market research— suggestions for new or improved products stem from research into cus- tomer's needs. Perform- ance and applications are prime considerations. Styling and design con- siderations regarded to be almost as important Sales and market testing an integral part of planning Packaging viewed as a sales tool in terms of its user- convenience and advert- ising and promotional effectiveness
SALES ORGANIZATION	Salesman regarded as an order-getter for the fac- tory Salesman lacks the pro- fessional status of the engineer, chemist, lawyer,	Salesman regarded as an order-maker who keeps the factory running and provides employment to production workers Salesmen accorded high status in the company and

Fig. 4.1 (cont.)

Function or activity	Production-oriented	Marketing-oriented
	or accountant. Less likely to be promoted to top management. Salesmen lack formal training. Tend to get left to their own devices as the men "out there." Motivation of the salesmen minimal	more likely to be promoted to top management positions Salesmen given formal and continuous internal and on-the-job training Motivation of sales organization given high priority. Chief sales executive regarded as part of the management team
ADVERTISING AND PROMOTION	Emphasis on cost rather than on the value of its contribution to the total selling effort Advertising and promotion regarded as an extra cost, not a basic cost like machines, or materials, research laboratories, etc. Not regarded as one of the skills required to run a modern business successfully. Advertising and promotion not looked upon as an important source of competitive differential advantage	Advertising and promotion is an integral part of the company's marketing effort and a basic cost Outstanding advertising and promotion considered to be as equally important to the successful running of a business as outstanding manufacturing technique, technical research ability or financial and legal skills. Advertising and promotion regarded as a potential source of competitive differential advantage, particularly when the differences in own and competitive products become less and less distinguishable

I know there are exceptions where an aggressive new entrant has seized an opportunity and beaten long established suppliers at their game; but as sleeping businesses are weeded out by increasingly intensive competition, the scope for such adventures is likely to decline. In this connection I shall have something to say about conglomerates.

Like many a lively idea, marketing probably arose from a single forceful insight: since the customer is always right, business should be managed in accordance with his interests; or simply recognition in commercial terms that necessity is the mother of invention. When illumination strikes with such intensity it can blind the converted to any other aspect of reality and marketing became the received wisdom of a generation, often unqualified by common sense. Recently there have been indications of uncertainty. In particular, marketing has been successively redefined; until now it is virtually just another word for business, encompassing the complete range of corporate activity—finding and meeting needs in a profitable way.

Marketing might be more modestly described as "market-oriented planning", but planning is indivisible and any bias is surely undesirable. What any company adopts in practice is total planning, embracing both the market and the exploitable resources.

Consumer and Engineering Products

Marketing grew up mainly in the consumer industries where its validity seemed indisputable. Applied in other industries, it becomes less apt, as is Newtonian mechanics in the wider context of cosmic space and time. The difference in emphasis between the consumer and engineering industries can be illustrated by reference to extremes.

Most consumer products are made in large numbers of identical items, and it is reasonable to suppose that plant can be designed for a specific product line, such as hulahoops, and written off over the sales life of the product. This is true to some extent even in the motor industry where car bodies are produced by pressing using highly expensive dies cut from hard metal on Keller milling machines. Clearly the cost of these dies should be recovered before a new model or design is introduced.

It follows that, in the ideal consumer product situation, only the potential market and the company's marketing resources need be considered.

The manufacturer of engineering products, on the other hand, builds up valuable technical experience and costly but rather more versatile facilities over a much longer period, usually optimized to a particular product mix. Since they are substantial, he cannot afford to disregard these assets when planning to diversify.

No one would set out to use assets simply because they are there; that would be like hiring a deckchair at the seaside and continuing to sit in it notwithstanding the onset of a thunderstorm just because the shilling has been paid. But a marine engineering company, which has recently installed a costly tape-controlled horizontal boring machine, would tend to prefer products making use of this equipment, since with any depression in shipbuilding there will be surplus heavy machining capacity and no prospect of reselling the machine at a reasonable price.

More important, the assets of a company (the talents of its people, the accumulated skills, location, outlets, customer contacts and material resources) are what give it a competitive advantage; indeed, the only durable competitive advantage which it has.

It would be no more desirable for an engineering company than for a consumer company to launch a product that the market does not need. Less obviously a product that fails to make optimum use of corporate assets is also likely to be vulnerable. In product development, therefore, the engineering company has more factors to consider.

The distinction is purely illustrative and only partly true, bearing as it does on the relation between numbers off and value per unit capital investment, and therefore not uniquely associated with consumer and engineering products. But it serves to emphasize the way in which a useful principle may have to be distorted when applied inappropriately elsewhere.

In practice, planning in every kind of company is an integrated activity. If only the market were considered we should all select the same business to be in, the same customers to serve, since the market is common to everyone, and there can only be one best market opportunity, one most profitable venture.

Two Questions

Fortunately common sense usually prevails. Most managements are conscious of the need to ask two questions when considering a possible new product: "Will it sell?" and "Is it consistent with the company's business?" In asking these questions, they implicitly acknowledge that a company is effectively reconciled with its environment through proper choice of products. Some years ago I received a letter from a Continental company seeking to place a licence in the United Kingdom. It began:

> Whereas we are manufacturers of lathe chucks and clamping tools, we have now developed an electric cow and horse cleaning apparatus, which does not really harmonize with our manufacturing and merchandising schedule.

The writer's reference to "manufacturing and merchandising" shows that he has grasped the two essential conditions for successful product development, namely internal resources and the external context.

Innovative Bias

It is sometimes said that product development in the United States is market oriented whereas in Britain commercial innovation has tended to be a byproduct of technical inquiry. The divergence is only a matter of emphasis, and both market and marketing research are commonplace in Britain as is inventive engineering in America. There have always been periods of industrial history when consideration of a company's resources or of the market environment has tended to be dominant. But what is needed is a fusion of the two.

Before the dedicated advocate of marketing dismisses the

technical innovator as commercially naïve, he should remember that Baird's work on television, Whittle's on the jet engine and Cockerell's on hovercraft, though substantially concerned with the solution of absorbing technical problems, led to commercially successful products. He might also bear in mind that Honda Soichiro, the Japanese industrialist, who for several years has dominated world motor-cycle markets, is essentially an engineer, "happier on the shop floor than in the executive suite" (*The Sunday Times*).

A success story recorded in *The Financial Times* in September 1967 underlined the scope for variation and went very much against the current grain. A Birmingham company, R. & A. G. Crossland, had been growing steadily and profitably, and in explaining this excellent performance the article reported: "Another principle founded on the comparative security of steady orders is the strictly subordinate role allotted to sales. Mr. Crossland believed sales must always be subject to production rather than the other way round." Presumably a supplier of components to a mass-production industry, such as motor vehicles, cannot afford to fail on either delivery or quality, since any interruption in the customer's production flow might result in crushing penalties. Over-zealous salesmen, who sell more than can be made to the necessary standards, would therefore not be tolerated.

In general the change from trying to sell what a company can make to making what the market needs is commendable. But there is no golden formula; every situation calls for individual study. Indeed, the dichotomy between technical and market orientation shrouds the issue. The problem, rather, is to exploit a company's existing and potential assets in the context of present and emerging markets with profit and survival in view. Planning essentially requires a comprehensive vision.

Guidelines for Decision

Because the future is uncertain and because a new venture almost always calls for considerable investment, planning decisions are difficult to take. Yet any procedure in business should lead to action or a decision to act. Decisions are made more easily if there are yardsticks, guidelines, pointers and precedents, and precedents in sufficient numbers constitute experience. If such experience can be coded or formalized, then planning becomes simpler.

Businessmen are insistently practical and often impatient with abstract ideas. But, unlike the present, which is here and now and concrete, tomorrow is by nature insubstantial. Any frame of reference for future planning must therefore be intellectual rather than tangible. At the same time it is assumed that the human mind prefers to work with manageable material and ideally in a sequence of steps.

The proposed framework contains two basic elements: a key concept, dynamic corporate identity; and a key procedure, successive focusing. Usually the first step in a management study is to define objectives; but in the case of planning there must first be a corporate identity to have objectives. It seems reasonable to suppose that deciding what you want is the first task in any exercise. But what you want depends on who you are, where you are and what you have or are ready to commit.

Dynamic identity is not simply an answer to the question "What business are we in?", but a more precise and useful formulation, where "dynamic" is applied in the sense of continuity with progressive scope for change and evolution. A corporate identity comprises one or several "dynamic product areas".

Successive focusing is essentially a dialogue between a company and its environment where the field of interest is narrowed by stages, as in artillery bracketing or ranging. A first salvo is seen to fall beyond the target; the range is reduced and the next salvo falls short; from the information provided by these experimental shots, the gunner is able next to find his mark.

Other aspects of dynamic planning include: preconditioned opportunism, cyclic programming, asset analysis, innovative marketing, synthesized projection, comparative evaluation, interleaving acquisition and binary management. Each of these concepts will be examined in later chapters.

Through a formal planning framework, data becomes more manageable and the alternatives more clearly seen. In conditions of partial uncertainty, in which planning inevitably takes place, an artificially imposed structure is indispensable, as form is to music and a rectangular frame to painting. None of these limitations inhibits planner, painter or musician, but simply focus their attention on what is important.

Planning is neither forecasting nor simply a definition of objectives. It is the formulation of purposeful future action in a context of incomplete knowledge.

Focused Innovation

The ideal innovative product is one which establishes a new harmony between a company and its environment, both being in a constant state of change. Technological capability and emerging market needs are reconciled through proper choice of products.

This dialogue, between a company and its environment, is the core of dynamic planning, which recognizes that commercial benefit only springs from innovation which is relevant and timely. By helping to promote and focus the creative process, dynamic planning serves to channel innovative energy towards commercial ends. As I have suggested, dynamic planning is the means whereby a company maintains its competitive position in a changing world by adaptation.

It calls for a clear definition of corporate identity, derived from a study of a company's technical and commercial strengths, or differentiated assets. Awareness of identity in relation to the external context enables a company to recognize those innovative opportunities best suited to its capability, looking at the outside world and asking, as each pertinent development emerges: "What's in it for us?"

Nothing lasts for ever, but in the planning situation, personal or corporate identity is the most enduring element. It is therefore taken in this book as the basic datum or fundamental premise. Though capable of change, identity continues to exist when plans, programmes and objectives have long been superseded.

CHAPTER 5

PRACTICAL DYNAMICS

In his book *Long Range Planning*, Ernest Dale, of the Wharton School of Finance and Commerce, rightly notes that the planning process provides a vital stimulus to the imagination, and goes on to say:

> In this connection, perhaps the most famous planning document is that developed by John J. Raskob, treasurer of Du Pont, when he urged his president, Pierre du Pont, to invest £17 million in General Motors on the following very persuasive grounds:
>
> The greatest economy after World War I will be that of the United States.
> The greatest industry will be the automobile industry.
> The greatest company can be General Motors.
>
> The initial investment grew approximately 40 times to over £700 million within about 40 years.

To me this recommendation is not planning but inspiration. A comment on the uncertainty of inspiration was provided by a chance reference I happened to see elsewhere. Writing in *History of the 20th Century* (Chapter 45, p. 1239; Purnell) on "The days of boom and bust", Professor J. K. Galbraith notes: "In 1929 one of the very largest of the Wall Street operators was John J. Raskob. . . . So far from calling for preventive measures, Raskob in 1929 was explaining how, through stock market speculation, literally anyone could be a millionaire." What is needed is some more controllable procedure than inspiration on its own, a procedure to focus our thinking, to help us think more usefully about the future.

At the same time we can no longer look to that doubtful and

discredited word "diversification", particularly if we mean diversification at random or into totally unfamiliar areas of business. It has left too many problems in its trail if only through the anti-trust laws, as in the case of General Motors and Du Pont. We need some way to give direction to our planning:

"Are you going out, Mr. Davies?"

"No, Mrs. Jones. If I were going out I would be pointing the other way."

Business advisers (and with diffidence I count myself as one) frequently take possession of common sense ideas, which everybody else has used for years by giving them impressive or formidable names. Dynamic planning is such a name and, if it seems like common sense, it will be good enough. It is based on the belief that selective mating of a company's resources with emerging market needs breeds commercial opportunities; and is also the process whereby a company and its markets can be progressively and continuously harmonized.

Conflicting Needs

Successful adaptation in a company is measured not only by the magnitude of current profits but also by longer term resilience, or net cash flow over a substantial period. A large dividend one year, followed by liquidation in the next, would give both shareholders and employees reason to complain.

A company is consequently faced by two conflicting needs: to optimize its current operations, and to make adequate provision for the future. In a manufacturing concern these aims can best be reconciled by continuity of product policy and proper emphasis on forward planning. As mentioned earlier, product and business planning are closely related.

It follows that product planning (or, more generally, business planning) may be defined as a creative function of management concerned with the forward development of a company, taking existing assets, facilities, resources and experience as the basic premise and relating or adapting them to changing markets

continuously and systematically. In other words, it is a process
of fitting a company to its environment, bearing in mind that the
company can also alter its surroundings.

Although continuity of product policy is essential, management
does in fact proceed by a series of decisions, each a discrete step
or change in direction. A procedure for product planning should
therefore not only enable a company to respond continuously and
effectively to a changing context, but should also progress by
stages, of predetermined length, at the end of which decisions
become due.

So many companies, conscious that they need to introduce new
products, review an endless succession of ideas and opportunities,
always believing the next that comes to light will be better than
the last, with the result that no decision is ever taken. Unless
substantial effort is concentrated on a sensibly related group of
prospects that can be studied intensively, their potential can never
be properly recognized or realized in a profitable venture.

Before suggesting a procedure for dealing with the future in
terms of present assets, it may be useful to describe the basic
change in corporate situation that has made such a procedure
necessary. The change has taken place so gradually that it has
hardly been apparent, with the result that industries have tended
to react intuitively rather than in any rational or systematic way.

The New Situation

In the first instance, a company is founded to exploit a new idea,
acquisition, property, invention, departure or development. The
object is clear: capital must be invested, men recruited, facilities
built up and markets explored in order to make the most of a
particular opportunity. Initially the company can afford to be
single-minded. Its product policy is ready-made.

As time goes by and the company expands, new products are
accumulated, in many cases simply because an opportunity
happens to present itself. More men, machines, experience and
other assets are assembled to serve these interests, until eventually

it is the resources themselves rather than any basic product or idea that has to be exploited. This is certainly true in many engineering companies.

Whereas the purpose of a company may once have been to develop some promising invention, today the object is to stay in business however frequently products are superseded or the market changes course. No longer are facilities and skills gathered round the product; products must be found to suit the facilities and skills.

It is at this point that companies are driven to reconsider their position, returning to first principles in order to redefine their purpose, policy and mode of operations. Although these remarks are made with engineering companies in mind, there can be few consumer companies to whom this situation does not apply in some degree.

Take a fictional entrepreneur who, in the eighteenth century, devises a mechanical saw. He builds one in his stable and sells it to a nearby industrialist. It works well and several local business-men also order saws. The inventor–entrepreneur may have to hire an artisan to help him build machines, forming the nucleus of a production unit.

His success leads him to consider selling his saws in Sheffield, Birmingham, Glasgow, Newcastle and London, but he now finds that he spends all his time travelling over dreadful roads in stage-coaches, so he recruits both a manager for his factory and sales representatives at strategic points throughout the country, leaving him to devote more time to thinking about the future of his already profitable business.

At about this time he or his son discovers that another company have caught on to the idea and is producing cheaper saws in competition. It is decided that a new improved mechanical saw must be developed and the son goes up to the Midlands to find a clever mechanical engineer—a Watt, Stephenson or Bolton—providing the beginning of a research and development depart-ment.

One day this engineer suggests: "You have been successful

with a machine based on a reciprocating cutting action, why not conceive another?" So they develop slotters, and shapers and eventually go into the big time by launching horizontal planers, then plano-millers.

By this time the company have assembled an enormous collection of plant, buildings, technologists, sales and marketing people, managers, accountants (often recruited at great expense), overseas agents and other resources. And it is these assets which must be kept profitably employed. The business formula has changed.

Cyclic Regeneration

Since the cycle of product replacement is so much faster in the consumer industries, it may be possible to learn from their experience, much as an accelerated film of airport operations can reveal conditions that at normal speeds may not be evident.

Consumer product development is usually so planned that something new is always ready to succeed the product that has passed its peak. Sales forecasts help to determine at what point the new product should be launched, though it is important to bear in mind that profits may begin to fall well before there is any diminution in total sales volume.

One simple curve, for unit sales and profit per unit sold, showing a typical life cycle for a new product from introduction to decline, appears in Fig. 5.1. Following an initial boost, which is due in part to intensive promotion, enthusiastic selling and experimental purchasing (competitors are buying the product to see if it works or represents a threat), the curve of unit sales droops slightly after the first surge of energy is over then recovers, continuing to climb towards maturity and saturation. In practice the forms of individual curves will vary widely.

Profit per unit sold begins below the zero line during the launching period, but rises rapidly as initial costs are written off and operations become more economical. Prices can be high, since at this stage few if any competitors have entered the field and the product holds a monopoly position.

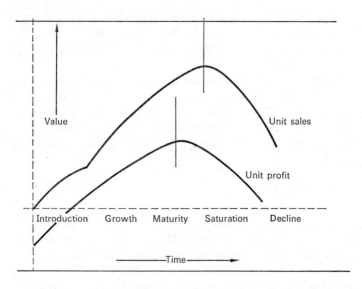

FIG. 5.1. Simplified product life cycle: curves of unit sales and unit profit showing stages in product sales life.

With the advent of competition, prices may have to be reduced quality improved or expensive services provided so as to maintain or increase the level of sales. Also selling costs increase as the radius of the sales area is extended (all things being equal, by the square of the radius) until, with entry into export markets, they may become very high indeed. It follows that unit profit will begin to fall long before the curve for unit sales has reached its maximum. To quote a friend of mine, the curve for unit sales corresponds to general health and that for unit profit to sexual vigour.

It is thus the second differential, or rate at which the slopes of sales, and particularly profit, curves are changing, that should be watched. Unfortunately, unlike a graph in space, the complete form of a curve in time cannot be known at any given moment: it stops dead at the present.

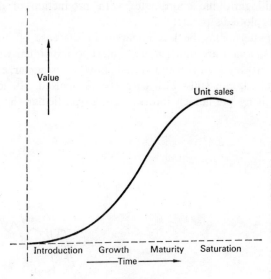

Fig. 5.2.

Also curves may take many forms. For example, Fig. 5.2 shows how sales resistance to a new product, which is simply a variation on products already on the market, affects the launching phase. Particularly in the case of consumer products, loyalty to existing brands has to be overcome and there may be no period of experimental purchasing. Variations in curve form, coupled with the data cut-off point (the present instant), makes interpreting these curves extremely difficult, as will be seen from the next two diagrams.

Figure 5.3, kindly prepared for me by the Economics Department of Courtaulds Limited, is a real (as distinct from idealized) life-cycle plot, showing United Kingdom production of viscose yarn and staple up to the middle of this decade. The graph is additive between the three products so that the spaces between the lines show the growth of the new products, staple and tyre yarn. Figure 5.4, also prepared by Courtaulds, gives the same data on semi-logarithmic coordinates with production of different products plotted separately.

The pattern may be less apparent in the case of industrial products, which are much more subject to individual variation, but the basic cycle of rise and decline, however irregular, extended or disguised, can still—with care—be recognized. An idealized curve, giving pre-launch information, in particular the cost of

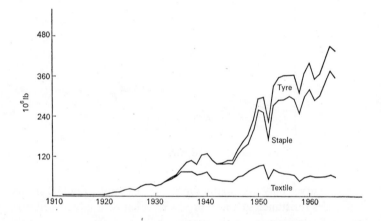

FIG. 5.3. Actual plot for production of viscose yarn and staple in the United Kingdom. Rayon is a viscose yarn.

engineering and development, with a line for the recovery of investment is illustrated in Fig. 5.5.

Without deep understanding of the underlying circumstances, it is easy to be misled by life-cycle curves. Put simply, rayon is produced by squirting one fluid into another through a fine nozzle. The size and configuration of the nozzle can be changed, as can other parameters, such as the composition, temperature and pressure of the two fluids, leading to a greater variety of possible combinations. Nylon also competes with rayon as a material for tyre reinforcement. It is conceivable therefore that the apparent life-cycle curve for rayon could follow the line in Fig. 5.6. As one form of rayon meets increasing competition from nylon, profit begins to fall; but just at that moment the development department discovers a new improved rayon, which again is more than price-competitive with nylon. The same pattern of events might then occur again.

Finally, Fig. 5.7 shows the effect on aggregate profit of delays in product launching. Given equal development costs Company

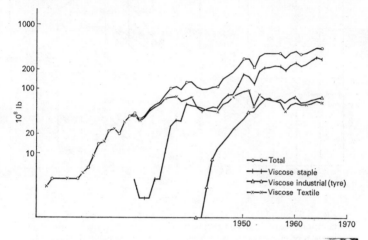

Fig. 5.4. Points are only plotted up to 1965, since when sales of staple have risen sharply, while textile and industrial sales have remained essentially unchanged.

C can never achieve the same net positive cash flow on a particular product as company A. On the other hand, in a real situation, it may be that company A will have spent a fortune on development (square lines show budgeted development expenditure) and in practice, company B, which may have found short cuts in the light of company A's experience, may secure the best net cash flow overall, especially if it quickly follows company A in launching.

Whatever the form such curves may take, products should ideally succeed each other continuously so that total company profit remains above a given minimum, as with the later curves in Fig. 5.8. But with a sales life of 50 years or more, as in the case of the steam locomotive, a manufacturer may well be taken by surprise.

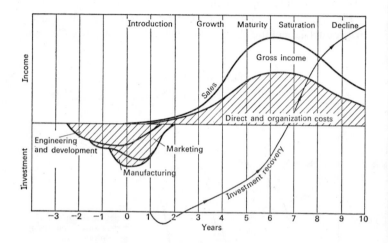

Fig. 5.5. Simplified life-cycle curve showing sales volume, various components of cost and recovery of investment. (Slightly modified version of curve taken from *New Product Development* published by Booz Allen & Hamilton, with permission.)

Identity and Role

With growing emphasis on the economic utilization of available facilities and the high rate of technical change, engineering companies, like consumer companies, are thinking increasingly in terms of continuing product succession and review.

It is therefore necessary to devise a procedure whereby a company's plant and experience may be related to emerging market needs or adapted to meet new situations. Any procedure for this purpose should assist a company to:

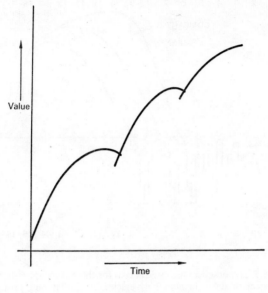

FIG. 5.6.

(1) Plan its future continuously and systematically.
(2) Make the most of its existing assets.
(3) Keep in close touch with its market environment.
(4) Make product decisions with the minimum delay.
(5) Exploit whatever unexpected opportunities may come to
    light.

The first essential in conceiving such a framework is to define a
company's role or corporate identity. Though I do not pretend
to understand everything that Marshall McLuhan writes, I was
struck by his statement in *The Medium is the Massage* that "roles
are now replacing goals". I felt that here was formidable support
for my reservations on planning by objectives.

To think usefully about its development, a company must have a
recognizable identity, a role known and understood both by the
company's employees and by the outside world, a lasting role that,

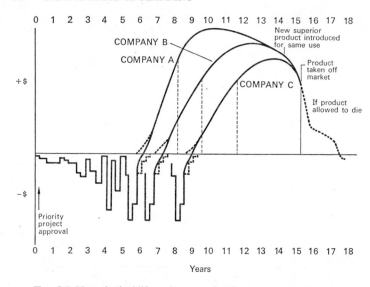

FIG. 5.7. Hypothetical life-cycle curves for three companies showing the effect of delay in launching essentially similar new products. (The diagram is reproduced, slightly modified, from a paper "Product strategy and future profits", by C. F. Rassweiler (Vice President for Research, Development and Engineering, Johns-Manville Corporation), published in *Research Revue* (April 1961, pp. 1–8.) and reprinted in *Product Strategy and Management*, edited by Thomas L. Berg and Abe Shuchman, Holt, Rinehart and Winston 1963.)

as far as can be seen, will not be overtaken by events or changes in the market—in other words a dynamic corporate identity capable of adaptation. Indeed, as I have already suggested, identity must precede objectives, since nothing can have a purpose unless it first exists.

Figure 5.9 shows how company identity can evolve in time. The identity may be visualized as an irregular prism, the cross-section of which changes over time; alternatively as the cross-section of an electric cable carrying various strands or conductors: the section can change its shape or size, as new strands join the main flux or diverge from it, but it preserves an essential continuity.

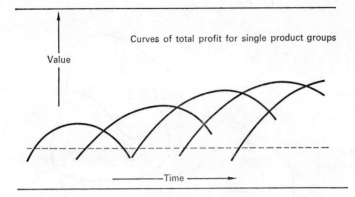

Fig. 5.8. Ideally, products should be introduced continuously so that a new product is always ready to replace the one beginning to decline.

A suitable role is the key to successful product planning and a big step towards meeting the five basic requirements enumerated above. It extends into the future; it can take account of existing reputation and experience; it provides a basis for a continuing market review; can simplify decision making; and offers scope for "planned opportunism".

Continuing Review

Bearing the company's role in mind, management is in a position to look at current news, technical innovation, commercial developments, social, political and economic change, and ask themselves "What's in it for us?"

For example, a company active in "separation plant", noting from the technical or daily Press the growing problem of pollution, would be prompted to inquire what part they could play in solving it. Knowing their own identity, they are quicker to respond to environmental change, recognizing potentially profitable opportunities germane to their experience.

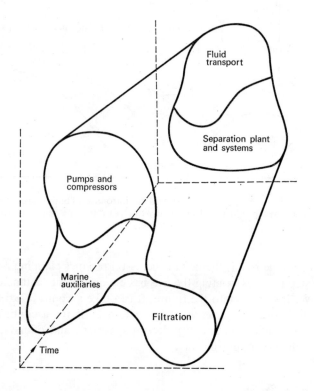

Fig. 5.9.

Again, consider a company that had traditionally supplied intrinsically safe flame- and explosion-proof equipment for use in coal-mines. Knowing that their business was threatened in that they had a monopoly customer in the United Kingdom, which was closing pits and contracting generally, the company would be anxious to introduce new products.

By adopting "electromechanical aspects of safety" as a more general field of continuing interest, the company can conduct a regular review of product opportunities, focusing on product ideas consistent with the company's resources and experience.

The management would be aware that during recent years there has been one long succession of disasters—earthquakes, floods, slipping coal tips, oil slicks, breached and overflowing dams, unprecedented damage due to fire, mining accidents, losses at sea and in the air, large-scale robberies and havoc on the roads. By reviewing these events, the safety-conscious company could hardly fail to discover some product opportunities.

To illustrate the process of conception through relating identity to world environment, I will refer to the Longarone Dam disaster. The lake behind the dam was surrounded by mountains and, following heavy rain, great quantities of soil and rock started moving down their slopes into the lake, which, like Archimedes' bath, overflowed.

Considering this calamity I tried to think what a safety-conscious company could devise to forestall any similar disaster in the future. Of the various ideas that occurred to me, the least apparently practical was a pencil-like probe, incorporating a transducer, which could be made in quantity and suitably distributed in the terrain round such a lake. Any substantial earth slide would then be detected, a warning signal sent to the dam, where the sluice gates could be opened in good time to release a sufficient quantity of water.

The technical and cost problems seemed insurmountable until quite recently I referred to the idea at a seminar and was told that a company had already launched a product of this kind.

In practice an area as broad as safety is far too comprehensive to use effectively. In the case of this study we eventually only explored prospects in the handling and transport of noxious, inflammable or otherwise dangerous materials. Because of the technical link between mining and civil engineering, we also investigated hazards on building and construction sites.

A review of opportunities based on corporate identity, with reference to events in the external world, can be conducted in an emergency to solve a one-off planning problem, but should strictly be performed regularly and allow for immediate, short-term and long-term opportunities, perhaps even on a scale of 15 years.

Dynamic Product Areas

It is convenient to subdivide a company's overall identity into several such continuing areas of interest or "dynamic product areas", as illustrated in Fig. 5.9, though only the upper or later section comprises genuine dynamic areas. Figuratively, a rounded personality is good for a company as it is for a human being. Exposed salients projecting into other company's specialities, unsupported by associated product ranges, can be very vulnerable.

Essentially, a dynamic area defines a class of activities or products in functional or general terms. It should be broad enough to embrace a great number of product ideas including many that have not yet been conceived but specific enough to be readily communicated and to focus a continuing review or product search.

A company may have several related or even unrelated dynamic areas, and it is emphasized that they are not simply generalizations of the company's whole activity, but must be carefully defined. It is neither true nor useful to think of GEC–AEI–EE or Westinghouse just as manufacturers of electrical and electronic products, or ICI as being in the business of chemicals. Such overall descriptions are unlikely to trigger potentially promising ideas.

Theodore Levitt's inspired question "What business are you really in?" has been a major landmark in the development of marketing philosophy, but it has to be used with caution, and the kind of answer being sought defined precisely.

When an American railroad was suffering from declining turnover and profit, the question was put to them, "What business are you in?" They answered naturally "The railroad business."

"But railroads are losing money. What business are you really in?"

After some thought, the reply came: "I suppose we are in the transportation business."

Given this answer they were able to consider whether in fact they should acquire an airline, or maybe a shipping line on the Great Lakes. It was the key to seeking substitution products or services that might sooner or later replace those already offered.

Now transfer the questioning to a shipyard on the Clyde or Tyneside. Following the same sequence the answer might be given: "We produce equipment and machinery for transportation." Such a response is unlikely to be very useful: who would consider making motor-cars or aircraft in a shipyard? The weakness of defining a business exclusively in market terms is evident.

Similarly, the definition "entertainment" could be too broad for a jukebox manufacturer or quite misleading for a company whose assets happen to be large or spacious premises in town and city centres.

Dynamic areas should as far as possible be timeless, so that a company's activities may be capable of indefinite regeneration— new products being introduced within an area as existing products become less profitable. Thus in the case of safety: whatever vicissitudes befall particular devices, safety equipment of one kind or another will always be required.

The word "dynamic" is used, not simply because it is a fashionable adjective, but with reference to the technical or scientific concept "dynamic equilibrium". As something leaves (becomes obsolete or uncompetitive), something else enters (is introduced) to take its place. Continuous product succession (or expansion) is therefore possible within an area.

A simple example of dynamic equilibrium is shown in Fig. 5.10. A vessel is full of water which is entering through an inlet at the top and leaving through an outlet at the bottom and at a rate such that the vessel always remains full. It is in dynamic equilibrium since, although the vessel is always full, the population of molecules is continuously changing. Perhaps a school is a better example in that pupils join at 5 or 11 and leave at 15 or 18, but since communities are growing, the population of the school will also gradually increase. What is more, since the fabric of the school is relatively permanent and staff tend to remain somewhat longer than the pupils, the school will retain a basic continuity of identity or character. Step changes may occur, as when the school goes comprehensive, but even then something will remain. Again, no school is packed to bursting point with pupils, and, if it is a grammar school, an element of selection is involved.

Similarly, no company should attempt to occupy the whole of a dynamic area, which should simply be used as a first broad guide

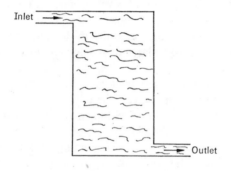

FIG. 5.10. Example of dynamic equilibrium.

in planning, with a view to choosing only the most promising ideas and opportunities brought to light within it, usually in conjunction with a screening checklist.

It is dynamic in the sense that, whenever any product is withdrawn, through obsolescence or changes in the market, there is always ample scope within the area for finding something else to take its place. If we print banknotes and are faced with the threat that some of our overseas customers want to print their own, we may perhaps adopt the broad dynamic area "security" based on our reputation for reliability and skills in protecting valuables. Study of the area may suggest countless other possible activities which would be worth considering, as shown in Fig. 5.11. Such opportunities would then be screened with reference to the market and the company's facilities and skills.

At the same time, banknotes could be embraced by other overlapping areas, as shown in Fig. 5.12, such as high-quality printing, but the higher the fewer, and such an area is unlikely to

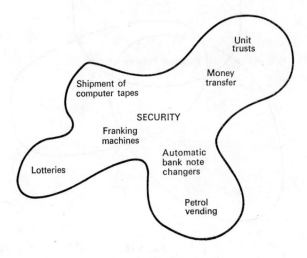

Fig. 5.11.

be prolific in product opportunities. Once a new activity in a particular dynamic area has been selected (say security transport), that area is reinforced and the others may begin to atrophy.

Function and Image

I conceived my first dynamic area in 1961. (Afterwards I personally delivered two of my four children, and realized that conception was the easy part.)

The group of companies concerned had an enormous range of products: pumps, compressors, auxiliary plant for ships and power

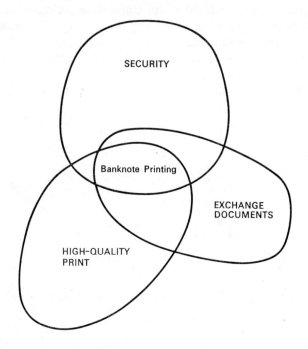

FIG. 5.12.

stations, evaporators, valves and even houses. Within this range I discovered there were de-oilers and de-aerators (for separating oil and air from boiler feedwater) desalination plant (for purifying seawater), arising from the company's flash-evaporator work; water-treatment plant; and an experimental pressure filter (for squeezing the moisture out of sludges or damp solids). The simple concept that embraced this miscellaneous collection of activities was "equipment for materials separation".

This definition bore some relationship to their existing knowledge of technology, manufacturing facilities and market outlets; but it also had the power to prompt new but relevant ideas—centrifuges, cyclones, diffusers, dialysis plant, gas-chromatography equipment and countless other opportunities, including some not yet invented or conceived. Many will be excluded straight away, but some items germane to the company's experience will almost certainly survive techno-commercial screening. Thus, although the dynamic area is based on the present, it has a foothold in the future. In other words, it is a wide net for products, from which a selection can be made, and a basis for opportunist planning.

It is dynamic in that any one diffusion process, evaporator, filter or centrifuge could become obsolete; eventually, with the advent of controlled thermonuclear power, it may no longer be necessary to separate the fissile isotope of uranium from natural uranium. But we shall always have to separate some material from another; and equipment for "material separation" is a dynamic area that can last virtually for ever.

Again, any one fastener may fall into disuse; buttons may be replaced by zips, rawlplugs by anchor bolts, but fastenings themselves are indispensable and therefore constitute a genuine dynamic area.

The dynamic area is, of course, a term of ranging application. It might refer to the exploitation of a particular material, nickel, say, or aluminium; to a service, such as conversion, including, for example, the conversion of cars, private houses, factories, ships and aircraft; or even to a personal talent—plus the essential information sources—for buying potentially profitable businesses.

It may not always be possible to express a dynamic product area in a few words, but the concept should be relatively simple. A company might, for example, specialize in producing "machinery for the rolling or otherwise continuous processing of sheet and strip material, including steel, aluminium, board and plastics".

A shipbuilder might have more difficulty in devising dynamic areas, consistent with his knowledge and resources. His instinct may be to consider novel forms of transport, but the field is limited and most other forms of transport are ill-suited to a shipbuilder's experience. He might then see one aspect of his skill as lying in the provision of accommodation and furnishing, but on examination he will find that his cost structure is such as to make any furniture he might produce beyond the means of even the most luxurious hotel. If then he looks at systems building he will discover that he is tackling a market where his experience is rudimentary and where his major competitors are very well established.

Perhaps the unique ability of a shipbuilder is to pack great complexes of plant, with interwoven wiring, piping, ducting and communication, into a confined space. It may be, therefore, that he could apply his experience to the design of self-contained and package plant (mobile or static, including, for example, drilling rigs) and to problems of automatic warehousing, high-speed construction of specialized turnkey projects, even such remote fields as urban congestion, city market gardening, underwater farming and prospecting, and the synthetic production of protein and other foods.

But, even more than the aircraft industry, shipbuilding is ill-adapted to diversification. The shipbuilder would be best advised to watch his own markets carefully, perhaps to specialize, to keep abreast of technical developments and equip himself to serve emerging needs. Even as I write, I see that Mitsubishi has turned down an order for a 300,000 ton super tanker, noting that to build it they would need to re-equip their yards. It may be that, following mergers on the Clyde, the leapfrog process is bringing business back to Britain.

The dynamic area should be defined to be just broad enough to afford a sufficient watershed for opportunities, but not so broad that it is unspecific or out of scale with the size or nature of the company. For shipbuilders, perhaps shipbuilding is the most dynamic area.

Apart from focusing a company's identity, the dynamic area serves a variety of other purposes. It can help to direct an immediate search for manufacturing licences or associates; it has a part to play in long-term forecasting; it can contribute in the selection of research projects.

It can also provide a company with a strong marketing image. If particular concerns are widely associated with separation, aspects of safety, fastening or conversion, any potential customer with problems in these fields will turn to them for assistance or advice. There may then be opportunities to sell their products. Again, if all a company's employees are aware of its identity, their suggestions may be better focused to its interests—and the potential product lists will not in every case be so curiously miscellaneous, covering the most improbable scatter of activities.

So many product planning managers observe that there is no problem in gathering ideas; it is screening them they find more difficult. I would submit that the trick lies rather in focusing the actual generation of ideas. Some years ago every company I visited, from iron founders and mild-steel fabricators to motor-component manufacturers and instrument engineers, had under-water fishing gear in their potential product list.

It is stressed, however, that the dynamic area has no organization role. No workshop, sales force or research department should be organized on dynamic area lines; each should be angled to its function, perhaps in terms of cost and profit centres. The dynamic area is simply a device for planning, a conceptual aid to focus forward thinking.

Criteria for Choosing Areas

A dynamic area may take many forms but, as already indicated, it must achieve a satisfactory balance between the too general and the too specific. Definitions based on "not too little and not too much", are seldom satisfactory, so I shall endeavour to be more precise. Ideally a dynamic area should:

(1) Be capable of continued application and usefulness, irres-pective of changing social, industrial and market needs. *Will it last?*

(2) Be likely to embrace a large number of individual products. *Does it afford enough scope for seeking products?*

(3) Not be limited to a single market, market area or industry. *Does it offer a sufficient breadth of market?*

(4) Be simple to identify and describe and sufficiently definite to focus a product search. *Can it be expressed in a few words and be readily understood?*

(5) Be in the general stream of social and industrial change. *Is it likely to yield new developments?*

(6) Not be strongly associated with another company or industry. *Is it unique?*

(7) Be consistent with a company's experience and image. *Does it embrace any existing products or activities?*

(8) Relate in some degree to markets in which the company are already well established. *Will it provide an opportunity to use the company's present sales facilities and outlets?*

These criteria should, of course, be treated with discretion. A good dynamic area may sometimes fail particular requirements.

Some of these criteria may be surprising. Limitation to a single market (item (3) above) is fine for an individual product or product group, but not for a continuing identity. It is convenient to to have an escape route, if existing markets show signs of recession or decline.

Over the past 10 years, I have heard at so many directors' dining tables the comment: "We must get into plastics (or petrochemicals or electronics, quarrying, road-making, construction, building or natural gas)." There has always been a tendency to jump on the bandwagon of what appear to be growth markets. If one man's intuition leads him to select a particular industry as a good potential market, it is not unlikely that his competitors will be looking in the same direction. After all, most businessmen read the same newspapers and journals.

Far fields always seem greener; but take another look to see how many other cows have got there first. Markets can become overcrowded and it is not worth tackling the more popular markets unless the company has assets or experience that can give it an advantage.

Interest in a particular chemical product has sometimes been followed by wholesale construction of new plants until there is massive surplus capacity. One company is reported to have started building a polyethylene plant when other companies were petitioning the Board of Trade to prohibit dumping.

Fortunately, such capacity problems in the chemical industry tend in time to solve themselves; and there is also a temptation to announce the construction of new plants—simply to discourage the others.

A good market is often regarded as more important than the company's own ability to sell or make the product. Vending machines, whatever the demand, are unlikely to support the overheads in heating, space, machinery, inspection and technical resources of an aircraft factory, though a combination of products might conceivably utilize all the company's principal facilities.

With reference again to the dynamic area criteria, the value of a simply worded area (item (4)) lies in its focusing capacity. As suggested earlier, if every employee of a company knows what kind of business he is working for, his chance of suggesting pertinent activities is much enhanced. Again, simplicity of definition assists in registering a company's image and facilitates a worldwide product search where language barriers exist.

Uniqueness (item (6)), is of course, difficult to achieve in practice. Dorr-Oliver and Sharples are already well established in the separation business, and GKN in fastenings. Nevertheless, an attempt to define an exclusive product area is, of course, desirable.

I have not referred separately to all the eight criteria, but the significance of most of them is I think self-evident.

Differentiated Assets

Where a company has no natural role or formulated product areas, a study of its resources and experience will often suggest lines of development. By thinking systematically about a company's assets and using certain guides, suitable dynamic areas can be conceived.

Assets are considered to be of two kinds: differentiated and undifferentiated. Undifferentiated assets are those common to many companies—land, factory space, general purpose tools, unskilled labour and money. Money is universal and perhaps the least differentiated asset of any. All commercial activities become more competitive as their exponents become more experienced and knowledgeable, and diversification is no exception. It follows that if a company treats capital as its primary asset when planning to diversify, it will do so in competition with every other business—from chain stores to heavy engineering groups.

The words differentiated and undifferentiated are in practice relative terms. For example, during a credit squeeze, access to liquid capital may well become a differentiated asset; and if the land a company owns is situated in the City of London, on Manhattan Island, near the port of Rotterdam, or in an area earmarked for development, say the shores of the Cromarty Firth, it may well become or constitute a differentiated asset.

But however they may be selected or defined, the differentiated assets, peculiar to a given company, form the proper basis for a business planning study.

Such assets may be of many different kinds. I remember that at one seminar I led for the British Institute of Management, two officials from the Home Office were in the audience. I was puzzled by their presence and perhaps even disturbed when I discovered they were from the Prison Service. By I think the third session I plucked up sufficient courage to ask their reason for attending a seminar on product planning.

"That is quite simple," answered one of them, "we believe that several prisons in this country could become self-supporting or even profitable establishments."

I thought their aim was most commendable and inquired if what I had been saying had any bearing on their problem.

"Yes, certainly," replied the other, "we have been thinking on very similar lines."

I wondered what they considered to be their differentiated assets and was told first, with a smile, that at least they had "a tied labour force". Someone observed that it was not always tied as firmly as the authorities might wish.

The prison official continued: "Another asset lies in the location of many British prisons. They tend to be old buildings and consequently industrial conurbations have grown up round them. They are therefore well placed for undertaking subcontract work."

"I trust you pay the union rate," remarked his neighbour.

Nevertheless, it seemed to me a reasonable and certainly desirable objective, and I continued to question them: "With regard to your tied labour force, what is roughly the distribution of your skills? I should imagine that you have a few mechanical engineers, like myself, who could no doubt turn their hands to forcing safes, and perhaps the occasional operational research scientist able to plan a great train robbery."

"Well, I don't know about that," said the official, "but we have a fair number of accountants."

On the best authority, therefore, I am able to emphasize that in defining corporate identity it is useful in the first instance to identify those assets which in combination distinguish an organization from every other. It is these assets that provide a business with any competitive advantage it may have. The market is common to everybody; a company's potential is unique.

At the same time it is necessary to examine the company's "differentiated liabilities", since they may represent a limiting constraint. Often, however, a liability may be associated with complementary assets. It is emphasized, for example, that those industrial establishments set up to provide employment for the blind need not regard blindness solely as a defect to be overcome. In particular, blindness can lead to the development of more acute senses of touch and hearing, and promote the development of worthwhile personal qualities—I am told that blind switchboard operators tend to be more sensitive, friendly and adept in their work than sighted people; and there is a well-known personnel-selection specialist who happens to be blind.

It is unlikely, on the other hand, that an organization could

operate effectively without sighted people in addition. Blind salesmen are seldom successful in the longer run, since there would be a
strong tendency for customers to buy initially on sympathy,
which after a time wears thin. Some compromise would be
essential, though compromise need not be looked upon as second
best; I have heard it described as "the appropriate course between
extremes". And a combination of human characteristics and
qualities can afford the same uniqueness of potential as a combination of any other differentiated assets—as Theodore Sturgeon
showed in his fascinating book *More than Human*, concerning
a telepathic composite of some ten unusual talents.

Characteristic Table

As a preliminary it is convenient to draw up a "characteristic
table" which is used to prompt ideas for product areas. A dynamic
area should transcend individual products and product groups, and
link as many aspects of a company's experience as possible.

The table is thus designed to provide a concise expression of a
company's resources and experience, which can therefore be
readily reviewed or even committed to memory. It normally comprises three columns as follows:

(1) Existing products, past products and products under
    consideration, though only potential products thought to be
    particularly appropriate should be included.
(2) Details of the company's experience, assembled from de-
    sign, production and research departments.
(3) Sales outlets, by trades, industries and sometimes individual
    customers where the customer's activities are readily
    identified.

Items within each column are not arranged to have any horizontal correspondence and the table in Fig. 5.13, based on a fictional
group of four companies, is a typical example. Tables may often
be far more detailed and elaborate, including a greater range
of headings.

FIG. 5.13. Characteristic table of products, processes and outlets. In compiling the table, special emphasis is placed on skills or knowledge in which companies have unique experience or are particularly advanced. The line in the processes column, divides design, research or technological experience from manufacturing facilities and skills. It will be noted that there is no horizontal correspondence between different columns.

Products	Processes	Outlets
Pumps	Dewatering	Domestic consumers
Air compressors	Crystallization	Hardware shops
Thermal driers	Control engineering	Department stores
Centrifuges	Hydraulics	Motor manufacturers
Finned tubing	Pneumatics	Garages
Evaporators	Combustion	Chemical concerns
Pressure vessels	Heat balance	Construction companies
Refrigerators	Rotation	Plant hire firms
Filters	Reciprocation	Builders' merchants
Lightweight diesels	Structures	Tonnage oxygen plants
Domestic heaters	Soil mechanics	Mining
Window fasteners	———————	Docks
Air-conditioning	Extrusion	Electricity undertakings
Winches	Deep drawing	Aircraft industry
Escalators	Copy turning	Research establishments
Cartridges	Broaching	Food processing
Dish washers	Chemical milling	Sewage and water boards
Car bumpers	Complex fabrication	Education authorities
Heated towel rails	Precision casting	The Services
Immersion heaters	Powder metallurgy	Hotels

Trigger Mechanisms

The table may help to prompt ideas for dynamic areas in a variety of ways. A few of those that have been used from time to time are as follows.

One approach is to take each item in turn and scan the remainder of the table to see if any relationships emerge. For example, a company might have among its products air compressors and air-conditioning equipment; be experienced in pneumatics; and supply equipment for tonnage oxygen plants. The links between these four items might suggest the product area "air handling and processing", embracing, in addition, air conveying, air cleaning, air filtration and distillation, pressure exchangers, fluid beds, air cooling and so on. If a broader area is required, then the word "gas" might be substituted for "air".

Another method is to consider each product (column 1) and endeavour to generalize it as a function. Thus a window fastener, which is a specific product, might be expanded into fastenings in general, which could form a dynamic product area; car radiators into small air-cooled heat exchangers; a filter or centrifuge into materials separation plant; escalators into short-range passenger conveying.

Not only functions, but also applications and outlets may be generalized. I remember being at a conference on one occasion and, to make conversation with my neighbour before the arrival of the principal speaker, I inquired as to his company's business. He said they made soap and I then asked his company's name. He mentioned a company which was unknown to me and I said that this was strange, since I thought I had heard of all the soap companies with their smooth-hand and bubble-bath advertisements on television.

He said: "We don't make that kind of soap; ours is a coarse soap for scrubbing floors."

"That's curious," I said, "I haven't seen anybody scrubbing floors for years, what with wall-to-wall carpeting, plastics tiles, polished wood and special finishes."

"No", he said sadly, "it's not a very good business."

I said that he looked quite prosperous and didn't appear to be suffering too badly.

"We're not," he answered, "we diversified."

I was interested immediately and prompted him to explain.

"Indirectly our business was in cleaning the floors of commercial and industrial premises." He went on, "So we decided to go in for floor maintenance and preservation generally. Now we are thinking of developing still further—into the maintenance of walls and ceilings."

Product areas can of course be based on manufacturing or

technical processes, and column 2 in the characteristic table may be scanned for suitable ideas. Companies can usefully present themselves as specialists in all aspects of extrusion or control engineering, high-quality casting or soil mechanics. Particular management skills might also be borne in mind, e.g. experience in negotiation with government departments or controlling a large export programme.

Engineering principles may likewise provide a basis for devising product areas. Thus a company making centrifugal pumps will be familiar with hydrodynamics and rotation, embracing a knowledge of bearings, glands and seals; in turn hydrodynamics and rotation suggest the further product area of fluid mixing. One product that resulted from a study of this kind was a jet mixer which, in fact, had no rotating parts within the mixing vessel, but the jet was produced by just the kind of pump the company already manufactured.

In summary: before any business can clearly distinguish its objectives, it is necessary to define a corporate identity. Otherwise, all companies would tend to have the same objectives. Identity should be dynamic in the sense that, though maintaining an essential continuity, it must be adaptable to the changing environment in which the company operates. Indeed, ideally, it should be capable of immortality. Again, given a suitable identity, it is necessary to be outward looking, so that the recognition of opportunities is almost automatic.

As I have noted earlier, a company might be advised as a father might advise his son: "Do what you are able to do well." But "Do what you do well" is not the same as "Do what you do now" or "Do what you have always done".

The Story of Specimen Industries

To outline the situation in which dynamic planning may be applicable, I will record the history of a near fictional concern. Perhaps it would be appropriate to call them Sample Limited.

ORIGINS

Set up in 1910 to package and distribute small portions of other people's produce, Sample Limited were one of the first companies to provide an independent marketing service. Founded on a single bright idea, they gradually acquired facilities to exploit it on a national scale. The scope was large since, whatever misfortunes befell particular clients, there would always be new products to be packaged and an insatiable demand for free samples.

At one stage, the company found that nearly half their business was in dairy produce, and the chairman, a keen farmer, suggested that they take up dairying as a new activity. Nobody dared disagree. Unfortunately, once they were in dairying they found their dairy sample customers disinclined to have their samples packaged and distributed by a company which was also their competitor. The sample business started to decline.

But the dairy business flourished and soon the company decided to manufacture dairy plant. Since they already owned 30 per cent of the dairies in the country and were acquiring more, they were not too worried about customers.

It was decided that the company needed new blood and the managing director, who was shortly due to retire, decided to recruit a personal assistant. A young man was appointed.

BAND WAGON DEVELOPMENT

He had already some experience as a junior manager and had been to a summer school in marketing. He had also read a paper by an American called Grace. Grace had carried out a study which had shown that demand for chemicals was entering a period of rapid growth. Grace Brothers went into chemicals; so Sample followed suit. "Cheese," said the young executive, "is no less sensitive to temperatures and pressures than complex chemicals, and our process experience would be invaluable."

The founder still exerted influence and, drawing attention to the company's name, he persuaded his colleagues that Sample Limited should specialize in producing specimen quantities of rare compounds and in the design of pilot plants.

It was about this time that Sample Limited became a public company, but under the more imposing title of Specimen Industries Limited. The personal assistant in due course became managing director.

He had also become a chartered engineer and ever since graduating had been fascinated by large-scale process plant. After a year or two, despite the founder's reservations, a chemical engineering company was taken over and integrated with the dairy plant department. The two sales forces were combined and a few small personal conflicts began to rear their heads.

SPREAD OF INTERESTS

Meanwhile the founder's son was appointed assistant to the company secretary, who was also getting near retiring age.

The company had grown extremely prosperous and were looking for new capital outlets. "What we need," said the future company secretary, "is a wider spread of interests". So Specimen Industries started acquiring profitable companies, whenever an opportunity presented itself; whatever the activities of the companies acquired.

Specimen Industries were now one of the largest groups in the country, and it was at this point that things started going wrong.

They had assembled considerable resources in order to exploit first the original bright idea, then the products and services which had sprung from it. They had accumulated wealth and used it to acquire a great variety of interests. And now it was these assets that had to be kept profitably employed.

OPPORTUNISM

The group's evolution had been opportunist and piecemeal, and had in consequence gradually diverged from the mainstream of social and industrial change. Their activities were no longer in perfect harmony with their market environment. Specimen Industries and the requirements of society had slowly grown apart. They had also become increasingly difficult to manage.

This did not mean that their products were no longer needed— by no means. The real weaknesses were much more complex.

First of all they were not the only company who had recognized opportunities in the chemical industry. At the time they entered the field, the oil and chemical industries were the main topic in almost every boardroom, as the building, petrochemical and gas industries have been discussed since then. Most businessmen read the same newspapers.

If one man's intuition leads him to select the chemical or quarry industry as a good prospective market, it is not unlikely that a competitor's intuition will guide him in the same direction.

THE SAME IDEA

Only recently Specimen Industries had brought on stream a new phthalic anhydride plant. When the decision to build was taken, it seemed a good idea: phthalic anhydride was an intermediate in many processes—in the production of pharmaceuticals, dyestuffs, plastics, plasticisers and other materials—so the requirement was likely to be substantial and comfortably spread.

Unfortunately, some eleven other companies had reached the same conclusion and the twelve plants now in existence represented an embarrassing surplus of capacity.

GROWING COMPETITION

The group's traditional activities were subject to increasing competition, both from well-established major companies and from newcomers.

The entry of young and energetic companies with low overheads into the fields which Specimen Industries had once monopolized was introducing slack, and many of their manufacturing facilities were under-utilized. Competition from abroad had likewise grown intensive.

They had sought subcontract work with only moderate success, since the whole country was going through a trade recession and companies who had at one time sub-contracted manufacture were now concerned to keep their own shops occupied.

OUT OF CONTROL

In attempting to spread their interests widely, Specimen Industries had acquired a large number of relatively small companies, and it was difficult to put over a strong corporate image, even for sectors of the group. Also, in distributing the available promotional resources among so many companies, their advertising tended to be ineffective.

What is more, opportunities for inter-company trading were being overlooked and the management was not adequate in numbers of experience to control the many activities to maximum advantage or to provide the economies of common services. Two of the companies, who had once been fierce competitors, were still at daggers drawn and through their rivalry were forcing down prices when there was no other competitor in sight.

Control was attempted by allotting holding-board directors to the boards of member companies, but no such group of men could possibly encompass the range of technical and commercial experience necessary to make control effective. As a result, profits that could have been retained within the group were slipping out between their fingers and into other pockets.

Each of these problems arose from the lack of any considered group or company product policy and failure over the years to study the market systematically.

EXCHANGE OF VIEWS

One of the two young men who had helped in building up the

group, but had by now acquired a few grey hairs, attended a seminar on product planning. He came back with a certain desperate enthusiasm and suggested that a product development committee be formed.

The first few meetings of the committee were abortive. Most contributions were entirely negative.

"You can't make anything but resins in a plant optimized for resin manufacture," said one plant manager.

"We're just coming on load," added another, "and I haven't time for panel games."

"Why can't we concentrate on selling our existing products more effectively?" remarked the sales director. "Why not, indeed," replied the managing director. "Let me know by Monday how you propose to set about it."

The next meeting was worse. The chairman began by asking if anyone had any bright ideas. Everyone started looking round the room for inspiration. A young man, who had been deputed by the sales department in one of the smaller companies to attend committee meetings and had previously been in die-casting, muttered: "I suppose we couldn't manufacture doorknobs— or window-fasteners—or light fittings?"

He was attacked from all sides. "Not a chance: mostly material, no added value and look at the competition—the big metal mass production companies on one side and backyard plastics boys with no overheads on the other. Anyway we haven't any outlets in the building industry."

TRESPASSING

The chairman called the meeting to order. "I realize the problem isn't easy", he said, "perhaps we are too diversified already and need to concentrate."

"There's no sense in entering fields where we should only pass for amateurs. I hear that shipbuilders are going into building; can they really hope to compete with Laings and Taylor Woodrow, Token, Turriff, Wates and Wimpey? Any new methods would surely have been spotted by the specialists, who seem pretty wide awake to me."

"The aircraft industry have learnt that lesson," put in the production director. "Making slot machines in an aircraft factory is just a waste of heat and space, not to mention expensive men and machines."

There were a few positive suggestions but no one was responsible for pursuing them and they were soon forgotten. Two quite good proposals were turned down for no good reason except that someone considered them outrageous.

NOVELTY RESISTANCE

Not only in Specimen Industries, but elsewhere too, people pay lip-service to new products, but any actual suggestion meets a negative reaction. It is either too unexciting; or so exciting it frightens the management to death. There is a tendency to fall between two stools. A product concept that is entirely new may yield big profits but involves considerable risk. Profit margins on a product with an established market that can be measured are likely to be small.

But after this initial experience, Specimen Industries began to take the problem seriously and embarked on systematic planning which led eventually to profitable action. They also decided on a definition: a product would only be considered new — and not simply a modification — if it was able to create a new profit centre.

CHAPTER 6

WORKING METHOD

ABSTRACT concepts have no place in management unless they can be converted into useful action. Dynamic planning—a continuous or intermittent process whereby a company adapts to its environment through proper choice of products—may be translated into action through a procedure I have called "successive focusing". It is little more than common sense—but all management methods and techniques of any value are simply accumulated common sense formulated in tranquillity.

No company is able to exploit every opportunity uncovered, every innovation brought to its attention, every unsatisfied commercial need. Effort is necessarily concentrated on selected opportunities, ideally on opportunities where the company's inherent capability provides some edge, some genuine competitive advantage.

Successive focusing, of which product screening is a minor example, is designed to make manageable any task which at first sight seems too large and complex even to be comprehended; and involves reducing the field of attention by stages, reiterating earlier stages when sufficient information has been gathered to make their content more significant.

In a limited sense, e.g. as applied to product screening, successive focusing means doing an increasing amount of work on a diminishing number of alternatives.

Successive Focusing

In dynamic planning a company is considered to be in constant interaction with its environment, evolving through adaptation, while maintaining an essentially continuous identity. In this context, successive focusing must therefore offer a procedure through which a company may be reconciled with its environment progressively. An abbreviated version of the process, shown as a dialogue between a company and its environment, appears in Fig. 6.1.

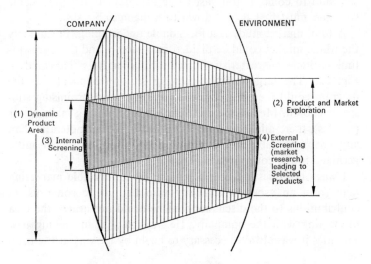

COMPANY   ENVIRONMENT

(1) Dynamic Product Area

(2) Product and Market Exploration

(3) Internal Screening

(4) External Screening (market research) leading to Selected Products

Fig. 6.1. Simplified form of successive focusing shown diagrammatically as a dialogue between a company and its environment.

A dynamic product area is first defined, using methods described in Chapter 5, as part of the company's identity.

Within the dynamic area a market exploration is conducted to identify emerging product needs (also usually a product search to ascertain in what degree these needs are already being met). Returning to the company, we screen the product opportunities discovered (often several hundred), with reference to the company's potential for exploiting them; and finally carry out depth surveys of the markets for the few remaining opportunities, hopefully selecting the one or two which show the greatest promise.

Starting with the Company

The company's resources and experience, as embodied in the dynamic product area, are considered first, since it is these assets that distinguish it from every other company and give it whatever competitive advantage it may have. Also the whole market, present and to come, is too vast to be explored in any practicable way and must first be cut down to a manageable size.

A total market study is a formidable undertaking. Presumably the whole market could be divided into sectors and their growth-times-volume characteristics calculated as naïvely indicated in Fig. 6.2. The largest fastest-growing sector (chemicals) in the diagram could then be subdivided and the most promising subsector chosen. Meanwhile, in the most unpromising main sector (textiles), there might be a subsector of far greater potential than any chemical subsector, containing opportunities much more germane to the company's experience.

I was once questioned at a seminar by a very able marketing man from an asbestos company who had made some useful contributions to the discussion, but he could not accept the idea of starting with the company. He insisted that in seeking new activities it was always necessary to begin by looking at the market.

He said that in his company, for example, it was recognized that asbestos was sometimes a substitute for concrete and sometimes for steel. They therefore kept their eyes open for applications in the environment or market where asbestos could be used in place of these materials competitively, as in channel, pipes, roofing, etc. As soon as he had made his point, he saw the answer as quickly as I did myself.

Subconsciously at least, he was assuming a corporate identity based on the exploitation of asbestos. I noted that it was a perfectly acceptable and sound approach; all I would suggest was that conscious attention be given to the definition of identity, which should be carefully structured and clearly understood, so that in the end it did not represent a limitation.

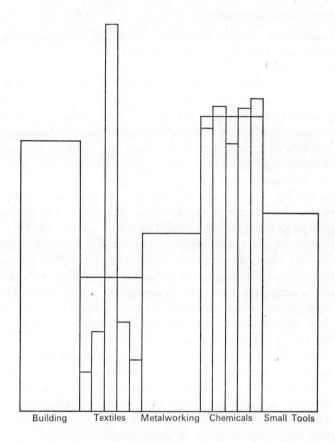

Building   Textiles   Metalworking   Chemicals   Small Tools

FIG. 6.2. Comparison of volume–growth values within and between industrial sectors. It is never practical to conduct an exploration over the complete market panorama; also, successive subdivision can be seriously misleading in that important opportunities may be overlooked. Vertical scale represents volume (£) times rate of growth, but the quantities do not correspond to any real situation. Thus if chemicals is selected for further study as the most promising sector, we may miss a first-class prospect suited to a company's potential in what at first sight appears to be the most unpromising sector, namely textiles.

Stepping-stone Development

Identity is frequently taken for granted and plays an implicit rather than an explicit part in company planning. The result is often a stepping-stone development, where the company jumps to the nearest stone, then to another and so on. If purpose has not been properly defined, it is a matter of luck whether the sequence of neighbouring stones leads to the opposite bank or to the bank from which the company started, or leaves them stranded in the middle. If their instincts are good, their evaluation procedures sound and half an eye is cocked to see where they are going, each step may represent a profitable move.

A leading European company, was established to supply products based on maize, and developed their business by examining the properties of this material. Later, they set out to adapt the properties to the requirements of the market. For some time, maize had been sold simply for animal feeds and the company then wondered if it could be converted into food for human beings. Unfortunately, the taste was unattractive, so they decided to isolate the starch and also made oil as a byproduct, sold in bulk to manufacturers of margarine. It was viscous and used for giving body to other products.

When next the company required new products they found they could hydrolize the starch with acids to produce sugar syrups of low viscosity, which could be crystallized into dextrose, thereby introducing a whole new range of applications. Hydrolysis by enzymes subsequently gave an improved yield and purer products, further extending the circle of consumers.

At this point, the company realized that they had an even more versatile raw material of high purity and considered selling it as a feed stock for the chemical industry since corn could be grown easily and in quantity. A byproduct used in the production of caramel, dextrose aldehyde, could be hydrogenized to form alcohol.

At the same time, starch itself had many qualities and was particularly suitable for adhesive and similar applications. It helped in binding together paper fibres and in sizing the surface to provide better printability. It could also be used for finishing fabrics and textiles and as a binder for foundry sand.

As time went by, the requirements of industry grew more and more sophisticated and starch-based materials were not always good enough. The main problem lay in modifying the starch, say by oxidizing and cross-linking, but the results were sometimes less than adequate.

By this time the company had built up a substantial market, in particular for adhesives, which, as much as access to the original material, represented a differentiated asset. They therefore switched to synthetics or a combination of products, wherever necessary, to retain their hold on these markets. Instead of supplying simply maize-based adhesives, for example, they supplied adhesives of any kind or origin. It was a successful policy, but the extent to which companies can engage in stepping-stone development will often depend on their size and overall resources.

In fact, each stage in a company's development must have a starting point within the company, if only in the whim of a chairman or managing director. It is better, however, to have a well-considered starting point, and there could be no more fundamental basis than corporate identity. I cannot believe that any real company, seeking new activities, could assimilate with equal facility the casting of prestressed concrete beams and the manufacture of electric-shaver motors or plastic toys.

Many companies will claim that they can make anything, given a first-class market opportunity, by acquiring the people and resources they would need. In practice, an alien product can always be introduced more quickly and economically by a company already more suitably equipped.

Finally, the market is universal, the company unique. And the planner is planning for a particular company, not some infinitely versatile concern. He is stuck with it. We should have little patience with a man who, offered the job of business planning in a company replied "If I'm to be responsible for planning, I would rather work for GKN or Standard Oil." He would again be like the Irishman who, wherever he was going, preferred to start from somewhere else.

Matching Capability with Needs

Definition of identity is only the first step in the procedure. At the same time, successive focusing will be of little help unless the process can be broken into tasks. To look at a company, scan the market and then conceive the ideal product calls for a talent that few of us possess. Something more systematic, more practical is wanted.

In the procedure I have found convenient in practice, after assessment of the company, the environment is explored for opportunities (products, market needs and acquisition prospects), which are then evaluated in groups, first with reference to the company and then to its environment through depth research. On the basis of information gathered, a course of action is finally decided.

The working framework may be shown as a succession of stages, summarized in Fig. 6.3, where a single study is involved, but it may also be regarded as a repeating cycle (cyclic programming) where a company is large enough to have a separate planning function. The stages are:

(1) *Pilot Review*, in which a tentative role would be defined, largely in terms of dynamic product areas, plus the intention of the study, terms of reference and provisional criteria for selecting new activities.

(2) *Search*, in which an intensive systematic worldwide search would be conducted to discover products already or on the point of being marketed, together with patented ideas, emerging technology and other information pertaining to the satisfaction of discovered needs, or opportunities for licensing, etc.

(3) *Exploration*, in which markets are explored in order to identify emerging market needs consistent with the com-

pany's role and immediate requirements as agreed in the Review.

(4) *Audit*, in which companies are considered with a view to

Fig. 6.3. Table showing stages for a single product-planning study summarizing the action to be taken in sequence or parallel. The question of acquisition is considered in Chapter 10.

Stage	Description
1. Pilot Study (Review or Planning)	Define say 10 functional dynamic areas, consistent with the company's resources and experience, embracing but not limited to their existing business, plus basic screening criteria
2. Search	Conduct a carefully defined and systematic world-wide search within the agreed dynamic areas for self-contained proprietary product opportunities which might be introduced under licence or some other acceptable manufacturing and sales agreement
3. Exploration	Explore corresponding sectors of the market in order to identify emerging or unsatisfied requirements and to check the probable demand for products discovered; also ascertain possible parallel requirements of present customers and diversification lines successfully adopted by competitors, at home and overseas
4. Acquisition (Audit)	Investigate prospects for acquiring companies or agencies, serving to extend or complement the company's product range, or to provide additional manufacturing or marketing resources necessary to exploit the products recommended
5. Evaluation	Evaluate the products brought to light, technically and commercially, and particularly with reference to competitive activity, through a procedure ranging from coarse screening to market research in depth
6. Action	Recommend a positive course of action and introduce proposed associates, with a detailed programme for implementation, showing cash flows and prospects for further innovation; also advising generally on the negotiation of agreements and indicating possible lines of longer-term development; resolve identity

acquisition as sources of additional facilities, e.g. an importing agency as a ready made sales force.

(5) *Evaluation*, in which products, markets and facilities are assessed in groups (comparative appraisal) in order to establish the most promising combination, as the basis for an integrated programme of development.

(6) *Action*, in which the information assembled is reviewed and a decision taken to proceed, withdraw or undertake a deeper study, and any negotiations are put in hand; also, the tentative dynamic areas are screened, in terms of the opportunities uncovered, to give a more definitive identity.

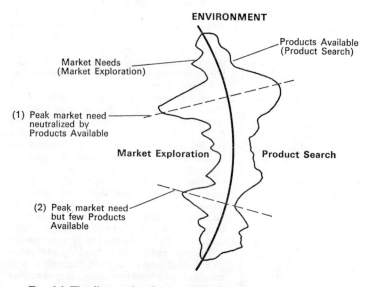

FIG. 6.4. The diagram is, of course, only illustrative and there could be no continuity of function as the two irregular lines might suggest.

It will be noted that stages (2), (3) and (4) are concerned exclusively with the environment and provide the opportunities for subsequent evaluation. The relationship between Search and Exploration is illustrated in Fig. 6.4, which shows the environment side of the successive focusing diagram enlarged, with profiles of emerging market needs on the inside and products currently available on the outside. A peak emerging need (say, where the advent of natural gas created a requirement for associated plant) is cancelled out by an opposing peak in product availability. Clearly, where there is a peak need and few products available to meet it, an important opportunity exists.

A typical working method is shown schematically in Fig. 6.5 and as a tabulated summary in Fig. 6.6 (at end of chapter). I propose to discuss each stage in some detail.

1. Pilot Review

The first stage of a product planning exercise is sometimes treated as a pilot study and is variously known as review, analysis or simply planning. It would not, of course, be put in hand until the company had ascertained that its existing products were being marketed to maximum advantage.

The stage comprises a detailed examination of the company's resources and present market environment in order to draw up a characteristic table of products, processes and outlets, as illustrated in the previous chapter. Using this table as a basis, several dynamic areas, or areas of search, are defined, and a brief literature search is carried out to determine growth sectors within these areas.

Also during this stage, tentative check lists and selection criteria are prepared for assessing individual products, prospective licensors and companies or agencies for possible acquisition or association. Figure 6.7 (end of chapter) is a checklist used by my own company for a preliminary review of a company's purpose in embarking on a product search, with other requirements and criteria. Brief supporting information is obtained using the checklist in Fig. 6.8 (end of chapter).

Typical aims in undertaking studies of this kind are enumerated in Fig. 6.9 (end of chapter) and lists of product criteria for different fields of engineering appear in Fig. 6.10 (end of chapter).

Also during the initial stage, it is usual to check whether

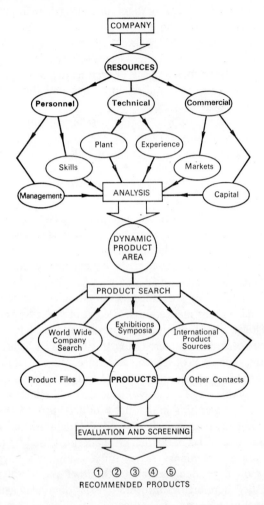

Fig. 6.5. A systematic procedure may be used for conducting an intensive worldwide product search. (A. E. Ansell, formerly of Proplan.) As illustrated, the process applies to a consulting study. Within a company internal research and development may partially replace the product search.

existing products are being fully and effectively exploited, not only in the company's traditional markets, but in potential markets which have not yet been explored.

2. Search

Also within the dynamic product areas a search is conducted in order to assemble a substantial list of product opportunities, perhaps several hundred in all, so that the probability of including a few first-class items is very high. At the same time, the allocation of internal research expenditure can be more effectively planned if it is known what other companies throughout the world have introduced or are currently developing. There is little point in spending half a million pounds on developing an improved carburettor if in Japan or Germany the last successful tests have been completed on an engine which does not need a carburettor.

Over the years it is possible to build up a comprehensive register of "product sources", listing engineers, consultants, patent and licence agencies, research foundations, development bodies and government establishments throughout the world who are prepared to forward product information. Such data can then be recorded on punched cards.

Another useful device is to assemble a library of exhibition catalogues, providing an up-to-date, reliable (with entries checked by the companies themselves) and readily accessible source of company names, and data classified by any number of product lattices. During a search it is necessary to make direct approaches to manufacturers, regularly attend conferences and exhibitions, and constantly review published information, economic data, import statistics and so on.

A thorough search of this kind goes a long way towards ensuring that no important opportunity is overlooked and that any product taken up is not superseded shortly afterwards. In one case a client was seeking details of dishwashers and had discovered a total of forty different models; a subsequent intensive search revealed forty designs in Italy alone.

On another occasion we believed that a client could complete his range of vacuum pumps at the less sophisticated end of the scale by introducing a water-ring pump. We suggested that a licence search might usefully be carried out, but were told that a competitor had recently acquired a licence in this field from the leading continental manufacturer. Nevertheless, we made some brief inquiries and discovered that both Siemens-Schuckertwerke in Germany and Burckhardt in Switzerland were both willing to license recently developed and thoroughly competitive pumps of this kind.

To take up a licence, perhaps as the result of a casual contact, without examining the available alternatives, may be very hazardous. I often wonder how many licence agreements are the consequence of chance encounters by chief executives in aeroplanes.

During the search, information is also gathered on the performance of products in their markets of origin.

3. Exploration

The purpose of a market exploration is to identify emerging or unsatisfied requirements within the product areas. In the case of "materials separation", for example, discussions might be held with buyers and chief engineers of mineral processing concerns, oil and chemical companies, plant contractors for the food industry and other likely users of separation plant, to ascertain what equipment is on long delivery; what features of present equipment are unsatisfactory or what new features could usefully be introduced; and what problems in separation are not adequately solved by any equipment currently available. It will also be important to record the properties of material already being processed or materials which may be processed in the future.

It is emphasized that in making such inquiries the interviewer may not know what precisely he is looking for and must therefore be sufficiently informed to recognize the significance of any unexpected comments he may hear. At the same time he should realize that informants will only be willing to spend time with him if the discussion is a genuine exchange of ideas and the interviewer himself can make a useful contribution.

I remember once when I was seeking to establish the demand for glandless pumps conducting an interview with a representative of Unilever. He said that he could give me little encouragement, but if I came across a satisfactory pump for handling abrasive materials in suspension, perhaps I would let him know. By chance my next interview was with a company who told me they had just developed such a pump and I was able to suggest they contact Unilever.

An exploration is not to be confused with a market survey, which is usually concerned with a single product or product group. The subject of a survey is known at the beginning; the object of an exploration is not.

4. Audit or Acquisition

Often the introduction of new products creates problems of manufacturing or sales capacity. Alternatively, the product may be taken up by acquisition of a company. A search for manufacturing concerns or selling agencies may therefore be carried out, usually within the same country as the company seeking to expand, but not invariably.

Sometimes a company may be acquired to increase the viability of an industrial group by vertical or horizontal integration or as a source of manufacture at some unspecified later date when production can be transferred to the parent company's facilities and the residual premises disposed of by resale.

In a product planning study, however, the purpose is usually to supplement existing sales or manufacturing resources.

Company searches are normally product oriented, since companies are prepared to publicize their products, but it is much more difficult to obtain financial information, particularly where the company is privately owned. Applying the principle of successive focusing, the first task in reducing the field is to identify companies making products of the right general character. The task of investigating a finite number of companies, selected in this way, is, of course, less formidable than covering the whole of industry.

5. Evaluation

All products, product ideas and companies are evaluated, using a full screening process, developed during the search and exploration stages from the checklist prepared in the planning stage. Market checks are carried out and potential competition is identified.

Generally, products are screened in groups, since comparative evaluation of similar products is not only economical, particularly where large numbers of products are involved, but also tends to be more reliable than assessment of a single product in isolation. It is clearly less costly in time to make inquiries about half a dozen products during a tour of potential customers in Birmingham, Sheffield, Glasgow and Manchester, than to conduct a series of market surveys for each product in turn, repeating the tour of customers.

6. Action

On completion of the cycle, the information assembled and analysed during the study should make a decision to proceed relatively easy. But implementation may be far more difficult. New products cut across familiar procedures, and executives, already overloaded, may regard a departure from established routine as the last straw that will break their backs.

If the product is to be launched effectively, someone with sufficient authority to cut through traditional practice must be charged with its success, usually reporting directly to the chief executive (see Chapter 11, Organizing for Innovation).

Any negotiations can then be initiated, royalties and down-payments agreed, and a programme prepared. Decisions are required on whether sales and manufacture are to be handled by existing organizations or whether the new activity should be isolated with separate costing and overhead structure. The project manager must participate in resolving these issues and share responsibility for the decisions taken.

Visual Aid

The six stages provide the core of any product study and the acquisition, evaluation and action or implementation stages are treated in greater details in later chapters. Meanwhile it may be useful to show a simplified version of the product-search process in schematic form. The diagram, reproduced in Fig. 6.5, was devised by my former Proplan colleague, Tony Ansell, and shows the analysis (review), search and evaluation (screening) stages.

It is, of course, essential to ensure that the aims and procedures of a study are clearly understood by all concerned. It is convenient to lay out an initial statement for a project of this kind under the following headings:

(1) Intention and summary (see Fig. 6.9).
(2) Appreciation (see Fig. 6.11).
(3) Criteria (see Fig. 6.10).
(4) Terms of reference (see Fig. 6.3).
(5) Programme and duration (see Chapter 10).

The appreciation is, of course, an elaboration of the company's intention, and typical paragraphs taken from statements for a considerable variety of companies are itemized in Fig. 6.11.

FIG. 6.6. Table showing a product planning study (as performed by a service company) is normally conducted in six stages, corresponding broadly with the summary in Fig. 6.3. Stages may overlap to some extent and are often modified in consultation during the progress of the work. As will be evident, the object is to carry out a blanket search in areas broadly related to the company's interest to ensure that at least a few sound opportunities are brought to light, and it would not be until the conclusion of the study, when the fruitfulness of particular dynamic areas are known, that a definitive corporate identity, concentrating on selected areas, would be adopted.

WORKING METHOD

1 Planning

1.1 The first task is to examine the company's facilities, skills, technical experience, special knowledge of senior executives, customer contacts, access to associated resources (including the know-how of existing licensors and other members of a group) and constraints, in order to draw up a characteristic table summarizing the company's assets and potential.

1.2 Review the activities of companies supplying similar products, serving similar markets or employing similar technology, to uncover any successful diversification programmes; also consider developments envisaged by competitors.

1.3 List typical self-contained proprietary products of appropriate character by reference to the technical and trade Press to help in establishing the scope of the inquiry; and collect information on technical developments pertaining to the company's business.

1.4 In the light of data gathered so far, a preliminary market exploration is conducted to establish possible areas of opportunity for further search and study, including new applications of existing products and other items selling to existing markets.

1.5 In consultation, perhaps ten dynamic areas would be selected, half-related in some way to the company's present lines, the others defined more generally in terms of their resources and experience; at the same time, comprehensive screening criteria would be established for evaluating potential new activities within the ten dynamic areas.

2 Search

2.1 An intensive worldwide search would be conducted within the agreed search categories in order to assemble a substantial list of products which (a) are available for manufacture under licence, long-term contract, joint company or other formal agreement and would appear to have sales potential in the United Kingdom market, (b) might be taken up through acquisition of an existing company either in Britain or abroad, or (c) could be independently developed.

2.2 In conducting the search, details would be gathered: through associates in United States, Japan, the major European countries and elsewhere; by reference to a register of product sources, which lists contacts with engineers, consultants, licence and patent agents, research foundations, government laboratories and development establishments throughout the world; by attendance at conferences and exhibitions; by scanning published information; and by direct approaches to relevant concerns.

2.3 The object in performing an intensive search of this kind would be to discover a large number of products, so that (a) no important opportunity is overlooked; (b) any product taken up is not on the point of being superseded; and (c) the probability of selecting several first-class products is high.

2.4 Approaches would be made to companies whose products are considered to be worth consideration in order to discover if they would be available to a British concern.

2.5 Any product brought to light outside the area of search but considered interesting would be drawn to the company's attention.

3 *Exploration*

3.1 During and following the search, a market exploration would be carried out in order to identify emerging or unsatisfied requirements in customer industries related to the areas of search. To save time, exploration is begun while the search is in progress, since during the search there are inevitably delays while awaiting reactions from potential licensors.

3.2 The work would be conducted largely by personal interview and would comprise a detailed elaboration of the study started in the first or planning stage.

3.3 The performance of products in their markets of origin would also be established, with spot checks of corresponding markets in the United Kingdom. Particular attention would be given to (a) the ability and willingness of potential licensors to service the licensed products with continuing development and applications data; (b) the nature and strength of competition; and (c) the kinds of customer involved.

3.4 On the basis of this information the market factors in the screening process would be defined and weighted.

4 *Acquisition*

4.1 In parallel with the exploration, inquiries would be carried out in order to identify companies active in fields corresponding to the search categories.

4.2 These inquiries would be product or service oriented, since such information is readily available even in the case of private companies, whereas financial and operating data or details of technical facilities, customers, etc., are likely to be limited.

4.3 Emphasis would be on smaller (usually private) companies with specific products or manufacturing facilities related to the inquiring company's own emerging pattern of development, including well-established sales agencies.

4.4 A coarse screening would be carried out to select those companies worth approaching with a view to acquisition or association.

4.5 Details would be assembled through visits and interviews and analysed in preparation for the evaluation stage.

5 *Evaluation*

5.1 All products and possible associates would be classified in groups and evaluated using the screening process developed in the planning and exploration stages.

5.2 Reference would be made to a standard check list of screening factors (approximately 80) to ensure that no significant consideration has been overlooked.

5.3 Products are screened in groups since it is more economical to do so and because comparative evaluation tends to be more reliable and objective than assessment of a product in isolation.

5.4 Where uncertainties arise or information is still inadequate to form a judgement, further inquiries would be conducted in the field or by reference to the company.

5.5 Each product group would be the subject of a report, containing details of products and companies together with an appropriate technical and commercial appreciation.

6 *Action*

6.1 In the last stage direct approaches would be made to the companies recommended as prospective licensors or associates and proposals put forward on the negotiation of licence terms and implementation.

6.2 The whole course of the work would be summarized in a final report, with positive recommendations for immediate action, marketing and subsequent development.

Fig. 6.7. Tabular checklist to assist in establishing the basic aims and criteria for a product planning study. Such a check list is seldom used as a questionnaire, but as a basis for discussion.

SEARCH CRITERIA

Answers to as many of the following questions as possible would be appreciated:

1. What is your company's purpose in seeking new products:
   (a) To occupy existing facilities and personnel?
   (b) To reduce dependence on a limited range of markets, component manufacture or subcontracting?
   (c) To permit series production with greater standardization, as a balance for other products required in a great variety of type and sizes?
   (d) To make and sell a proprietary product, with better profit margins?
   (e) To establish a measure of vertical integration, retaining a greater proportion of overall profit within the company?
   (f) To introduce a supplementary source of turnover and meet a target for expansion?
   (g) To secure a foothold in markets with a high rate of growth?
   (h) Some combination of these, or some entirely different reason?
2. How much additional turnover does your company require from a new product and what minimum return on capital?
3. What total investment would be considered acceptable, given the return were adequate.
4 What is your company's present annual turnover approximately?

5. How is annual sales value currently broken down among:
   materials and bought-in items
   direct labour
   overheads
   profit?
   What are your company's current operating ratios?
6. Would you be prepared to set up entirely new facilities, or would you wish to assimilate a new product within your present manufacturing and sales framework?
7. Could you devote any design and development effort to the introduction of a new product?
8. Would you expect to recruit new sales staff?
9. How soon would you wish to launch the new product?
10. Can you define, in general terms, the technological experience of your company, e.g. in mechanisms, gas dynamics, process design, heat transfer, hydraulics, electronics, systems, etc.?
11. What materials are machined, formed or otherwise processed in your shops?
12. What size and weight limits should a new product fall within: say an envelope one-foot cube, and weighing not more than 100 lb? (crane-lift?)
13. Roughly, what should be the cost per unit?
14. How many items per batch or series? Annual production?
15. What is the minimum acceptable percentage added value?
    What is the range of sales price per pound or ton?
16. What is the normal sales life of your existing products?
17. What markets do your company serve at present?
    What are your channels of sale?
18. Would you wish to export? To what countries?
    Corresponding to what proportion of your turnover?
19. Are your existing products subject to a seasonal or other cycle of demand?
20. Have you any reservations about licensing, joint-company agreements or company acquisition?

Fig. 6.8. Table showing detailed checklist of company information. Full information is seldom obtainable or necessary, but particular items may be important in any given situation.

COMPANY DATA SUMMARY

Information on companies (potential clients, prospective licensors, etc.) is reviewed under the following headings:

1. *Identity*
   1.1. Name and address (tel.)
   1.2. Managing director
   1.3. Contacts and dates
   1.4. Ownership and associates
   1.5. Shareholding
   1.6. Competitors
   1.7. Literature and sales promotion
   1.8. Nature of business and history

2. *Management*
2.1. Composition of board
2.2. Composition of executive corps
2.3. Prior experience
2.4. Organigram
2.5. Responsibilities

3. *Facilities and Skills*
3.1. Site and factory area
3.2. Employees, subdivided
3.3. Production facilities, crane lift
3.4. Machine schedule: capacity, age, condition
3.5. Shop layout and flow plan
3.6. Tolerances and inspection
3.7. Design facilities, personnel
3.8. Development facilities, research
3.9. Sales organization, staff

4. *Financial Background*
4.1. Capital: authorized, issued, employed
4.2. Assets: fixed, current
4.3. Indebtedness
4.4. Turnover and margins
4.5. Direct labour: materials: overheads
4.6. Deliveries and stock position
4.7. Cost accounting practices
4.8. Depreciation practices
4.9. Analysis of balance sheet

5. *Business Ratios*
5.1. Margin on sales
5.2. Net income on sales
5.3. Sales on net worth
5.4. Net income on net worth
5.5. Receivables on sales
5.6. Inventory on sales
5.7. Inventory turnover (each line)
5.8. Current ratio
5.9. Sales to working capital

6. *Labour*
6.1. Composition of work force
6.2. Union affiliation
6.3. Labour relations
6.4. Labour practices
6.5. Restrictive practices
6.6. Hourly rates
6.7. Method of payment
6.8. Lost time record

6.9. Last (first) in first out?

7. *Contract Practices*
7.1. Duration, size, type, number
    cost plus FS
    cost plus per cent
    cost plus bonus
    penalties
    escalated fixed price
    fixed price
7.2. Collection period
7.3. Default rate

8. *Products*
8.1. Designations: past and present
8.2. Description, specs, drawings
8.3. Functions, applications, users
8.4. Special features, advantages
8.5. Age, development status
8.6. Manufacturing requirements
8.7. Components and bought-in items

9. *Commercial and Marketing*
9.1. Markets, subdivided
9.2. Outlets, channels of sale
9.3. Price structure, discounts
9.4. Turnover per product
9.5. Turnover per salesman
9.6. Dealers: number
    place
    location
    size of staff
    other lines
    inventory
9.7. Salesmen: number
    training
    salary and commission
    territory
    field
9.8. Service: facilities and staff
9.9. Export performance

10. *International*
10.1. Representation
10.2. Associations
10.3. Competition
10.4. Licences granted
10.5. Licences taken up
10.6. General experience of licensing
10.7. Patents, numbers, dates, where?

FIG. 6.9. Table showing typical aims of a product planning study.

PRODUCT SEARCH OBJECTIVES

A company may wish to embark on a programme of product development or controlled diversification for many reasons, for example to:
1. Meet a target for expansion, without prejudice to their existing business, by introducing complementary new activities (The turnover or profit needed from supplementary lines may be determined by what is known as "gap analysis," where the "gap," shown graphically, is the difference between the rate of growth expected from existing products and the rate of growth desired.)

2. Offset any decline in turnover or profit, which may occur through innovation, market saturation or a change in operating practice.
3. Strengthen and extend their product range so as to present a broad and complete front to the market, and increase the number of items selling in parallel with present lines, improving their marketing efficiency.
4. Reduce their dependence on military, aircraft or marine work, with their attendant fluctuations; on customers with massive buying power such as the motor industry or a nationalized concern; or a single vulnerable activity exposed to heavy competition; or on jobbing, subcontracting, or the manufacture of specials or components in a great variety of types and sizes, with poor market control and profit margins.
5. Make profitable use of surplus manufacturing capacity and personnel released by rationalization, better production methods or a decline in the company's traditional markets, and improve their viability by economies of scale and integration.
6. Exploit their accumulated technical experience and provide stimulating work for a good development team, so keeping it intact.
7. Increase their total sales within a geographically limited market through a greater but sensibly related variety of products based on indigenous materials.
8. Provide a firm base for continued development and growth by extending the company's foothold in expanding markets, with the accretion of other compatible products in the longer term, and utilize their capital resources at least as profitably as if invested elsewhere.

Fig. 6.10. Examples of preliminary selection criteria for aero-electronics, heavy-engineering, process-engineering and instrumentation companies. Such criteria are assembled on commencement of a study, sometimes as basic terms of reference. Keyword tables are used to prompt ideas, and it is emphasized that the cases shown are fictional combinations from several sources, with possible anomalies.

PRELIMINARY SELECTION CRITERIA

CRITERIA (AERO-ELECTRONICS)

To ensure that the project is started on the right lines, the following tentative criteria are submitted for consideration. Any product put forward should ideally:
1. Fall in the fields of light current and electronics, precision mechanisms or possibly engineered plastics.
2. Sell as a complete product or assembly, possibly through agencies, direct to users or plant contractors, preferably in a standard range of types and sizes.
3. Yield turnover in the region of £250,000 per annum within 2 or 3 years.
4. Involve minimum investment, though limited capital resources would be available for a first-class proposition, and make an adequate contribution to overheads.

5. Be novel in concept, of advanced design or cheaper to produce than present alternatives; or offer some other marked competitive advantage.

6. Require little or no development and be ready for marketing within 18 months.

7. Exploit, though not necessarily be restricted by, the division's product and design experience as in:

light current	electronics	instrumentation
transducers	pneumatics	gauges
radio frequencies	hydraulics	probes
thermocouples	control	measurement of:
thermistors	modules	extension
potentiometry	micrologic	compression
remote indication	coding	deflection
synchronization	sensing	strain
miniaturization	detection	creep
digital techniques	amplification	position
analogue conversion	calibration	direction
analogue computers	circuitry	inclination
network analysis	wiring	temperature
precision mechanisms	piping	potential
inertial guidance	panels	time
gas bearings	cubicles	frequency
gyro-devices	tanks	reliability
synchro-devices	vessels	sensitivity
servo-devices	containers	speed
heat transfer	viscosity	lightness
systems design	corrosion	embedment

8. Employ to some extent their knowledge of materials, for example:

copper	silicone rubber
copper alloys	glass fibre
Constantan	polyester resins
Chromel–alumel	solid-wall plastics
Thermocoax	honeycomb plastics
stainless steel	coated metals

9. Utilize the division's production facilities and skills, particularly in electronics assembly, precision machining and fitting, circuitry and wiring, fine soldering and welding, printed and potted circuits, encapsulation and vacuum techniques.

10. Comprise in general small items (inches in overall dimensions rather than feet), though complete assemblies up to 20 ft across can be accommodated.

11. Be suitable for manufacture in batch sizes up to a hundred off, rather than thousands, with a substantial added value.

12. Permit some stock accumulation, to allow for fluctuations in other work.

13. Have an average unit cost of approximately £250, ranging from perhaps £50 to £1000, with complete projects in the region of £10,000, or large single orders of £40,000 (600 items).

14. Sell in a limited number of expanding markets, possibly including:

research	process control
building	civil engineering
mining	machine tools
gas	water distribution
nuclear	electricity supply

15. Not create insuperable marketing problems or involve excessive promotional expenditure.
16. Afford opportunities for export, with the prospect that overseas sales may eventually be twice home sales in value.
17. Be available for manufacture under licence or other acceptable agreement, with an exclusive franchise embracing a substantial territory, including the United Kingdom.
18. Have already proved successful in the market of origin but be new to the markets covered by the franchise.

CRITERIA (HEAVY ENGINEERING)

Any product, plant or process put forward for consideration by the company should ideally:

1. Comprise a complex mechanical assembly, self-contained system or coherent group, involving medium to heavy precision engineering, and be complementary to the company's existing business.
2. Sell as a finished unit, assembly or installation, preferably direct to users, possibly tailor-made to their requirements.
3. Contribute additional turnover exceeding £500,000 per annum, preferably within 18 months, and be capable with other complementary products of generating new business in the region of £4 million per annum in the longer term.
4. Involve minimum investment in additional fixed assets and utilize available liquid capital more profitably than if it were invested elsewhere, maintaining the company's present return on capital of at least 15 per cent.
5. Be novel in concept, of advanced design, or cheaper to produce than present alternatives; or offer some other marked competitive advantage.
6. Constitute a fully developed product (certainly not a prototype) and be ready for marketing within 12 months, though some design effort would be available for subsequent expansion or improvement of the range.
7. Utilise as far as possible the production skills of Tyneside Engineering and Warren Foundry, and also the company's machinery and factory space, with resources for:

milling	planing	sheet copper work
turning	platework	moulding
boring	flamecutting	coremaking
drilling	levelling	melting
grinding	welding	casting

gearcutting	brazing	shot blasting
fitting	tube bending	finishing
assembly	pipe coiling	quality control

with particular emphasis on heavy machining, jig milling and boring, and non-ferrous centrifugal casting.

8. Employ some materials with which the company is familiar, such as:

mild steel	gunmetal	copper alloys
stainless steel	aluminium	aluminium alloys
alloy steels	white metal	nickel alloys
cast steel	cast iron	wood and plastics

though preferably excluding gunmetal and other copper-based alloys, but including the welding of aluminium.

9. Exploit, though not be restricted by, the company's product and design experience, as in:

prime movers	metallurgy	heat transfer
propulsion	bearings	steam cycles
mechanisms	shafting	steam balance
reciprocation	transmissions	thermal economy
rotation	gearing	evaporation
automatic control	glands	reheating
space conservation	valves	combustion
package plant	lubrication	fluid dynamics

10. Have a substantial added value, with a design and direct labour content exceeding 20 per cent, say in accordance with the following breakdown of sales value:

Materials	40 per cent
Direct labour	15 per cent
Overheads	25 per cent
Profit	20 per cent

giving an added value well in excess of 100 per cent on materials.

11. Permit some batch production (five to ten units per batch), though variations on a theme would be acceptable.

12. Weigh at least three tons finished and installed, but embody no single prefabricated component weighing more than 20 tons, and fit within an envelope 25 ft cube.

13. Cost at least £15,000 per installation and preferably between £40,000 and £50,000, though a cost of £5,000 per unit would be acceptable if the added value were exceptionally high.

14. Sell in several expanding markets outside the boiler industry, possibly including some with which the company already have connections, for example:

power	paper	mineral processing
chemicals	textiles	oil industry
fertilizers	paint	breweries, distilleries
metallurgical	construction	heating contractors
steelworks	architects	civil engineering

15. Not create insuperable marketing or stock control problems, or involve excessive promotional expenditure; also not be subject to trade cycles, though a limited fluctuation out of phase with boiler work might be acceptable.

16. Afford opportunities for export, especially to the Continent of Europe, Australia, South America, Africa and the Far East.

17. Be available for manufacture under licence or other acceptable agreement, with an exclusive franchise embracing the United Kingdom and at least one other substantial territory, such as the British Commonwealth, the American Continent or the Continent of Europe.

18. Present no legal difficulties or conflict of interest, particularly with other members of the group, and not involve excessive dependence on deliveries by subcontractors.

19. Have already proved successful in the market of origin, but be new to markets for which the franchise is available.

20. Provide scope for sustained sales over at least five years, with good prospects for development and the introduction of complementary products.

CRITERIA (PROCESS INDUSTRY)

Any product put forward for consideration should ideally:

1. Fall broadly within the company's area of operation, say in the continuous processing of thin, preferably plastics or fibrous, sheet or strip material, possibly with subsequent treatment or conversion.

2. Contribute turnover not less than £500,000 per annum, with the possibility of building up to four times this value within 10 years.

3. Involve a capital investment not greater than £2 million, providing that the eventual return is maintained at 15 per cent or more.

4. Have a high value-to-volume ratio, selling at prices exceeding £300 per ton, with added value in the range 50 to 60 per cent.

5. Utilize the company's management and technical resources, their present staff and, if possible, their existing manufacturing facilities.

6. Exploit, though not be restricted by, the company's technical experience, for example in the fields of:

chemistry	film and sheet	polyester
physics	foamed plastics	polyethylene
mechanics	fibres	polypropylene
electronics	cellulose	polyurethane
plastics	synthetics	resins
delicate webs	gelatine	epoxies
hydrodynamics	wire gauze	phenolics
suspensions	bonding	silicones
dispersions	decoration	nylon
fluid systems	coatings	rayon
alkali solutions	textiles	natural fibres

7. Be advanced in concept, either through substituting more advanced plastics for materials at present used, or in terms of an entirely novel formulation; or offer some other marked competitive advantage.

8. Employ at least some aspects of the company's manufacturing know-how and equipment, represented by:

feeding	process plant	distillation
sorting	continuous production	chromatography
cutting	instrumentation	automatic counting
digestion	pilot projects	dosing and measuring
beating	pressure vessels	quality control
washing	water treatment	wax engraving
bleaching	effluent disposal	plaster casting
straining	recycling/recovery	die making
moulding	power generation	electrodeposition
filtration	steam raising	embossing
sizing	precise registration	presswork
impregnation	sheet trimming	machining
drying	automatic feeding	fabrication
calendering	sequential control	transportation

9. Call for production quantities of not less than 500 tons per annum (£20,000) for any one converted product, though batches of 20 tons would be acceptable.

10. Sell in several expanding markets, with ample scope for sales in the United Kingdom and good opportunities for export, particularly to countries where the company are already well known, as in:

India	African Continent	Indonesia
Pakistan	South America	Australia
Thailand	Middle East	Commonwealth
Burma	South East Asia	Scandinavia

11. Not create insuperable development, production-planning, stock-control, marketing or other assimilation problems, though the company would be ready to embark on technical development, take up licences, acquire facilities and build up or buy a sales force, were the opportunity sufficiently promising.

12. Provide some turnover at an early date, either through ancillary production, provision of services or handling, but be ready for large-scale introduction within two years.

13. Present no legal difficulties or conflict of interest, particularly with present customers, other members of the Synthesis group, or companies engaged in large-volume production of medium or low priced synthetics.

14. Permit sustained sales over at least ten years, with good prospects for development and growth, and the introduction of complementary products.

CRITERIA (INSTRUMENTATION)
To meet the company's immediate requirements, any product selected should ideally:

1. Fall broadly in the field of instrument engineering and be complementary to the company's present business.

2. Sell as a finished product or assembly direct to users, in a limited range of types and sizes.

3. Contribute turnover in excess of £100,000 per annum within 18 months, and £250,000 within three years.

4. Involve minimum investment, though capital resources would be available for a first-class proposition (up to say £50,000).

5. Be novel in concept, of advanced design, or cheaper to produce than present alternatives; or offer some marked competitive advantage.

6. Require little or no development and be ready for marketing within 12 months.

7. Exploit, though not be restricted by, the company's product and design experience, as in light current work and:

instrumentation	control	systems design
electronics	pneumatics	electromechanical design
diodes	transistors	circuit design
relays	switching	potentiometry
reliability	interlocks	intrinsic safety
simulation	modules	unit construction
alarms	pushbuttons	illuminated panels
monitoring	memories	data handling
scanning	blending	sequence control
telecommunications	telemetry	remote indication

8. Utilize to some extent the company's production skills, for example in:

bench fitting	brazing	engraving
assembly	welding	presswork
circuitry	evacuation	turning
soldering	encapsulation	drilling

9. Employ at least some materials with which the company are familiar, such as:

sheet steel	enamel	inert gases
light alloys	self-adhesive tape	extruded plastics
copper alloys	semiconductors	perspex
gold plating	mercury	melamine
epoxy coatings	dry hydrogen	polyurethane foam

10. Weigh a few pounds, or if a cabinet or console, less than three tons, fit within a ten-foot cube and cost at least £50 per minimum sales unit.

11. Be capable of batch, not series, manufacture.

12. Have a substantial added value, with a direct-labour content exceeding 15 per cent.

13. Sell in several expanding markets, preferably in the process industries, for example:

oil	chemical	food
gas	paint	sugar
coal	paper	sewage
nuclear	steel	pipelines

also motor car and gas turbine manufacture, ship builders and research establishments.

14. Permit sustained sales over at least five years, with good prospects for development and the introduction of complementary products.

15. Afford opportunities for export, particularly to Belgium, Holland and Australia, where the group are already well established.

16. Sell, if possible, through present channels, using for example their existing sales force and that of the construction group to which they belong.

FIG. 6.11. Table showing paragraphs taken at random from planning statements and suitably disguised. They form part of a section in such a statement conveniently known as the Appreciation.

APPRECIATION

---

1. For merchant-ship propulsion the diesel has virtually superseded the steam-turbine, being cheaper to install and operate, with repercussions on the sales of gearing and marine boilers. The water-tube boiler market is in any case highly competitive. Also, the market for marine diesels is over-subscribed since most are made under licence and none of the licences are held exclusively. At the same time, other manufacturers have cut margins to a minimum so as to keep their facilities employed and the technical trend towards the medium-speed diesel for marine propulsion is leading to a further deterioration in the company's position. (Note: steam-turbines are said to be returning for use in supertankers.)

2. Although the company are large, their markets are geographically limited and they are only able to sell effectively in the Republic, where their main plants are situated. Problems of import quotas and tariffs arise, in that any products manufactured must predominantly utilize indigenous raw materials and not depend significantly on components bought in from abroad. Since the total market is restricted, the volume of products selling to this market must be substantial, and therefore in considerable variety. On the other hand, it is clearly undesirable that any channel of sale should carry a small (and hence unprofitable) traffic.

3. As the industrial arm of an aerospace company, the company have two

key problems. The existing product ranges, being derived from aircraft developments, are random, isolated and diffuse. The sales organization, which is accustomed to multi-million pound projects, is ill adapted for marketing a relatively small volume of industrial products. It follows that the company should reinforce these ranges with complementary products selling to the same or similar customers, and create a sales organization more in keeping with the company's industrial activities.

4. Over 90 per cent of their output is sold directly or indirectly to the coal-mining industry and the company have therefore been seeking to increase their exports and diversify their markets. There are, however, certain limitations. The company are geared to manufacture specialized equipment, which commands relatively high prices, and it is only where there are special circumstances that such prices can be competitive. Outside the mining industry these special circumstances are likely to be thinly spread, and few industries will have comparable replacement and maintenance requirements. It follows that the company must compromise between selling in a wide range of markets (placing a virtually intolerable load on the company's sales organization) and selling in a single market. Initially, it is recommended that explorations be confined to five selected industries, selected so as to optimize turnover from old and new products combined.

5. Specialization makes the department vulnerable during the sudden fluctuations in aircraft procurement imposed by changing government requirements. Attempts to diversify outside the aircraft industry have been hampered by two main problems. Since their engineers worked for many years in isolation, there is only limited awareness of emerging needs outside the aircraft industries. Secondly, other sections of the group have pre-empted several fields outside the aircraft industry where the department's experience could be readily applied.

6. The increasing unit size of power-station plant is one of several technical and economic factors which have led to major changes in the markets which the company previously served. There has been a sixfold increase in the value of a single project, leading to a marked decline in the engineering and sales content of annual turnover. Again, the percentage of their work for power stations has doubled over recent years, leaving them vulnerable to the demands of a single monopoly customer.

7. The company's markets for materials have been threatened by a number of technical developments. Defence requirements for components of reduced weight and size, coupled with the development of solid-state devices and packaged circuitry, with overall miniaturization, have reduced the quantities required. Substitute materials with advantages in manufacture (thermo-plastics) or in operation (glass epoxy grades) started to replace the company's existing products. With increasing labour costs and longer production runs, materials which could be formed using less labour tended to become more attractive, even when the unit cost of the alternative materials and the associated tooling costs were higher. For these reasons, the company have decided to adopt a broader and better balanced operating base.

8. The company are critically dependent on subcontracting, which normally has the disadvantages of vulnerability, low margins, high sales cost and excessive variety. They are also anxious to occupy new premises and present staff released by rationalization within their group.

9. Conscious that an interrelated or integrated pattern of activities yields (synergistic) economic and commercial advantages, the company are planning their development as a logical extension of their present business, based on their strong worldwide sales resources, marketing experience, technical knowledge and manufacturing facilities. At the same time, increasing competition in their traditional markets from countries like Japan, where labour costs are low, has made the introduction of additional lines particularly urgent.

10. Their products seldom wear out and the market may already be nearing saturation, particularly for their high-profit lines. They supply a wide variety of customers, serving to limit the effect of individual market fluctuations, but calling for a major selling effort per unit volume sold.

11. The combination of small volume, low contribution to the final added value and strong competition weakens the company's position. Frequent modifications and the need to tailor-make equipment to customers' requirements result in short production runs, high design costs and acute service problems. They are therefore planning a change in strategy, whereby they will exploit their technical knowhow, not simply by producing machines, but by making and selling the end products of these processes.

12. Much of their output is sold through manufacturers of air compressors, so the company are highly dependent on a single class of outlets, which they are unable to control to any great extent. At the same time, a history of insatiable demand, a small number of customers, the level of customer negotiation, the volume per order and the company's own dominant position had made it unnecessary to create a sales force. They would therefore welcome a proprietary product, ideally taken up by acquisition of a company with good marketing resources but poor manufacturing facilities.

13. The existing sales facilities could handle a wider range and larger volume of products than are currently available to them, and in addition, their operations might usefully be extended into Europe. The company would therefore consider development involving licensing, acquisition or joint ventures.

14. The most vulnerable sector of the company's activity is on the aircraft side, where a high rate of product obsolescence reduces net growth and sales are subject to changes in national policy. Also, products are not readily adaptable to industrial markets. Nevertheless, it is considered that the experience associated with aircraft and allied activities could be applied in the industrial field, provided that the operation were divorced from the aircraft operation.

CHAPTER 7

SEEKING AND SCREENING PRODUCTS

PRODUCTS (or services) are the key link between a company and its environment, as I have noted in an earlier chapter. As the market changes, so must the product portfolio, which itself can only change in step with available assets and experience. Since products are fundamental to any business planning exercise, it is appropriate to consider the tasks of seeking and screening them in detail. In the selection of new products, it will be assumed as before that businesses are most competitive when they do something they are well equipped to do.

It is sometimes thought that the business of seeking new products is relatively new, if it is distinguished from the normal process of invention. I was therefore interested to read in a copy of *Knowledge*, borrowed from one of my children, that in 1438 Johann Gutenberg, believed to have originated printing using movable type, entered into a partnership with the expressed object of "exploiting new ideas". In return for financial support, Gutenberg was to instruct his partners in "new arts". Unfortunately, with the death of one partner a court case was brought against Gutenberg for the recovery of the money invested, but I was glad to learn that the court decided in his favour.

Random Diversification

Product acquisition has often tended to be opportunist and piecemeal, and some companies have pursued diversification until control has become virtually impossible, leading to inefficient manufacture and uneconomic marketing.

Often products have been taken up or companies acquired when the management of the acquiring company have had neither the technical nor the commercial experience to judge the performance and potential of the product or company acquired. In one case a building-project business was purchased by a consumer-product company, and a new construction process was launched before it had been technically proven, resulting in some indignant and disaffected customers.

Appalled at the losses of their subsidiary, the acquiring company decided to liquidate their acquisition, just at the point when life testing of the product had been successfully completed. Another company, with complementary knowledge and resources, picked up the pieces separately at a very modest cost.

Growth markets soon become bandwagons, and it is worth bearing in mind that businessmen tend to read the same books and periodicals. Some years ago the evident attraction of the building industry led several companies to venture into competition with the specialists, sometimes with no knowledge of the market and often with disastrous results.

More thoughtfully, a leading tobacco company observed the failure of a predecessor to break the potato-crisp monopoly. Crisps have a relatively brief shelf life and successful marketing depends not only on distributing the packets, but also on retrieving unsold packets after a given period (stock rotation). Otherwise soggy crisps may lead to disenchanted customers. The tobacco company, having some experience with products which deteriorate if inadequately packed or left too long, acquired a crisp business and effectively established themselves. At the same time, their existing contacts with public houses, supermarkets and similar outlets for tobacco no doubt provided other differentiated assets.

Successful product innovation usually depends on discovering a new relationship between a company's special assets and a market, and dynamic planning is based on the belief that selective mating of a company's resources with emerging market needs breeds commercial opportunities.

Sidestepping p 88

Contributory Studies

Applying this principle, a company may use a variety of individual methods to link its past experience with new activities. Some examples follow.

Parallel diversification. A company planning to extend its range of products might conduct a study of other home and, more particularly, overseas concerns which have diversified from the same initial field, selecting products that have proved successful and are consistent with their own experience.

Substitution. Manufacturers should keep their eyes open for substitution products. Where a product or a service is threatened by a strong alternative, the alternative should be considered. A company making jig borers should investigate the prospects for spark erosion; a manufacturer of rock drills the use of plasma and water jet techniques; a supplier of power generating plant the development of magnetohydrodynamics; a fabricator of light-gauge metal sheet the application of plastics; and an iron-founder the fabrication of heavy components from steel plate.

Parallel and series. Complementary products selling to the same customer as an existing product may sometimes be taken up, such as an accelerator pump for central heating by a company already making pressure burners for central-heating boilers. Similarly, process extension involves finding new products falling into the same process sequence as an established line. Thus a thermal drying unit might be supplied in addition to a filter.

Applications development. It is often useful to explore new applications of existing products or develop applications for a byproduct or available material. Fly ash from power stations has been turned into lightweight building blocks and the nickel companies have played a major part in the development of stainless and heat-resisting steels. Again, it was proposed that a company making a wide range of pumps for marine and power applications consider the introduction of screw, canned-motor and certain other types of glandless and semi-glandless pumps, with a view to securing their position in the food, chemical, oil and nuclear industries.

Gap filling. An existing range of products might usefully be studied to ascertain if there are any gaps. As noted in a previous chapter, it was recommended that a company making vacuum pumps consider the addition of a water-ring pump to meet demand where modest vacuum was required.

Redeploying assets. Manufacturing resources can sometimes be redeployed in new activities. A French company making radiators for motor-cars, and hence familiar with the transfer of heat from one fluid to another, was recommended to consider plate heat exchangers since the same company also made vehicle bodies and had access to the heavy presses necessary for forming the heat exchanger plates.

Multiple assemblies. A company geared to manufacture and assemble in quantity might carry out a search by numbers. Having prepared a list of mass or multiple produced end products—vehicles, machine tools, vacuum cleaners, refrigerators, traffic signals, small arms, welding equipment, parking meters, etc.—the company could check if there were any self-contained sub-assemblies which could be improved or were in short supply, e.g. clutches, motors, switching, control devices and similar equipment.

Tool and product. Occasionally a new production tool or process is developed which can itself be used for manufacturing a product with unique advantages in utility or price. A company might buy a machine for welding pipe helically or longitudinally from stainless steel or aluminium strip, the pipe being suitable for applications where imperfections were acceptable provided that the pipe were very cheap. Or, by purchasing a gear-rolling machine, developed in the Soviet Union, which employs induction surface heating and is said to make gear of adequate quality without further processing, at low cost, a newcomer might secure a foothold in the gear-production business.

Stepping-stones. Existing products or reputation may trigger off a sequence of thought leading to potential new activities. Figure 7.1 is a fictional chart, sketched in an hour and a half and based on a method that has been used by Wilkinson Sword. Particular attention would be given to activities linking several different routes, e.g. holders and fixtures in the diagram. Again, a manufacturer of sporting guns investigated the prospect for various other cartridge-operated devices—humane killers, girder punches, cable cutters, fixing tools, rock-breakers and explosive-forming, for example.   Maizena p. 88

Functional analysis. Where a company serves a particular class of customers, the activities of those customers may be analysed to identify fresh ways of serving them. A German company building graders and pavers for roadmaking reviewed the whole process of *Autobahn* construction and discovered a need for a special machine capable of laying edge sections continuously. Other companies have studied the housewife's day or the gardener's toil to identify new products.

Most of these approaches are based on the logical extension of an existing product range or the wider exploitation of present assets. They do, of course, represent methods of adaptation rather than complete mutation or diversification.

Invitation to a Brainstorm

Some methods of generating ideas have already been described, but the direct application of the procedures described in Chapters 5 and 6 may be illustrated with reference to a particular study. I have no great regard for brainstorming, believing that private concentrated thought is more productive than random conversation, though, of course, it has its place. Also, in that brainstorm-

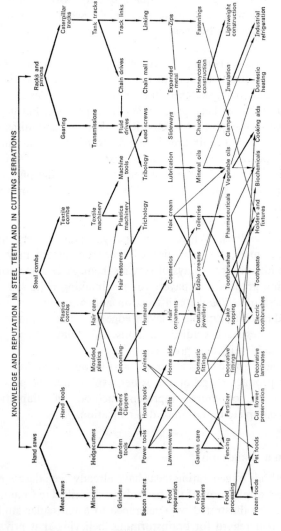

Fig. 7.1. Provided that ideas are screened with reference to the company's assets and items are selected to reinforce, rather than diffuse, the company's strengths, this procedure can be very fruitful. The thick lines show the sequence of thought; the thin lines the reinforcing links subsequently discovered. This procedure might be regarded as a one-man brainstorming session.

ing requires the participation for several hours of five or ten imaginative people, it can be very costly.

When, therefore, I issued my first "Invitation to a Brainstorm" in 1962 while employed by Martech Consultants Limited, I was careful to prepare the ground.

The participants were asked to contribute in three ways: first to suggest broad areas of potential activity prompted by the characteristic table shown in Fig. 7.2; second to review or discern changes taking place in the environment under the ten headings listed in Fig. 7.3 (change sectors: see Chapter 9); and third to relate each activity area with each change sector to see what product opportunities might be appropriate to the company concerned.

FIG. 7.3. Table listing environmental or change sectors circulated in advance of a meeting the purpose of which was to draw from the people taking part current knowledge and imaginative projections of developments within these sectors.

1. Food	6. Production methods
2. Territorial development	7. Time and labour
3. Energy	8. Communications
4. Materials	9. Accommodation
5. Goods and services	10. Safety and security

It was a detailed application of the principle: What's in it for us? First identify the product areas, then the changes taking place in the environment, and finally, the points of overlap or interaction.

I am embarrassed to recall that my report of the session was distributed under the somewhat pretentious heading "Encephalogram". The list of product areas, which were not all strictly "dynamic", appears in Fig. 7.4, and the commentary on change or environmental sectors in Fig. 7.5. The results of the discussion on change sectors is of historical interest, since it mentions several possible developments which would still be regarded as current, shows some over-optimism in projection and includes a number of ideas such as canned television (pre-timed home television recording for playback on some more convenient occasion), which have since materialized.

FIG. 7.4. Table showing proposals for product areas generated during a discussion session and based on the characteristic table in Fig. 7.2. Many are not in fact genuine dynamic areas in the sense of my earlier definition (see Chapter 5).

PRODUCT AREAS

1. Locks, switches and spring mechanisms
2. Chains and flexible drives
3. Connectors
4. Packaging, boxes and containers
5. Tanks, vessels and containers
6. Pollution and waste recovery
7. Air treatment
8. Filtration
9. Air-cooled heat exchangers
10. Self-contained process plant
11. Process control
12. Control engineering
13. Meters and instruments
14. Electrical and thermal insulation
15. High pressure technology
16. Woven wire and wire mesh
17. Expanded and foamed metals
18. Films, coatings and surface finishing
19. Intricate fabrication in special materials
20. Metachemicals
21. Multi-material technology
22. Advanced materials technology
23. Plant for processing advanced materials
24. Materials and components for new forms of transport
25. Machinery for producing new building materials
26. New building materials
27. Building
28. Domestic and leisure equipment
29. Surgical and medical equipment
30. Agricultural equipment

FIG. 7.5. Table showing minutes of a discussion meeting with developments and projections prompted by the change or environmental sector keywords in Fig. 7.3. The meeting was held in the offices of Martech Consultants Limited in June 1962.

ENCEPHALOGRAM

1. FOOD is a basic change area since growing population places an increasing stress on world food resources. There are three immediate subdivisions: production, storage and distribution.

   Concentration of population calls for more efficient methods of *food storage* and *food distribution*.

   Industrialization, particularly in such areas as the United Kingdom, and reduced supplies of food from overseas will lead to the development of *new food growing techniques*. Thus *Chlorella* grown in brightly sunlit water is said to have a yield of $17\frac{1}{2}$ tons per acre with 50 per cent protein content as against wheat at 1 ton per acre with 12 per cent protein content. The protein yield per acre is even lower with cattle; thus as pressure on acreage increases, meat is likely to form a diminishing portion of our diet. However, by using *Chlorella* or other high-yield algae foodstocks, meat production can be maintained. Submarine food growing and fish farming are other promising developments.

Protein extraction from leaves, grasses and bagasse is another aid to food production that is likely to become increasingly important (edible cellulose).

Weather control may help to make the seasons more reliable.

Where food is plentiful, as it is in Europe and the United States, demand for *luxury foods* will grow, since where there is abundance variety is needed to stimulate the appetite. Technical aids to oyster and caviare production are already in existence. Foods with concentrated nourishment will become increasingly popular. Luxury in general moves downward through the population.

With the advent of nuclear submarines, space flight and the systematic exploitation of desert areas, *portable food-producing plants* (hydroponics or the production of food in tanks) may need to be developed. On the other hand, preservation offers a simpler solution.

2. TERRITORIAL DEVELOPMENT is likely to receive increasing attention with the opening up of new continents.

Special vehicles for rough terrain, hovercraft, tractors and sausage-roller trucks, will be required.

There will also be a need in the short term for *lightweight sectional equipment* that can be carried to the heart of continents by air.

In particular, *cheap and simple farm implements* will be wanted, possibly using tithe system of financing. (Farm carts have been handled in this way with great success.)

Note: disillusionment with underdeveloped countries as markets and fear of nationalization may in fact present substantial opportunities to a company prepared to study the problem and tackle it systematically. Thus a large number of small subsidiaries set up to yield a quick return will spread the risk of entering a young nationalist country. Assembly would normally be sufficient to meet any regulations concerning local manufacture.

In the longer term, large-scale agricultural projects will call for *massive rugged single-purpose farm equipment*, as forecast by the chairman of Massey Ferguson ("The trend is towards large high-powered specialized tractors").

Road building and other public works projects will continue to require large numbers of *civil engineering ancillaries*, e.g. hydraulic jacks in tunnelling.

Tropical and arctic engineering are fields of potential opportunity. Buildings in *reinforced plastics* are being made for use in the Antarctic.

3. ENERGY requirements usually grow as a compound function of increase in population since the number of kilowatts consumed per head also increases.

It follows that *energy conservation* will become more and more important. Thus demand for heat transfer equipment will continue to expand and particularly *regenerative heat transfer*.

However, it is highly likely that within 10 or 15 years the controlled release of energy from light nuclei will have been achieved. After a number of false starts, development now appears to be moving in the right direction and *fusion power* is becoming a practical possibility. Limitless energy from seawater will change the whole balance of industrial society. Although the capital cost of generating plant will probably be high and distribution costs will initially remain unaltered, energy is the basic condition of all industrial activity, and feedback through every manufacturing process will produce cumulative effects.

One consequence of increased availability of energy will be *new techniques of materials extraction and separation*, e.g. electrical smelting.

Another likely development in the energy field is the *direct conversion* of fuel to electric power, probably by magnetohydrodynamic techniques.

Both fusion and magnetohydrodynamics will call for new *temperature resisting materials*, particularly ceramics and cermets.

Cheap electric power will lead to growing application of the *heat pump* for domestic and industrial heating.

Also, as conventional fuel supplies diminish and society depends increasingly for energy on large static power plants, *new mobile power sources* will be required, probably depending on the conversion of electrical to chemical energy and reconversion in the vehicle. The fuel cell is an example.

The need to store energy will bring increasing use of *accumulator devices*, including hydraulic accumulators.

Meanwhile, in the shorter term, *marginal energy sources* are likely to be tapped increasingly. Synthetic oil from limestone (carbon) and water (hydrogen) may be produced, and already the gasification of low-grade coal is in hand. Other methods of using coal mines are likely to be developed.

As mines become more mechanized, increasing quantities of *pulverized coal* will be produced, bringing flotation techniques and piped supplies.

For these reasons and because of its increased availability from other sources, *gas* of one kind or another is likely to represent a major source of energy during the next 10 years. The Government have decided that 10 per cent of British gas supplies are to be provided by natural gas from the Sahara. With the construction of large gas-producing plants, gas is expected to become cheaper and gas demand in industry is already growing. Also *liquefied petroleum gases* are becoming more available, and on the Continent are widely used for vehicle propulsion.

It follows that *gas transport* by ships or pipeline will become increasingly important, as will new methods of *gas storage*.

4. MATERIALS always represent a limitation on development, both in availability and properties.

New sources of materials are therefore likely to be exploited. The Mohole project, for example, may demonstrate the possibility of pumping molten magma from beneath the earth's crust.

Seawater, which contains reasonable quantities of magnesium and other elements, as well as combustible hydrogen and heavy hydrogen for nuclear fusion, is another promising source.

Water itself is likely to be in short supply before long, at least in the United Kingdom. The shortage is largely a result of growing industrial demand.

Seawater treatment will almost certainly expand. Already fresh water is distilled from it for drinking purposes, and salt (for chlorine production) obtained by crystallization. Once one material is extracted, it becomes more economic to separate others, and it is probable that multi-material separation plants will be established in many coastal areas.

Current interest in the biological sciences may release many new techniques. One of them is *biological concentration of materials*; an example is the concentration of iodine from seawater by seaweed, but this is a rudimentary process compared with some considered to be possible.

Chemical processes involving bacteria are likely to be developed as the requirement for complex materials increases.

The increased availability of *vacuum techniques* will mean their wider use for separation of materials.

Ultra-strong materials, using metallic whiskers, is a promising long-term development, while less remote are a wide range of corrosion, abrasion- and temperature-*resistant materials* involving both metals and ceramics.

The advent of temperature-resistant polypropylene may permit a breakthrough in the use of plastics, e.g. in cooking utensils.

Recent developments in the bonding and even welding of dissimilar materials may lead to the widespread application of *materials in combination*.

As pressure on materials resources increases, *conservation of materials* will become increasingly important with a strong incentive towards *waste recovery*.

Recovery of metals, e.g. scale from stainless steel, is already practised widely, but *recovery of valuable trace metals*, such as tungsten from spent electric bulbs, may also become necessary.

Next will follow *recovery of organic wastes*. And as a consequence of all these requirements more systematic and detailed *recovery of domestic wastes*.

Recovery of sulphur in usable form from smoke is now understood to have become practicable.

Government action on *river pollution* and *clean air* will create a situation in which recovery will become more economic. As in the case of seawater, recovery of one material will support the recovery of others.

5. GOODS AND SERVICES are particularly subject to social change. Material shortages, for example, will halt the prodigal usage of resources that has been the pattern in the past.

The affluent (or satiated) society has also created a reduced rate of increase in the demand for goods, but a growing call for *services*, which may, of course, involve certain kinds of product.

There is also a swing away from the prewar–postwar scramble for possessions towards a greater interest in the *public sector*. (Even conservative Britain has introduced NEDC with its implied acceptance of planning).

Maturing populations are becoming less concerned with fashion and impatient with unnecessary obsolescence (note the success of the immutable Volkswagen). As a result, there is a growing taste for *products that endure*. The desire for durability may lead to the acceptance of plastics wall facings instead of paint or wallpaper.

Maintenance equipment for home, factory, public services and other applications is almost certain to find growing use, for similar reasons, likewise *anti-corrosion technology* will be increasingly applied.

Another expression of the same trend is *do it yourself*, which also partly springs from growing leisure.

Coupled with garage dissatisfaction, it may create requirements for such substantial items of *private engineering plant* as domestic battery chargers and air compressor packs. Cars, particularly Land Rover models, are likely in future to be fitted with power take-off points.

More leisure will also mean an increasing need for satisfying diversionary activities, with a consequent demand for certain classes of *leisure and sporting equipment*.

6. PRODUCTION METHODS will almost certainly be affected by social evolution and the need to conserve materials.

One consequence of the situation outlined under Goods and Services is a trend towards *replacement manufacture and design*.

The electronically controlled milling machine, for example, illustrates the application of automation to *production in small numbers*.

New methods of metal forming will be developed; already work is being carried out on electrochemical, electrohydraulic, chemical and spark erosion, explosive and magnetic-field techniques.

New methods of metal fabrication are also being introduced. *Electroslag welding* of thick plate, and swedging, which involves the pinching of webs in the surface of sheet to strengthen it, are two examples. *Adhesion* as a substitute for welding may also become more common.

7. TIME AND LABOUR are also under pressure, since, although increasing population gives extra hands, it multiplies by many times the demands made on these hands and their associated brains.

The affluent society also makes certain jobs, like mining, unacceptable. In addition, union pressure and the high cost of labour increase the need for *automatic and control equipment*.

On the land the situation is particularly serious, creating requirements for *mechanical and automatic methods of planting and harvesting*. Non-bruising fruit is being bred with the avowed purpose of facilitating air-blast picking.

Mechanization in the building industry, where speed is particularly important, is also likely to expand. An attempt is now being made to mechanize plastering.

Chemical plants are already highly automatic, but certain processes, such as brewing, have still to be adapted successfully to *continuous operation*.

In addition, there are still substantial requirements for *continuous process recording*.

Remote recording of gas and water supplies, remote monitoring of oil wells and *remote control* in ships are likely to find growing application. *Automatic warehousing* and automatic loading and unloading are other promising fields.

Shortage of teaching staff may call for a wide variety of *teaching aids*.

8. COMMUNICATIONS are expanding at a rate approaching the square of the growth in population, since as the number of individuals increases, the number of links joining them grows at a far greater pace.

    Transport and *distribution* are aspects of communication which are particularly in need of new solutions.

    Congestion is a consequence of the growing requirement for communication in conflict with the tendency for population to concentrate in cities.

    Congestion in the city may lead to the introduction of multi-decker roads with separation of pedestrian traffic, distribution of traffic into channels classified by speed, vertical parking, passenger conveyors between stations as in Rotterdam and *compact personal transport*. (One can envisage a two-wheel enclosed vehicle with outriders for balancing when stationary and single-lever control.)

    End connections, both for freight and passengers, travelling by rail, sea or air, offer considerable opportunities for ingenuity.

    A promising solution to the rail freight end-connection problem is the *transferable body*.

    Fast inter-city transport is also likely to be worth investigating. Monorail systems have been suggested, together with air-cushion rail vehicles (Ford) and fast roller roads designed to carry ordinary vehicles (Westinghouse).

    Methods of *handling or avoiding distribution peaks* will become increasingly important, e.g. in power supply, travel, shopping, etc.

    Underground gas storage is planned so that gas produced in the summer months when demand is low can be stored for winter.

    Distribution of materials by *pipeline*, including gas, liquefied gas, coal and oil, is almost certain to increase. Pipelines are particularly suitable where there is concentration of consumption and can deliver large quantities at short notice, irrespective of weather conditions. Trunk pipelines and interconnected networks are already planned or building.

    The advent of the Common Market is likely to give an impetus to *port development*, and hence to certain classes of *mechanical handling* and to *operations research*.

9. ACCOMMODATION needs increase more rapidly than population since each person requires space at home, office or factory and places of public entertainment. The demand also increases with increasing prosperity.

    Building is therefore a major growth industry.

    Time is particularly expensive in the building industry, and *prefabrication* is almost certain to increase. Speed of construction is claimed as an advantage for *mortarless bricks* which are also said to give greater flexibility.

Capacity to cope with requirements seems likely to be inadequate, particularly in *private housing*, and the immediate solution may be *conversion of existing property*.

Packaged bathrooms and kitchens, embracing recent innovations, are believed to be a promising field of inquiry.

The advent of the second car may create a demand for *folding garages*.

With increasing prosperity and growing problems of noise, dust and fumes, *environmental control* could usefully be tackled as a composite exercise, embracing *central heating, air conditioning* and *acoustics*.

Prosperity also means more money for purchasing *domestic aids*. There are limits to this requirement, but the growing use of thermostatically controlled *self-heating saucepans*, frying pans and kettles in America and on the Continent may be followed in this country. Demand is stimulated by the housing shortage, since many young couples occupy cookerless rooms in other people's houses. A *self-stirring saucepan* would also be welcome.

Perhaps the last requirement in personal entertainment is *canned television*, with chronologically preset recording. Corresponding to a record player, the CTCPR would enable us to watch the programmes that we wish to see and not the ones that dominate peak viewing hours.

10. SAFETY AND SECURITY measures become more common as prosperity increases and economic margins become less critical. The occasional risk or hardship only justifies expenditure on precautions if there is ample money to spare.

More is likely to be spent in future on *defences against flood, fire, burglary, hurricane, or ice and snow*, not to mention *civil defence*. The military budget also falls within this category but is presumably fully stretched. British Railways may even install devices for *defreezing points*.

The difference between a dynamic area and a change sector is purely notional in that a dynamic area relates to the company and a change sector to the company's environment. Some are in fact interchangeable, and one outcome of the study, I recall, is that the company explored "environmental control", embracing central heating, air conditioning, acoustic control, etc., as a dynamic area.

Product Sources

In seeking new products, one factor is of critical importance, namely the urgency of the company's requirement. Are they already running short of profitable work? Have they foreseen some impending technical development or market change that will affect their pattern of activity within the next few years? Or are they simply planning their longer term development?

The approach is very much determined by the situation. If time is short, then the only solution may be subcontracting, from local manufacturers, who themselves may well be underloaded in times of general recession. Rarely, subcontracting may not be limited to jobbing work, and occasionally a sizeable contract has been secured from a process engineering company who are already building, say, an oil refinery, and have been let down by another subcontractor.

In the medium term a licensing, sales, merger or joint-company agreement may provide a satisfactory answer, though there are many pitfalls in acquiring products in this way.

Long-term planning is very much more difficult and the company is here dependent largely on its own resources. It must foresee changing requirements within its field of experience and undertake original development. In any case, licences and similar sources of developed products are only likely to be a stop-gap; and companies or countries that rely too much on licensing may find that royalty payments so reduce their margins that they cannot continue to compete. On the other hand, it is sometimes better to be second in the field, when the costs of hit-and-miss technical research and developing a market have been absorbed.

Manufacture and marketing under licence has long been a popular solution to a medium-term product problem and a systematic worldwide product search may be required. But even where a company prefers to develop products independently a knowledge of what other companies are doing elsewhere can be important. To commit massive expenditure to the development of an improved float valve when a breakthrough in petrol injection is imminent in Turin or Coventry might not be wise. Although they have impressive research facilities, Dunlop were not too proud to buy a licence from Pirelli for radial-ply tyres.

Sometimes a new product is introduced, possibly under licence, as a nucleus for further expansion of activities. For example, a company concerned with shell-and-tube heat exchangers decided to develop what came to be known as the "Platecoil" method in which recessed channels are embossed on sheets of steel. Thus, when two sheets are pressed together they become a self-contained heat-transfer element with contained flow paths. Although the company had thought initially in terms of steam and water, the development provided them with a bridgehead into the general process industries and gave them scope for developing such products as agitators, mixers, driers, evaporators and freezers.

A small company developed a range of high-speed cut-off blades for use with automatic tools, which enabled them to enter the entire field of machine-shop accessories, including such additional products as vacuum chucks. Development of a turbulence amplifier provided another company with a foundation in the business of fluid logic and pneumatic control systems.

Worldwide product searches are conducted using a variety of channels. Having defined its dynamic areas, a company may identify through directories and exhibition catalogues all companies active in the fields of interest. Direct approaches may be made, using a carefully worded letter to elicit information on the products that the respondents themselves consider to be interesting. The essence of a product search is to spread a wide net so as to catch the unexpected opportunity. If one knows in advance what kind of product one is looking for it is unlikely to be very exciting, and a search is hardly needed.

A second major channel is through established intermediaries distributed throughout the world. They may be patent agents, licence brokers, product consultants, merchant banks, commercial attaches, sponsored research organizations, such as the Illinois Institute of Technology and Battelle, the spin-off departments of major companies (particularly the aerospace corporations of the United States), also NASA, national bodies, such as the United Kingdom Atomic Energy Authority, the National Engineering Laboratory and the National Research Development Corporation, and the licensing organizations in Communist and Socialist countries, including Licensintorg (USSR), Polytechna (Czechoslovakia), Polservice (Poland) and Nikex (Hungary).

Literature searches, given access to a large library of periodicals and other current published information, may be both economical and fruitful. Carried out in parallel with searches through the other channels, it can help to make the coverage exhaustive. A brief list of journals devoted to new products or with new product sections appears in Fig. 7.6.

Fig. 7.6. Magazines and journals devoted to new product information of containing a regular section on the subject.

NEW PRODUCT JOURNALS

Clipper Cargo Horizons
  Pan American World Airways Inc.,
  Pan Am Building,
  New York,   Lists worldwide marketing and
  NY 10017, USA   licensing opportunities
Engineering
  36 Bedford Street,   Illustrated paragraphs on new
  London, WC2   engineering products under "Engineering ways and means"

Industrial Bulletin
  450 Ohio Street,
  Chicago 11,
  Illinois, USA
Industrial Equipment News
  Tothill Press Limited,
  161 Fleet Street,   Details of new American industria
  London, EC4   products
International Licensing
  Pinner,
  Middlesex   Lists worldwide licences offered
Inventions and Designs Licensed to Industry
  United Kingdom Atomic Energy Authority,
  11 Charles II Street,
  London, SW1
Inventions for Industry
  National Research Development Corporation,
  Kingsgate House,
  66–74 Victoria Street,   Details of new inventions under sub-
  London, SW1   ject heading—mainly British patents

FIG. 7.6. (cont.)

New Equipment Digest Penton Building, Cleveland, Ohio, USA	
New Product Newsletter 135 E. 44th Street, New York, NY 10017, USA	Worldwide details of new products
Newsweek Kinbex House, Wellington Street, Slough, Bucks	Page devoted each week to new products, both consumer and industrial
New Technology 42 Parliament Street, London, S.W.1.	Prepared by Ministry of Technology and the Central Office of Information
Patent Abstract Series Office of Technical Services, Washington 25, DC, USA	
Product Licensing Index Industrial Opportunities Limited, 13–14 Homewell, Havant, Hants	Worldwide licences available
Production Equipment Digest Hulton Publications Limited, 55 Saffron House, London, EC1	New British products
Products List Circular Small Business Administration, Washington 25, DC, USA	Details of American patents
Soviet Technology Bulletin CIS Limited, 6 Greenway Park, Galmpton, Brixham, Devon	New methods and products from Soviet articles
Technical Digest Spalena 51, Prague 1, Czechoslovakia	Translations of Socialist countries' magazines and details of new products and processes.

Sources of new products within a company itself have to some extent already been considered but should not of course be overlooked. A detailed summary of sources, both internal and external, appears in Fig. 7.7.

The reference to historical reiteration in Fig. 7.7 reminds me of a recent incident when I was addressing the Ship and Boat Builders National Federation. I suggested that a review of long obsolete products could sometimes yield ideas and, not very seriously, proposed the construction of Golden Hinds for American millionaires. I was told by the chairman shortly afterwards that a member of the Federation was already building them—perhaps subconsciously I had noted a reference in the Press.

Some people seem particularly successful in spotting products when they travel overseas. My own discoveries in recent months include a splaid (combined fork and spoon with cutting edge for use at cocktail parties); ratchet rollers, which only release two sheets of toilet paper at a time (Australia); flowered toilet paper (South Africa); push-button flushes (Switzerland); pressurized flushing cylinders (France) and photoelectric flushing (Sweden)—sounds like an unhealthy pre-occupation, but when travelling on business it is almost the only place to sit and think.

In that the net is wide, a product search yields many opportunities of no immediate interest. It is courteous to let the correspondent know, but it is also desirable to record the opportunity for future reference. Here lies the scope for a consulting company who in the course of time may complete many product searches. Rejected products can be recorded on punched cards, providing access under a variety of headings suitably coded.

For this purpose the Universal Decimal System and the Standard Industrial Classification are not very useful. They readily respond to the demand: "supply any information available on masonry drilling bits"; but fall down when asked to identify "products available for licensing in the United Kingdom, not more than 5 tons in weight, employing complex control systems, incorporating hydraulic components and selling to the plastic or metallurgical industries". Systems have been developed for this purpose.

It must be noted that such information becomes rapidly out of

Fig. 7.7. Table showing checklist of product sources and sources of ideas. The list is not homogeneous in that it includes both organizations and methods. Molecular (or critical) examination concerns the tailoring of chemical molecules to give desired properties.

INTERNAL AND EXTERNAL PRODUCT SOURCES

Existing products
  New markets
  New applications
Existing markets
  Adapted products
  New products

Research departments
Marketing departments
Market research departments
Brand managers
Advertising departments
Advertising agents
Planning departments
New product departments
Purchasing departments
Sales staff
Production staff
Other employees
Customer requirements
Written enquiries
Written complaints
Distributors and agents
Competitors' customers
Component suppliers
Original equipment manufacturers

Sales literature
Trade and technical journals
Product journals
Mail order catalogues
Press releases
Inventors
Patent agents
Licence brokers
Industrial designers
Merchant banks
Consultants
New product centres
Exhibitions and fairs
Exhibition catalogues
Board of Trade

Departments of commerce
Commercial attachés
Government departments
Embassies
Government laboratories
National agencies
Foreign trade organizations

Sponsored research laboratories
Research associations
University research departments
Trade associations
Makers of complementary products
Byproducts of other companies
Spin-off departments
Companies relinquishing products
Companies for sale
Potential acquisitions
Existing partners or licensors
Monopoly breaking

Patent office files
Patents expired
Foreign patents

Parallel diversification
Precursor markets
Historical reiteration
Import statistics
Market exploration
Functional analysis
Molecular examination (chemicals
Substitution products
Multiple assemblies
Complementary products
Gap filling
Tool and product
Characteristic tables
Brainstorming
Foreign travel
Technological forecasting
Science fiction

date, but a particular manufacturer might be expected to develop successor products basically similar in character. Potential licensors should therefore be reapproached whenever a new search is put in hand.

As my former colleague John Howard frequently observed, it is also important to know the country in which a search is carried out, and national differences can be quite important. Although we think of the United States as big-business oriented, some 85 per cent of American corporations are relatively small concerns, operated in many cases by their owners. America has therefore been a fruitful source of licences. Japan, though a major innovating nation, is more difficult to tackle in that the bulk of industry is concentrated into large, highly diversified groups, and it is seldom easy to identify the proper correspondent for a given product area.

Licensing has something in common with a blind date, and the would-be licensee must court the licensor. It would be convenient if the character of licensee and licenser could be fed into a computer to judge compatibility. I am reminded of an adventurous colleague who decided to try her luck with a computer dating bureau. Her qualifications proved to be so impressive that the managing director of the computer firm dated her himself. I only hope our product searches are equally successful.

Joint Ventures

There has been a tendency in recent years for American companies in particular to favour joint ventures in preference to licensing agreements. Having suffered from unfortunate experiences in licensing, they believe that joint ownership will give them greater control over the operation and that each partner would have an equal interest in making a success of it.

For example, a British and a United States concern could set up a 50:50 company in the United Kingdom to market products manufactured by the British partner to the American company's designs. The British company might undertake the funding of the joint subsidiary as effective payment for the product knowhow, securing a return not only in proportion to its holding but also as a mark-up on manufactured products supplied to the subsidiary.

The sense of control comes from the view that marketing is the key to a successful business and that the joint sales company is partly owned or even sometimes controlled by the product-providing overseas partner. On the other hand, the joint subsidiary may be vulnerable to the performance of the partner responsible for manufacturing.

It is often complained that a licensed product may represent too small a fraction of the licensee's business for him to take it seriously or to devote sufficient effort to exploiting it. "If we licensed our portable winch to Massive Industries, it will be left in a corner and forgotten." Such a situation may arise when the licensee comes under pressure of demand for other independently developed and totally controlled products, which may then be given precedence. Precisely the same weakness may apply to a product handled on a joint-venture basis, but here the situation may be even worse, for with different profit centres under entirely separate managements, the manufacturer may not be adequately motivated to give the sales subsidiary most-favoured-buyer treatment.

The whole success of such a venture depends on the care with which the original agreement is defined. Unhappy licensing agreements are likewise often the consequence of ill-considered licence terms, and a properly worded licence agreement may be as effective and far simpler than a joint company, particularly when there are problems of corporate law, taxation and the export of capital. Long-range auditing is always difficult, and corporate legislation, with certain notable national exceptions, may make it easier to obtain a fair return from a joint venture than from a licence where it is sales turnover rather than overall returns which must be audited. Against this argument it may be said that a licence can be made reasonably secure, through a proper balance between initial payment and, say, a diminishing rate of minimum royalties.

Product Licensing

I remember a case where a thin-film evaporator was licensed to a British company and, during discussions, the licensor observed that the whole problem of auditing could be removed if the licence were bought outright for a single initial payment. The prospective licensee jumped at the suggestion and, in consequence, had no continuing access to the licensor's evolving knowledge and experience. Perhaps a year afterwards, the licensor totally revised his designs to give radically improved performance and the licensee was left with an obsolete product. It is emphasized that a licensee should retain direct contact with the licensor, not only for technical development but also for emerging applications. If the licensor discovers new markets for a special mixer, say, it is clearly desirable that the licensee should be in a position to exploit these markets also. The right partner and the right agreement are essential.

A checklist used by my own company for reviewing licence opportunities appears in Fig. 7.8, and the typical content of a licence agreement is shown in Fig. 7.9. The second list (Fig. 7.9) has been drawn from a paper presented by Edwin M. Burrow and Dudley B. Smith ("US licensing relations with UK and EEC") presented at a joint Licensing Executives Society and British Institute of Management Conference on 13–14 June 1968, in London.

A more general list of factors affecting international operations (as in granting licences or setting up joint subsidiaries overseas) employed by several major companies is reproduced in Fig. 7.10, and Fig. 7.11 is another checklist of questions relating to licensing or technical assistance agreements, drawn from a paper by Mr. W. F. Spengler, managing director, United Glass Limited, presented at the conference organized by the British Institute of Management and the Licensing Executives Society.

Whether or not the fashion for joint ventures continues, licensed manufacture and sale remains a common means of transferring knowhow from one body (individual or corporate) to another, often but not always across national frontiers. Such knowhow may be covered by patents or simply embodied in the product or manufacturing process and exploitation is usually restricted by territorial franchise. The commentary (p. 142) on licensing practice considers manufacture and marketing under licence, the negotiations of licence terms and the implementation of agreements.

Fig. 7.8. Table showing checklist for reviewing licence and other product opportunities, noting, first, key questions to be answered, and then, other data to be gathered.

CHECKLIST POTENTIAL LICENSORS

As a first step in placing any licence a general description of the item would be required, together with answers to the following three questions:

- (A) In what significant respects does the equipment show advantages over corresponding United Kingdom (or European) products?
- (B) How is the implementation of the licence likely to be affected by questions of patent cover in the United Kingdom?
- (C) Are the scale and conditions of application suited to the United Kingdom (or European) situation?

To assist in presenting the case for an association, as much of the following information as possible would be appreciated:

1. Drawings, diagrams and photographs of product.
2. Full descriptive literature and specification, indicating:
    - (a) identification: type marks and serial number;
    - (b) function of the equipment;
    - (c) the principles involved;
    - (d) leading dimensions and weight;
    - (e) capacity, output, speed of operation and performance;
    - (f) distinguishing features, advantages and novelties;
    - (g) nature, quality and characteristics of any end product.
3. Approximate cost per unit or installation and component costs.
4. Cost of any end product.
5. Production requirements for manufacturing the equipment including:
    - (a) quality of engineering and degree of precision required;
    - (b) type and size of production plant needed;
    - (c) number of employees in plant where equipment is made at present;
    - (d) special requirements: tools, skills, processes or material involved.
6. Date of introduction: prototype, first production model, current improved version.
7. Numbers sold to date: also in each of last three years.
8. Industries or types of user to which equipment is supplied.
9. Channels of sale: in home country and abroad.
10. Representation in the United Kingdom or Europe.
11. Names of any other companies known to be making similar equipment and principal competitors in home country and abroad.
12. Patent coverage with patent numbers, dates and territories.
13. Existing licensees or associates throughout the world.
14. Preference for form of association in present case:
    - (a) manufacturing licence with local selling rights;
    - (b) manufacturing licence with sales handled by licensor or his representative;

  (c) cross-licensing agreement;
  (d) joint company;
  (e) other form of agreement.
15. Proposed licensing terms:
  (a) downpayment;
  (b) royalties;
  (c) territorial franchise;
  (d) any special conditions.
16. Any further points of interest or questions to be put to prospective licensee.

FIG. 7.9. Table showing checklist for the content of a licensing agreement drawn from a paper presented by Edwin M. Burrow and Dudley B. Smith ("US licensing relations with UK and EEC") presented at a joint Licensing Executives Society and British Institute of Management Conference on 13–14 June 1968 in London.

CONTENT OF LICENSING AGREEMENT

1. Identity of parties—address of each.
2. Whereas clauses—representation licensor owns patents/knowhow/trademark.
3. Definitions of keywords such as "net sales", "field", "patent", etc.
4. Grant clauses—scope of that which is given to licensee.
  patents/knowhow/trademark.
  existing rights only or include future developments?
  sublicence rights or not (affiliates?).
  exclusivity or not (can be semi-exclusive).
  territorial limits, if any.
5. Royalty clauses—minimums, downpayment, running royalty.
  paid up total fee.
  (some royalties are tied to a price index.)
6. Reciprocal grants—licence to licensor or outright grant of title patents/knowhow.
7. Infringement clauses—who sues and what happens if a third party infringes some question *re* defending licensee if he is sued.
8. Confidentiality—scope and term of years.
  if know-how only, should individual employees agree to secrecy.
9. Admission of patent validity—for how long.
10. Term of licence and conditions for termination—effective date.
11. Accounting and right of licensor to inspect accounts—currency.
12. Arbitration (sometimes provided).
13. Law of what country governs and language which governs if dual language.

14.   *Force majeure.*
15.   Assignability of licence.
16.   Due diligence.
17.   Notices sent to whom at what address.

FIG. 7.10. Table showing factors affecting international operations as when granting a licence or setting up a joint subsidiary abroad. (Table used by several large concerns, but original source unknown.)

INTERNATIONAL FACTORS

1. General Climate
   Political situation and how it affects your business
   Market forecast
   Government attitude toward foreign investment
   Amount of foreign investment, names of key companies
   Indicators of market size for 126 countries
2. State Role in Industry
   Controls
   Nationalization policy
   State-owned industry
3. Organizing
   Controls on investment and how to obtain approvals
   Establishing a local company or a branch
   How to avoid government red tape
4. Rules of Competition
   Government policy and local practices
   Monopolies and mergers
   Freedom to sell
   Resale price maintenance
   Price controls
5. Remittability of Funds
   Exchange controls
   Transfer of profits
   Repatriation of capital
   Guarantees against inconvertibility
6. Incentives
   How to qualify
   Incentive zones
   Corporate and personal tax incentives
   Tariff incentives
   Capital incentives
   Incentives for investment abroad
7. Labour
   General situation—size and skill of labour force
   Unions and work stoppages
   Wages and fringes

Limitations on foreign nationals
Potential trouble spots
8. Licensing
Patent and trademark protection
Government controls and how to get agreements approved
Taxes on royalties and fees
9. Taxes
Corporate income taxes
Depreciation
Excess profits
Capital and capital gains
Dividends and interest
Foreign source income
Turnover, sales and excise taxes
Personal taxes
Tax treaties
10. Capital Sources
Where to get short, medium- and long-term loans in local currencies
Stock and bond financing
Public and semi-public sources
11. Foreign Trade
Trading patterns
Import controls
Tariffs and import taxes
Non-tariff barriers
Free ports, zones
Export incentives
Export credit and insurance

Fig. 7.11. Table showing short list of questions relating to licensing and technical assistance agreements, drawn from a paper by Mr. W. F. Spengler, managing director, United Glass Limited, presented at a conference organized by the British Institute of Management and the Licensing Executives Society.

TECHNICAL ASSISTANCE AGREEMENT

Questions to be put to a prospective licensor with whom a company is proposing to negotiate an agreement for technical assistance might include the following:

1. Is the licensor free of potentially compromising alliances?
2. Is he experienced in servicing technical assistance licensees?
3. To what extent is he likely to seek equity participation?
4. Do you know and like your management counterparts in the licensor company?

5. Have you examined all available data on him for the past five years, particularly research and development expenditures and other reported activities?
6. Will his R & D likely lead to other product areas of mutual interest?
7. Have you made patent searches in the prospect's country to get an indication of his inventive ability? Is he an innovator?

Summary and Benefits

Licences granted by one manufacturer to another usually involve an initial payment plus a subsequent royalty on sales. The initial payment is designed to cover the transfer of knowhow, drawings, etc.

Sometimes the royalty payment may be high for an initial period, diminishing to a fixed value after, say, one, two or three years. There may in addition be a condition regarding minimum royalties which must be paid whether or not the stipulated sales are achieved. This condition may be introduced to prevent the licensee from merely suppressing the product, e.g. where it competes with his own design.

Occasionally a licensor seeks to place his licence for a lump sum and no royalty. In very rare cases only, will this arrangement be of advantage to the licensee, who may find himself cut off from his source of information and may even be unable to proceed, for example when the licensor replaces the licensed model with a new design.

A licence may or may not involve a reciprocal agreement for the exchange of technical information on subsequent development, which is usually to the advantage of both parties. Such exchange may also cover applications, experience and practice.

A product suitable for licensing need not necessarily be covered by patents, particularly where there is considerable knowhow in the design, method of production or application. A licence may embrace complete manufacture or be confined to assembly, with components supplied by the licensor.

For the licensee, a licence serves to buy time, whereby he may quickly catch up or overtake his competitors. But it can only be a stop-gap, since without new technical development there cannot be new licences. Profits are inevitably reduced by royalty payments (though sometimes even more by technical research) and sales are usually confined to certain territories by the terms of the agreement.

For the licensor, the advantages of granting a licence may be as follows:

(1) It brings additional income without additional capital outlay, factory space, plant or personnel.
(2) The risk is comparatively slight, effectively an opportunity risk in that some other course may have yielded more return.
(3) A licensee, unlike an agent, will have interests closely coinciding with those of the licensor.
(4) The licensee has a sales force on the spot and a knowledge of local conditions.
(5) Local service is available and transport costs are minimized.
(6) Customers usually prefer a home-product or a product supplied by a local manufacturer.
(7) Licences can lead to a valuable exchange of technical information.
(8) The effect of any tariff barriers and trade restrictions is substantially diminished.

With regard to the final point it is necessary to bear in mind the effect of monopoly, anti-trust and restrictive practice legislation, particularly in the United States and European Economic Community (Treaty of Rome).

Calculating Fees

Licence terms involve a variety of factors, but fees are usually divided between an initial or engineering charge and subsequent royalties on sales. The initial payment is normally related to:

(1) Research and development costs incurred by the licensor in developing the product.
(2) Number of licences already granted or proposed.
(3) Territorial franchise.

Thus if the cost of developing a product has been £100,000 and the number of licensees were ten, each with a franchise for his own country (providing that the country is industrially developed and populations are approximately equal), then a reasonable figure for initial payment would be £10,000. It would, of course, be necessary to consider the possible granting of further licences by the licensor, but providing the licensee's territory is properly defined, he need not be concerned.

Royalties are, of course, calculated as percentages of sales. Where there is any substantial initial payment, royalties seldom exceed 5 per cent, depending on the estimated size of market and the cost of the product. In some cases, however, an initial royalty as high as 17 or 18 per cent may be proposed.

Licences may be used to buy time, to fill a gap in a product group, to satisfy a demand that is intimately linked with a company's existing products, to overtake a competitor, or to lay the foundation for a diversification programme. They can seldom sustain a company indefinitely. These points are developed in more detail below, where use is made of notes I took in discussion with Dr. Basil J. A. Bard, United Kingdom Chairman of the Licensing Executives Society and Director, National Research Development Corporation.

With regard to the financial aspects of licence negotiation, it may be noted that in the development of an invention there may come a stage when interest has been established but practical application is still insufficiently certain to justify the actual negotiation of a licence. At this point an option may be granted and an option fee negotiated.

Such a fee may be split such that half is paid immediately and half later, when the prospective licensee decides to exercise his option. His purpose may be to examine the potential of the invention before finally committing himself. Such an option might be subsequently extended for a further given period by payment of a modest but not insignificant sum.

The second half of the option fee could conceivably be the licence fee itself. It is pointed out that "an agreement to make an agreement" has no place in law.

Terms

The content of a typical licence agreement is shown in Fig. 7.9, but in negotiating a licence, there are four essential factors to consider, namely:

(1) Duration.
(2) Royalty rate.
(3) Guaranteed minimum royalties, if any.
(4) Each party's right to terminate.

If a licence agreement is exclusive, a minimum royalty will almost certainly be required to guard against any failure to exploit the licence, though such a condition might be omitted in the case of a non-exclusive licence. An alternative means for applying pressure to the licensee could be a break clause; notably, if the royalties paid during a given year do not amount to an agreed figure, then the licensor would be at liberty to break the agreement. Such a clause represents a threat or a spur to encourage full exploitation of a licence and discourage taking up a licence for purpose of suppression.

There may alternatively be situations when either party can ask to convert a non-exclusive licence into an exclusive licence, or conversely.

The royalty rate should be the key to a licence agreement, since it is central and everything else revolves around it. Royalty rate relates to turnover and the whole licence agreement will depend on the royalty rate decided.

All licence agreements are negotiated, but it is helpful if the parties have a common base on which they can negotiate. In other words, it is desirable that there should be certain agreed guidelines.

It will be found that for particular fields of activity there are prevailing opinions on royalty rate, usually depending on the innovative content of the final product. Thus for heavy engineering, where the price of the final product is made up largely of hardware irrelevant to the inventive aspect, royalty rates tend to be low. Typical rates are as follows:

Scientific instruments	$7\frac{1}{2}$ per cent
Pharmaceuticals (freely negotiated)	5 to 6 per cent
Agricultural machinery	$2\frac{1}{2}$ to $3\frac{1}{2}$ to 4 per cent

In the case of pharmaceuticals, rates as high as 20 per cent have been secured in court, as compensation for loss of profits, where the law requires that licences be granted to competitors. The rate for agricultural machinery is low, since the hardware content is relatively high, and in such cases it may only be possible to secure a good rate on the essential invention.

A variety of licence situations exist, but there are two particular types of situation where licensing applies, namely:

(1) The licensor is the innovator—he is developing the idea, but will require someone else to market the product.
(2) The licensor has himself been making or selling the product, but wishes to exploit it in markets or territories which he cannot reach.

In the first example, risk is high and royalty rates may be relatively low. In the second case, the product is already proven and there is a better basis for establishing favourable terms.

Often much can be linked with a patent licence, including agreements for technical assistance and other services. In a mature situation (i.e. where a market has already been demonstrated) calculation is easier, and, with greater confidence, better business terms can usually be negotiated. Thus the licensor may already know that he is making 20 per cent profit and could reasonably claim a fair percentage of a similar profit likely to be achieved elsewhere. A fifth to a quarter of the estimated profit is reasonable, though it is emphasized that the actual agreement will be based on turnover, not profit.

Negotiation

If the licensor has himself developed the product (which may be the case in either of the situations numbered above), the licence agreement should be such as to allow for amortization of development. Thus, the cost of development might be divided among the franchise territories in proportion to the sizes of corresponding markets, as suggested earlier.

A period of 6 years for amortization may be proposed, but it could then be argued that the patent has, say, 10 years to run and amortization should be at a lower rate. The other party may next insist that the market can only last 4 years, to support the case for a higher rate.

In negotiating a mature licence, it is usual to make separate charges for drawings, development and technical aid. A licensor can afford to be generous in this respect, with a view to creating and maintaining goodwill, and may charge only 75 per cent of the actual value, say £7,500 instead of £10,000.

Although licensing is inevitably a matter of negotiation, it is desirable for each party to decide in advance what his main aims are and stick to them, though showing greater flexibility on second-order points.

An immature and hence uncertain licence might command a smaller scale of fees, balanced perhaps by the advantage of being first in the field. It follows that sometimes a two-stage royalty rate may be negotiated. There are cases where the royalty rate is 6 per cent on sales up to a given value, with a smaller rate on sales beyond this value. Conversely, the reverse might apply where the licensee is struggling to establish a product on the market.

A royalty may occasionally be replaced by a flat fee, but such an arrangement is of course vulnerable to inflation. It may be that a proportional increase will be allowed to compensate for any changes in the relative or purchasing value of currencies. Alternatively, there may be an agreement to renegotiate the fee at reasonable periods.

Downpayment and Minimum Royalties

It may be possible to secure a downpayment instead of a minimum royalty if the licence is exclusive. In such cases, the licensor may be prepared to forego royalties in the first year, in recognition of the downpayment, or agree to a suspended break clause, say up to three years. Downpayments may be in respect of a technical report, drawings and continuing assistance.

It is emphasized that in any licence negotiations, there is always a dominant party (a "king–suppliant" relationship), but the dominant party should not overplay his hand and downpayments ought to be realistic.

Similarly, guaranteed minimum royalties are often necessary, especially when a licence is exclusive, but they should be consistent with realistic expectations. For example, a guaranteed minimum royalty might be not less than 33 per cent of the anticipated market share. Thus if the market is estimated to be £600,000, then a minimum royalty calculation might be based on a market of £200,000.

A licence agreement needs to be constantly monitored, and it is common practice to require yearly reports from licensees.

Evaluating Products

As the result of an intensive product search, anything from 50 to 300 products may be found, available for licensing, through joint ventures, by company acquisition or under other forms of manufacturing and marketing agreement. As noted earlier, the ideal product is one which best reconciles the company with its environment. The successive focusing procedure by which this reconciliation may be accomplished is described in Chapter 6, but detailed evaluation needs to be treated in somewhat greater detail. Some years ago I reviewed *Product Analysis Pricing* by

Wilfred Brown and Elliott Jaques for *Engineering* under the heading "Pitfalls in evaluating products", rather naïvely and unfairly, but some of the points are relevant to the present subject. I recall that my comments were broadly on the following lines.

Before introducing a new product a manufacturer should ask himself two questions: "What is the least that I can make it for?" and "What is the most for which it can be sold?" The difference between these quantities is a measure of the extent to which the project is worth while, if worth while at all.

Unfortunately, the questions cannot be posed so simply. Selling price and sales volume are interdependent. More people will tend to buy the product if its price is lowered, but how many more is problematical. The expense of manufacture will likewise depend on numbers. Even assuming that numbers made and numbers sold are equal and the price elasticity is easily determined, the optimal price at any time, in any situation, with any product mix, is difficult to ascertain.

What the market will bear is particularly hard to judge in the case of an entirely novel product or products made to specification. There is seldom scope for trial and error. Once the customer smiles, perhaps rather too quickly, and says "done", you may kick yourself for not adding another 10 per cent, but by then it is too late. The innovator is always at a disadvantage, and only his successors can learn from his mistakes.

The distinguished authors of *Product Analysis Pricing* are well aware of the problem, but they are much more concerned with the inadequacies of standard costing, which admittedly are real. For the traditional elements of unit cost with attributable overheads, they have substituted elements of utility, summing them to arrive at an overall value to the potential customer. By adding together price coefficients for features, properties, materials and "product surround", they provide a measure of intrinsic worth.

They were certainly right to question the method of standard costing, since it confuses manufacturing cost with what the market will bear. As frequently applied, it is little better than the labour theory of value, in which the worth of a product is the aggregate of all the contributory labour involved, from mining the raw materials to final delivery. When I was in Russia in 1957, I noted that the director of a Moscow factory, when asked how he arrived at a selling price, stated that something was allowed for materials, something for labour, something for plant depreciation plus 3 per cent.

Although they would hesitate to ask for such a modest profit, it is clear that many industrialists are also Marxists at heart. Their prices are reached by a similar process, effectively cost plus. But there is something slightly improper in adding on the profit in advance—and it certainly takes away the fun.

Product analysis pricing also has its limitations. Relative value of one product with reference to another may be easy enough to measure, where, for example, both are bearings. Even then the monetary value to the customer of the interval between two divisions on the Rockwell hardness scale must be difficult to estimate without exact knowledge of the application. For new products, where there is little basis for comparison, evaluation on these lines might well be meaningless.

Take a piece of stone, chisel it purposefully for several months. Even if your stone came from the marble quarries of Carrara, the result is unlikely to be worth one tiny fraction of a similar piece of stone chiselled (perhaps to the specification of Pope Julius) by Michelangelo. Yet, according to both Russian and Western practice in calculating price, the value would be very much the same: materials plus man hours plus tool depreciation plus a predetermined margin.

Mr. Brown and Dr. Jaques, on the other hand, would take each feature in turn, the shape of a thigh, the swelling of a muscle, the texture of the polished stone, the significance of an outstretched arm, and add the component values all together. They are clearly attempting something very difficult. The market value of a product can surely best be found by study of the market, not of the product alone.

At the same time, the difference between production cost and market price cannot be determined without reference to the company. Ideally, one should evaluate, not the product itself, but the performance of the company, bearing the market in mind, first with and then without the product, since the incremental capital investment required in introducing the product is difficult to calculate. What part of existing capital invested is applied to the new product? How much of any new capital invested is devoted exclusively to the new product?

To provide an absolute evaluation of a product in isolation, say in terms of the return on incremental investment it will yield, is such a mammoth task as to be almost hopeless. Where the number of opportunities are great, therefore, ranking products in order rather than rating them on a quantitative basis may be more meaningful and practical. Most screening processes pretend to be quantitative, including the one described below, but if the weaknesses are borne in mind they can be useful.

Screening

It is often noted in product planning that anyone can choose a horse, but few can pick the winner. Percentages quoted in different papers for the success of products introduced vary very widely. An American investigator working in the field notes that one product in twenty taken up in the United States has proved successful. Others say one in a hundred. I imagine that the variation arises from differences in definition of success, what constitutes a new product and at what stage it is considered to be launched; also from differences in consumer and industrial practice.

A typical screening process, which has been supplemented over several years, comprises a standard checklist of nearly eighty factors, divided into eight factor groups. Again, the procedure involves successive focusing, in other words, an increasingly intensive study of a progressively decreasing field.

These factors can be used merely as a checklist to ensure that no significant consideration has been overlooked or, by introducing a weighting for each factor, as a basis for quantitative rating, with the reservations I have noted.

Quantitative ratings should be treated with suspicion. No practical range of weightings can adequately cover the differential importance of particular factors.

If an electronics engineer conceives a new device while working for a major manufacturer but cannot persuade his management to adopt it, he may decide to set up in business on his own. To raise the necessary funds, he may obtain a second mortgage on his house, borrow his wife's savings or ask his friends for loans. A year or so later he enters into production and immediately finds himself threatened with a patent suit by Philips Electrical or Standard Telephones and Cables. He is forbidden to market his device and may lose his whole investment.

In a case of this kind, weightings for factors concerned with patent coverage would be very large indeed. Also, to use a quantitative process subjectively without gathering information in the field can be very hazardous, but I have known product planning staff to apply screening processes, checking off points intuitively, without emerging from their offices.

Selection Criteria

The key question, therefore, in choosing new products or processes is how to distinguish the more promising from the less promising. A sequential method employed by my own company for sorting product ideas is in three parts: first, a coarse screening using criteria assembled during the initial appraisal of a company's facilities (see Figs. 6.6 and 6.7); a second review involving information gathered from prospective associates and licensors; and a full assessment based on the standard checklist.

Thus simple selection is followed by coarse screening and successively finer screening, until the surviving proposals are few enough in number and sufficiently attractive to be the subject of detailed market research. As noted previously, products are usually screened in groups since comparative evaluation tends to be more economical and objective than isolated studies of single projects. Stages may be added or omitted, depending on the number and the range of products considered. In this way, the risk of overlooking some vital consideration is minimized, and the relative importance of different factors properly appreciated. It is worth considering the three stages in detail.

Basic Factors

First it is desirable to conduct a rapid qualitative check against a list of factors drawn from a preliminary study of the potential licensee to eliminate unacceptable ideas. These basic criteria are agreed on commencement of a study and are also used in conducting the product search. Typical headings, adapted by a former colleague in Martech, Courtenay Lindsay, from the criteria (see Figs. 6.7 and 6.10) detailed in the previous chapter, are as follows:

1. General Factors:
   1.1. Product philosophy, role and product areas.
   1.2. Preferred forms of association or agreement.
   1.3. Legal conditions or limitations.
   1.4. Investment available; factory space.
   1.5. Contribution to overheads; services to be utilized.
   1.6. Novelty, uniqueness and product leadership.
2. Production Factors:
   2.1. Product experience and design content.
   2.2. Type and quality of manufacture.
   2.3. Materials of construction.
   2.4. Dimensions and weight.
   2.5. Cost per ton, labour content or value added.
   2.6. Numbers off; size of batch or series.
3. Market Factors:
   3.1. Turnover required, profit margin, growth.
   3.2. Cost per unit or installation.
   3.3. Markets to be served or avoided.
   3.4. Competitors and customers.
   3.5. Sales organization and channels available.
   3.6. Country of origin and franchise.

These headings cover most circumstances, but special provisions can easily be added. Some factors are interdependent, e.g. 2.6, 3.1 and 3.2, but it may be possible to eliminate a product on one of these grounds without full knowledge of the others. Where possible, criteria are expressed numerically, but few should be regarded as critical at this stage.

Coarse Screening

When a sufficient list of products or possible associates has been assembled meeting the basic requirements of the first stage, they can be arranged in approximate order of suitability and promise by assigning numerical values to various factors, and comparing the totals.

The resulting sequence can then be used as an approach list whereby prospective associates may be contacted in logical order. Alternatively, the top twenty or thirty may be taken as the basis for detailed study.

In arriving at a cumulative rating for each prospective associate, the object is not simply to evaluate the product but to judge the opportunity. In other words the total for each item is a measure of the extent to which an immediate approach to the company is likely to prove worth while. Thus if a possible licensor with a promising product is lukewarm in his reaction to the client as licensee, the overall rating will be accordingly depressed.

Products are normally treated in categories, even where a prospective associate makes items falling into several, so that like can be compared with like.

It should be emphasized that the ratings are not by any means conclusive, and the relative standing of individual items may have to be modified in the light of further information received from correspondents or gathered in conducting market checks. Details are normally obtained from prospective associates using two questionnaires: one to obtain information on the product or products; the other on the company itself (see Fig. 7.8). It is preferable that the questions be put at a personal interview rather than submitted with a covering letter, though an inquiry by correspondence may occasionally be necessary.

The factors are listed below but may have to be adapted or augmented for particular situations. The component ratings are roughly weighted by marking out of 5 or 10 as shown.

INTEREST (10)

The interest of the prospective associate in reaching an agreement is marked out of 10 since it is critical to the success of an approach and subsequent negotiations. His interest is measured by the amount of information supplied, perhaps including a definite proposal; whether or not he has visited the prospective licensee or invited representatives of the company to visit him; whether he is acting through a licence agent and has a number of alternative licensees in view; whether he is prepared to proceed immediately or suggests an approach at a later date; and whether he has expressed general interest in licensing or particular interest in the inquirer's company. If, for example, an American company has stressed its interest in entering the European market, it may receive a low rating, since Britain may not always be regarded as a good base for this purpose.

NOVELTY (10)

The uniqueness of the product is also heavily weighted, since novelty of some kind, whether in the product or method of producing it, is a key consideration in taking up a licence. Novelty has been assessed in terms of the whole product or particular features; whether it is covered by patents or has been licensed elsewhere; whether it is an entirely new departure or simply an improved version of an established line; whether it is already familiar in the United Kingdom or only just becoming known in its home market; whether its styling is up to date or old fashioned; whether it is at the beginning of its life cycle, or has already reached maturity; and whether it is in a rapidly developing or stagnant field of engineering.

PROSPECT (10)

Again an important factor, prospect is compounded from the estimated size of the market for the product or product range, and its likely rate of growth. Weighting may be qualified by lack of information necessary to give an authoritative assessment, which could only be obtained by means of a full market survey. Ratings are based on the product's breadth of application; the growth pattern of the industry to which it sells; the extent of the range offered for licensing; where known the level of sales and success of the prospective licensor in his home market and his current performance and prosperity; the number of competitors in the field and degree of market saturation; and the likely territorial franchise.

SUITABILITY FOR MANUFACTURE (5 or 10)

The extent to which the product is adapted to the manufacturing facilities of the interested company is usually weighted relatively lightly, since products unsuited to these facilities have normally been rejected by this stage. At the same time, production facilities can often be extended where necessary and the company may not wish to miss a good commercial opportunity on these grounds. Also, the information available on any product is generally not adequate to permit a detailed and authoritative evaluation. However, where the utilization of idle plant is a prime consideration, the factor can be rated out of 10. Ratings are allocated by inspection of drawings and photographs; similarity to existing products; and, where possible, information on required methods of production supplied by prospective licensors.

SUITABILITY FOR SALES (5 or 10)

Whether or not the client company can sell the product easily and effectively is an important factor, but may be rated relatively lightly, since an undistinguished product which happens to coincide with an existing line would necessarily be awarded full marks both on suitability for marketing and suitability for manufacture, yielding a misleadingly high rating if not otherwise depressed. Products are rated by the extent to which an existing sales force can be utilized; the prospect of selling to present customers and through existing outlets, in particular to or through other members of any group to which the company may belong; whether the product can be easily handled by a relatively small number of distributors or a licensor's existing agent; and whether the sales of complementary products will benefit. Where no suitable facilities exist, the rating will reflect the ease with which they can be created.

STATE OF DEVELOPMENT (5 or 10)

The cost of introducing a new product and the speed with which it can be placed on the market will depend on the extent to which it needs adaptation or development. The importance of this factor is governed by the urgency of the company's requirements and whether the search has already tended to exclude underdeveloped products. In any case a few longer-term products may be worth considering. Ratings take into account whether the product has already been sold successfully in its home market or is simply a prototype, laboratory model or perhaps merely an idea embodied in a patent specification; whether it needs to be converted from metric to English units or adapted for the United Kingdom and western markets (as in the case of Soviet products); whether complete designs, drawings and technical advice a re likely to be supplied; whether some technical or applications development work will be necessary; and whether the company will have to acquire new staff and experience to make and service the product effectively.

OPINION OF MANAGEMENT (5 or 10)

If a product is to be taken up and exploited successfully, it must have the confidence of the company's senior executives. Their views are therefore of considerable importance, quite apart from any special knowledge they may have. The company's reaction will be particularly important when the product is being chosen to fill a gap in an existing range. Ratings depend on whether executives have indicated strong or tentative interest in a product or associate; whether they regard a prospective associate as a competitor, have found him unreliable, or have had unhappy dealings with him in the past; whether they fear that putting the product on the market will damage their relations with existing customers; and whether the product is in accordance with their own programme of development.

INFORMATION (10)

Some overseas companies tend to be poor correspondents and replies are often late or inadequate. The validity of the other component ratings depends substantially on the details supplied, and, since an approach to any prospect can only be recommended if there is sufficient information to justify a decision, this factor is heavily weighted. Ratings are a measure of uncertainty and reflect the detail in which information has been supplied, in particular literature, leaflets, brochures, catalogues, technical papers, patent specifications, photographs, samples, price lists, content of letters, figures for turnover, sales, etc., the specificness of any proposal, or the submission of definite licensing terms. This factor is, of course, related to the first, but the two in combination are considered to be critical.

Full Assessment

Detailed screening and assessment involves the examination of seventy-six factors for each short-listed product, grouped under the following eight headings.

(1) Performance factors (5).
(2) Stability factors (10).

(3) Growth factors (9).
(4) Assimilation factors (14).
(5) Marketability factors (14).
(6) Development factors (8).
(7) Production factors (10).
(8) Legal factors (6).

Over the years these factors have been progressively expanded and elaborated as fresh studies have highlighted new points to consider, but I think they were based originally on a list of 39 prepared by W. R. Grace & Co., and published by the American Management Association. Legal factors, though mentioned last, are often crucial, but a product does not normally reach the screening stage unless it has been cleared in this respect. Assimilation factors are those pertaining to the ease and speed with which the product can be taken up and established on a profitable basis.

The seventy-six factors can be used either as a check list for qualitative screening or elimination, particularly where the number of products remaining after the initial stages is still comparatively large; or as a quantitative method where there are only a few products to be studied. In any case the screen can be applied in increasing detail with finer and finer grids. Again, products rejected in the early stages should be reviewed in the light of information gathered in the later stages.

It will be apparent that various factors overlap with one another. It is this intrinsic duplication of factors and the problem of defining satisfactory weighting ratios which make quantitative assessment of this kind extremely unreliable. Particular products can, of course, be studied with reference to a selection of the more critical factors, and attempts should be made to give the individual factors proper emphasis.

RATING

For each factor, the product idea is assigned a rating of very good (2), good (1), average (0), poor (−1) or very poor (−2).

In early screenings, the ratings are plotted on a profile chart for each factor group and connected by a profile line.

When a chart has been completed for each group of factors, the entire profile of the new product is assembled for examination. Too many poor or very poor ratings show up vividly, and the product can safely be discarded. A profile that alternates back and forth, mainly on or near the average line, can be shelved for possible

SIMPLE PROFILE CHART

	R	W	P
1. Durability of market	(−1)	(3)	(−3)
2. Breadth of market	(0)	(3)	(0)
3. Possibility of captive market	(−1)	(2)	(−2)
4. Effect on product spread	(−2)	(1)	(−2)
5. Complementary cycle	(−1)	(0)	(0)
6. Stability in economic depression	(1)	(1)	(1)
7. End product or component	(2)	(3)	(6)
8. Difficulty of copying	(1)	(3)	(3)
9. Favourable supply position	(0)	(0)	(0)
10. Purchasing volume	(1)	(2)	(2)

FIG. 7.12. Simple profile chart for the ten stability factors. The figures in brackets represent rating (R), weighting (W) and weighted rating (P). Unweighted ratings are shown in this diagram, but also see overall weighted profile chart (Fig. 7.13).

re-examination later, if there is a shortage of really promising ideas.

A simple (unweighted) profile chart appears in Fig. 7.12, and is concerned with a single factor group. Each factor represents one aspect of product or company stability.

Thus if the market is durable, sales are likely to be secure for a considerable period; if the market is broad, then the decline of any particular market sector will not be critical. Products sold to associated companies would be less exposed to the idiosyncracies of customers than those selling on the open market. If a new product adds to the product spread, has a sales cycle complementary to the cycle of existing products or is independent of economic fluctuations, it will increase the company's stability. An end product gives a company more latitude than a component; while a product with good patent cover, made by a difficult or secret process, cannot easily be imitated. If the raw materials are readily available or components are purchased in sufficient volume to command the supplier's favour, again the company will be less vulnerable.

WEIGHTING

It is not feasible to give a numerical weighting for each factor appropriate to all projects, but in the early screenings judgement may be used to discount any very poor or very good ratings which seem to have relatively minor importance in the particular product search.

In the final screening, weightings, appropriate for the project, are introduced for each factor. The weighting takes the form of a numerical multiplier, 3 (essential), 2 (desirable), 1 (contributory), or 0 (irrelevant), allocated to each factor; 0 is used, of course, where the factor plays no part in the particular project under consideration or has no significance for the company concerned. By taking the profile chart rating for each factor, multiplying it by the weighting, and summing the result for all seventy-six factors, each product under assessment can be given an overall score.

The comprehensive chart in Fig. 7.13 covers all factor groups and is based on weighted ratings. The stability section corresponds to the values in the simple profile chart. For reasons already indicated, the shaded aggregate or average at the left-hand end is of very doubtful value.

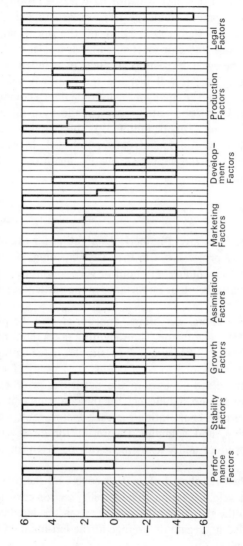

FIG. 7.13. Overall weighted profile chart. Quantitative evaluations of this kind, though indicative, should be used with particular caution but may be helpful in highlighting and comparing the particular strengths and weaknesses of different products. Weightings and weighted ratings for the ten stability factors are shown in brackets on the first chart (Fig. 7.12). Intrinsic duplication of factors and the problem of defining satisfactory weighting ratios make quantitative assessment extremely unreliable.

SIGNIFICANCE

It is emphasized that this overall figure is not absolute, since both rating and weighting are relative within the context of the particular product study. Also a single factor may be critical; for example risk of patent infringement may rule out a given product absolutely. In this case the weighting should logically approach infinity.

Care should be taken to understand the underlying significance of the scoring, which may be seen more clearly in terms of individual factor by means of a weighted overall profile chart. Comparison is sometimes simplified by super-imposing on the one chart in different colours the weighted overall profiles for several products.

Such an approach, however crude it may appear, ensures that no vital factor is overlooked. Intuitive judgement is guided and defined, and becomes in consequence all the more effective. The resulting assessment is thus more balanced and less prone to error than would be possible with any less systematic method.

FACTOR GROUPS

The screening factors that enter into the construction of a complete profile are as follows (developed from W. R. Grace & Company's list):

1. *Performance Factors*

1.1. *Turnover.* A product unlikely to secure more than a given fraction of a company's existing turnover, say 10 per cent, will be rated very poor (-2). The product will be rated very good (2) where a convincing estimate for turnover substantially exceeds an agreed minimum figure.

1.2. *Profit.* Where a product on sale overseas is already yielding profit on turnover above the company's present average, it will be rated good (1). If it is also likely to provide the company with a high return on investment over a long period, the rating will be raised to very good (2).

1.3. *Sales record.* Where a product is selling well in its home market and sales are still expanding rapidly, the rating will be very good (2).

1.4. *Capital utilization.* If the product is capable of putting idle capital to work in a profitable way, it will be rated good (1) or very good (2), but if it calls for excessive investment, either during its introduction or in the longer term, it will be rated very poor (−2).

1.5. *Overheads.* A product that is able to make a substantial contribution to overheads will deserve a good rating (1). Producing tin-tacks in an airship hangar would be costly in heating, lighting and capital depreciation, and the rating very poor (−2). A product that introduces heavy additional overheads will also be rated poor (−1) or very poor (−2).

2. Stability Factors

2.1. *Durability of market.* A basic component or material for which there will always be uses, such as $\frac{1}{2}$ in. copper tube or sulphuric acid, will be rated very good (2). A component intended for a steam locomotive or other end product which is almost obsolete will be rated very poor (−2).

2.2. *Breadth of market.* A product sold both nationally and abroad to a wide variety of customers will be rated very good (2), while another used in just one step of a process peculiar to a small number of manufacturers located in one geographical area will be classed as very poor (−2), unless the position may be improved by favourable long-term contracts with reliable purchasers.

2.3. *Possibility of captive market.* A product which has a market within the company or group will be given a very good (2) rating; one which has a potential use but can be bought from outside suppliers at such favourable prices that the return on investment for the manufacturing facilities would be borderline will receive an average rating (0).

2.4. *Effect on product spread.* A product that, added to a company's existing range, increases the company's viability and resilience in the face of market fluctuations, will be highly rated.

2.5. *Complementary cycle.* A product with a sales cycle complementary to the company's existing seasonal pattern will rate very good (2). A leading shipbuilder is said to have noted that when marine-engineering work was depressed, the company took the opportunity to install new machine tools. Assuming that other marine-engineering companies acted in a similar way, the company decided to enter the machine-tool market, in order to even out the fluctuations in their operating cycle. A product that tends to accentuate the present peaks and troughs will of course be rated very poor (−2).

2.6. *Stability in economic depression.* The rating will vary with the elasticity of demand. Where the purchase of a product can easily be postponed, such as a machine tool, it may receive a very poor (−2) rating (unless it is of a unique or advanced type such that its introduction will lead to large cost reductions for the customer). On the other hand, a new economical type of food container would be assessed as very good (2). Fluctuations due to the outbreak of war or other national emergency should also be borne in mind: demand for electronic control instruments would be reinforced, but machines for knitting fully fashioned stockings and other inessentials would be rated unfavourably.

2.7. *End product or component.* A finished product that a company can make, assemble and sell direct to customers will rate good (1). A component or subcontracted item that the customer can readily manufacture for himself when times are hard will be rated very poor (−2).

2.8. *Difficulty of copying.* A unique product or process involving a great deal of complicated know-how will be rated very good (2), particularly if covered by patents; while a simple device, not readily patentable, which could easily be copied by other companies, will be classed as very poor (−2).

2.9. *Favourable supply position.* A secure supply of materials and prompt delivery from a reliable contract source warrants a high rating.

2.10. *Purchasing volume.* If the new product's level of sales is likely to increase the company's requirement for certain components or materials, so making possible favourable purchasing contracts, the rating will be good.

3. Growth Factors

3.1. *Unique character of product.* The rating given will depend on how far the product is fulfilling an important unsatisfied need, or replacing a higher priced or higher cost product. This is a difficult assessment to make except on the basis of reliable technical and market information concerning the application and competing products or processes.

3.2. *Demand–supply ratio.* The product for which the demand is likely to exceed the supply will get a very good (2) rating, whether or not the product is unique.

3.3. *Expanding market.* A product that sells in growth sectors of the market will be rated very good (2); whereas one selling in declining markets will be considered very poor (−2).

3.4. *Export possibilities.* The rating will depend on the prospects for export sales. Excellent export potential but excessive dependence on export markets may get an average (0) or poor (−1) rating.

3.5. *Rate of technical change.* If there is a wave of change approaching on which the new product can ride, it draws a rating of very good (2). A good rating will similarly follow if a technical breakthrough or the appearance of new materials has recently opened the way to major developments in design or application. On the other hand, a product which is unlikely to experience growth more than commensurately with the growth of population and standards of living will be classed as average (0). One which is losing ground technically will be regarded as very poor (−2).

3.6. *Scope for technical advisory service.* If a product, alone or in conjunction with existing products, could lead to the creation of a technical advisory service, which in turn may promote the sale of other products in the company's range, the product will rate highly—particularly if the service can be readily defined and so easily put over by advertisement or other means.

3.7. *Ancillary sales.* Where a product offers the prospect of selling considerable quantities of related products made by the company, for example, auxiliary equipment and other complementary items, or opens up new possibilities for manufacture, the rating will be high.

3.8. *Useful byproducts.* Where a new process has useful byproducts which may help to swell the company's business, they should be taken into consideration during the appraisal.

3.9. *Utilization of management.* A new project will rate very good (2) if it offers an opportunity to enlarge the responsibilities of potential managers, with chances of promotion. The high rating would be offset if existing products were unduly deprived of their essential management, or if top management's time and effort were unreasonably taxed.

4. *Assimilation Factors*

4.1. *Relation to product policy.* A product that is in character with the company's evolving product philosophy and corporate identity will be considered favourably.

4.2. *Time to become established.* The product which can be put on a commercial footing most rapidly, or before there is any serious change in economic, technical or competitive conditions merits a good (1) or very good (2) rating.

4.3. *Company affiliations.* Where associated companies can assist in establishing the product, either as sales outlets or suppliers of components, the rating will be very good (2). Where they introduce restrictions or create problems of acceptance, the rating will be very poor (−2).

4.4. *Adaptation and development.* A product that is fully developed with detailed drawings and requires no modification or development will be highly rated (2). If it needs conversion to British standards, units of measurements or practice, or has a long difficult period of development ahead, it will be rated poor (−1) or very poor (−2). Where it is simply an idea or a designer's sketch it will also receive the lowest rating (−2).

4.5. *Applications engineering.* Where an existing well equipped laboratory can study and develop applications for the new product the rating will be very good (2). If new and different facilities are required the product would be classed as very poor (−2).

4.6. *Provision of assistance.* Where the prospective associate or licensor offers to provide sales and production engineers to assist in launching the product, it will be rated very good (2).

4.7. *Cost accounting.* If costs can be readily calculated in advance and the product fits the present cost structure it will be rated very highly (2).

4.8. *Operating margin.* Where the likely selling price considerably exceeds the estimated manufacturing, overhead, sales and other costs, thus providing a safe margin during the trial period, the rating will be good (1) or very good (2).

4.9. *Value added.* The more the total processing or manufacture can be carried out effectively by the company, the higher the rating.

4.10. *Internal availability of components.* If components or raw materials are available within the company, then the new product will be easy to assimilate and will also create increased requirements for existing products. It will therefore receive the highest rating (2).

4.11. *Types and sizes.* If the product can be made initially in relatively few types and sizes, the licensor supplying other items in the range and possibly components, the product will be rated very highly (2). Where a complete range must be provided from the start, the rating will be very poor (−2).

4.12. *Stock handling.* A product that can only be marketed successfully if large stocks are held will be rated poor (−1), particularly if the company cannot afford to do so and has little storage space (−2). A product well adapted to an existing stock control system will be rated high (1) or very high (2).

4.13. *Complementary products.* If a product depends for success on the sale of complementary or ancillary products which the company does not or cannot manufacture, it will be rated very low (−2).

4.14. *Transport access.* If the product cannot be readily despatched from the present factory because suitable transport facilities are not available, for example if the product is too large or too delicate, the rating will be low.

5. *Marketability Factors*

5.1. *Sales features.* If the product has advantages in price, quality, performance or durability, it will be marked average (0), good (1) or very good (2).

5.2. *Relation to existing markets.* A product which can be sold to existing customers rates very good (2). One which calls for an understanding of an entirely different market would be dismissed as very poor (-2).

5.3. *Reputation in allied fields.* If the company is highly regarded in neighbouring fields, though not necessarily in the field to which the new product immediately belongs, the rating may be very good (2).

5.4. *Proximity to market.* The product will earn a high rating if it can be sold easily in an area close to the factory of manufacture.

5.5. *Volume with individual customers.* A rating of good (1) or very good (2) will apply if few customers buy a large volume, or if customers are sufficiently concerned to provide evaluation facilities. This factor may be balanced to some extent against the breadth of market factor in the stability group.

5.6. *Channels of sale.* If existing distributors, agents or outlets can be used for marketing the product, it will be rated very good. If new channels of distribution are required, the rating will be very poor.

5.7. *Sales organization*. Where the product can be sold effectively using the existing sales organization and facilities, it will be rated highly. If an entirely new team must be recruited the rating will be poor.

5.8. *Availability of service*. If the product's servicing requirements can readily be met by the present service department, the rating will be high.

5.9. *Maintenance requirements*. If the product is likely to create serious maintenance problems, it will be given an unfavourable rating.

5.10. *Delivery schedules*. A product that accords with the company's existing practices on delivery will receive a good rating (1).

5.11. *Promotion*. A product calling for excessive promotional expenditure will be rated poor.

5.12. *Relation to customers' products*. Rating of poor (−1) or very poor (−2) will be given if the same or similar products are made by the company's existing customers, or if, though of a different type, the product tends to take business away from them or detract from the profitability of their activities.

5.13. *Anticipated competition*. Competitive standing determines the rating. If other well-entrenched suppliers not only serve their customers well but buy from them as much or more than they sell to them, the product will warrant a rating of very poor (−2).

5.14. *Freedom from periodic fluctuations*. Rating depends on the extent of predictable short-term cyclic and seasonal changes in demand. This factor is not to be confused with stability in economic depression (see above), but is concerned rather with peak and base load consideration as they affect the market and supply situation.

6. *Development Factors*

6.1. *Relation to development programme.* A project that is closely related to the main lines of a company's development programme and will broaden the knowledge fundamental to its development activities will secure a higher rating than a project that is out of line with them.

6.2. *Development costs.* Can the cost of development be written off on sales over a reasonable period? If not the rating would be very poor (-2).

6.3. *Utilization of existing knowledge.* The more familiar the technical areas to be explored, the greater the chances of success and the better the rating.

6.4. *Utilization of test facilities.* A project that employs existing experimental plant saves time and money, and merits a high rating.

6.5. *Availability of research personnel.* Lack of suitably qualified and able personnel within a company and the difficulty of acquiring them are factors to be weighed carefully and rated accordingly.

6.6. *Availability of design staff.* A product that calls for large additional design resources will be rated very poor (-2).

6.7. *Design for manufacture.* If the product has to be redesigned in order to simplify production, or to reduce costs, it will receive a poor rating.

6.8. *Variations in design required.* A requirement for a wide range of units, tailormade equipment, or special versions, resulting in high design and manufacturing costs, small series production and stock problems, will deserve a very poor (−2) rating, especially if frequent changes are likely to result in obsolete stocks.

7. Production Factors

7.1. *Utilization of idle equipment.* A product that can make full use of equipment that would otherwise be idle and places no demands on plant already occupied justifies a high rating.

7.2. *Balanced utilization of plant.* If the product itself makes balanced use of existing production facilities or contributes with other products to an equable distribution of work, its rating will be high. This factor differs from the first production factor. In that it involves a more comprehensive consideration of a factory's manufacturing resources and transfers emphasis from the short to the longer term.

7.3. *Standard production tools.* Where a product calls for the introduction of special-purpose machinery, additional production tooling, or novel plant it will be graded poor (−1) or very poor (−2), though if such special tools are likely to represent a unique facility, the grading may be high.

7.4. *Use of familiar materials.* A product that involves the working of materials foreign to the company's previous experience would be given a poor (−1) or possibly very poor (−2) rating.

7.5. *Use of familiar techniques.* Products which can be made using techniques and processes familiar to the company, and to existing standards of precision, thereby avoiding the cost of training personnel, will be classed as good (1) or very good (2).

7.6. *Availability of suitable labour.* Account should be taken of the local labour situation. If the product calls for large numbers of skilled production and maintenance workers or special skills not available in the district, it will receive a low rating.

7.7. *Redeployment of production plant.* If a product calls for a reorganization of factory layout, with major alterations to the production lines and flow routes, the rating will be low.

7.8. *Product size.* Consideration should be given to the size of the product and the convenience of handling it and transporting it within the existing factory building, using the cranes and mechanical handling plant available. A product of approximately the same size as most of the existing products would receive a high rating.

7.9. *Freedom from hazard.* Products that involve danger to plant or personnel will be classed as very poor (-2).

7.10. *Scrap and waste disposal.* Should a product introduce problems of scrap or waste disposal it will be assessed accordingly.

8. *Legal Factors*

8.1. *Patent protection.* Where sale of a product may risk infringing the patent or licence rights of another company, it will be rated very poor (-2). A product covered by patents in the licensee's country, and in the countries where he plans to sell it, will be rated highly (2). If the patents have only a short period to run or have long since lapsed the marking may be average (0) or poor (-1).

8.2. *Strength of patent.* Where a patent covers a feature not easily defined, overlaps with rival patents, or can readily be broken, the product will be rated poor (-1) or very poor (-2). If the product is covered by a unique, isolated and well drafted patent, it will be considered good (1) or very good (2).

8.3. *Licence position.* Where the contractual conditions and obligations arising from a licence are clear and satisfactory, the product will receive a high rating (2); where there are conflicts of interest, difficulties concerning trade mark or trade name, restrictions on sublicensing, or some doubt as to whether the would-be licensor is in fact at liberty to grant a licence, the rating will be poor (−1) or very poor (−2).

8.4. *Territorial franchise.* Where an exclusive territorial franchise is clearly defined and embraces good markets, the rating will be very good (2). A non-exclusive licence or one limited to an unprofitable territory will rate very poor (−2).

8.5. *Export as component.* Where there are restrictions on the export or the product as a component in a larger installation, the rating will be very poor (−2). Absence of restrictions on export or sale will merit a high rating (2).

8.6. *Marketing agreements.* Care should be taken that there are no marketing agreements that conflict with the full exploitation of the product. Obscurities in selling rights may call for an average (0), poor (−1) or very poor (−2) rating.

A simple checklist embracing all the above seventy-six factors appears in Fig. 7.14 and a profile adapted for a chemical concern in Fig. 7.15. It will be apparent that many factors overlap or reinforce each other and care should be taken to avoid double counting. In defining the legal factors (and also in connection with the section on licensing) I had the help of a friend and former colleague, John Hagon.

Most of the factors in Fig. 7.15 are self-explanatory, but it may be useful to elaborate on complementary cycles. Often a company seeks to introduce a product with a cycle of demand complementary to that of its existing products in order to fill the cycle troughs. As mentioned in paragraph 2.5 above, a group of marine engineers noticed that they were buying machine tools at the time that

Fig. 7.14. Table showing checklist of factors for screening new products. The significance of each factor is explained in the text.

SCREENING FACTOR CHECKLIST

1. *Performance Factors*
   1.1. Turnover
   1.2. Profit
   1.3. Sales record
   1.4. Capital utilization
   1.5. Overheads

2. *Stability Factors*
   2.1. Durability of market
   2.2. Breadth of market
   2.3. Possibility of captive market
   2.4. Effect on product spread
   2.5. Complementary cycle
   2.6. Stability in economic depression
   2.7. End product or component
   2.8. Difficulty of copying
   2.9. Favourable supply position
   2.10. Purchasing volume

3. *Growth Factors*
   3.1. Unique character of product
   3.2. Demand–supply ratio
   3.3. Expanding market
   3.4. Export possibilities
   3.5. Rate of technical change
   3.6. Scope for technical advisory service
   3.7. Ancillary sales
   3.8. Useful byproducts
   3.9. Utilization of management

4. *Assimilation Factors*
   4.1. Relation to product policy
   4.2. Time to become established
   4.3. Company affiliations
   4.4. Adaptation and development
   4.5. Applications engineering
   4.6. Provision of assistance
   4.7. Cost accounting
   4.8. Operating margin
   4.9. Value added
   4.10. Internal availability of components
   4.11. Types and sizes
   4.12. Stock handling
   4.13. Complementary products
   4.14. Transport access

5. *Marketability Factors*
   5.1. Sales features
   5.2. Relation to existing markets
   5.3. Reputation in allied fields
   5.4. Proximity to market
   5.5. Volume with individual customers
   5.6. Channels of sale
   5.7. Sales organization
   5.8. Availability of service
   5.9. Maintenance requirements
   5.10. Delivery schedules
   5.11. Promotion
   5.12. Relation to customers' products
   5.13. Anticipated competition
   5.14. Freedom from periodic fluctuations

6. *Development Factors*
   6.1. Relation to development programme
   6.2. Development costs
   6.3. Utilization of existing knowledge
   6.4. Utilization of test facilities
   6.5. Availability of research personnel
   6.6. Availability of design staff
   6.7. Design for manufacture
   6.8. Variations in design required

7. *Production Factors*
   7.1. Utilization of idle equipment
   7.2. Balanced utilization of plant
   7.3. Standard production tools
   7.4. Use of familiar materials
   7.5. Use of familiar techniques
   7.6. Availability of suitable labour
   7.7. Redeployment of production plant
   7.8. Product size
   7.9. Freedom from hazard
   7.10. Scrap and waste disposal

8. *Legal Factors*
   8.1. Patent protection
   8.2. Strength of patent
   8.3. Licence position
   8.4. Territorial franchise
   8.5. Export as component
   8.6. Marketing agreements

their marine work was on the downward grade. They therefore decided to acquire machine-tool companies in order to compensate for fluctuations in their work load. In practice it is not easy to achieve this result; but sometimes the same cause, such as a credit squeeze, can be responsible for fluctuations which are out of phase with one another in different businesses. For example, restrictions may affect both house construction and the sale of furniture, but owing to differences in completion and delivery periods, the impact on the two industries may not coincide.

National Variations

Screening, though depending ultimately on judgment, serves to eliminate the pitfalls of a purely intuitive approach. Thus in examining American, Japanese or Soviet equipment available for licensing, it should be borne in mind that circumstances in other countries are often very different from those in Britain. Scale of operations may be particularly important.

The Russians have, for example, devised an interesting process for prefabricating in a factory the cylindrical body of a storage vessel, rolling it up into a scroll, transporting it to site, unrolling it and completing a simple final weld, thereby reducing the cost of site-work, which tends to be very high.

Although the method appears most attractive, a prospective United Kingdom licensee would be advised to ask the following questions. How many factories are serving the whole Soviet requirement? In other words, are they able to operate a centralized industry? Do British tank fabricators have work on a nationwide basis or simply serve local needs? Is the annual demand in Britain commensurate with the cost of the necessary capital equipment? Or is construction limited to a relatively modest replacement market? Is the thickness of plate employed consistent with Western practice and standards, particularly those of the American Petroleum Institute? Could the scrolls be readily transported on British roads?

The screening process described above is shown visually in Fig. 7.16. The result might be four or five products, recommended in order of preference.

Unexpected Opportunities

Product decisions are difficult to take and companies have sometimes rejected promising opportunities on grounds which in the event have proved invalid. Almost every likely company in the United States and Europe rejected the process which was later so successfully exploited by Xerox and the Linz-Donau (LD) method of steelmaking, using tonnage oxygen, was apparently turned down by several United Kingdom companies, though it has perhaps in turn been superseded.

Products are no doubt discarded for mistaken reasons as often

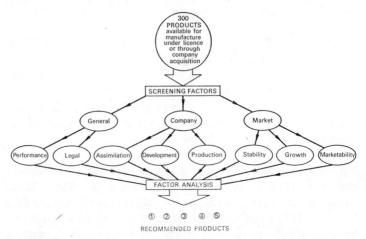

FIG. 7.16. Visual representation of screening process for handling a haul of several hundred products. The main company, market and general factor groups are shown. (A. E. Ansell.)

as they are adopted, emphasizing once again that purpose should be the greater part of planning. Supposed trends can be deceiving. Few would have foreseen the post-war resurgence of the gas industry or have believed that control systems based on pneumatics (fluid logic) could take the place of electronics in certain applications.

In practice it is the project rather than the product which has to be assessed in quantitative terms. Dr. A. Peisl of the German company Siemens, who has given considerable thought to the problem, uses the following formula:

$$nl + nm + nb + D + J + M + ns + ng + P = np,$$

where n is the number of units to be made (normal, minimum or maximum), l is labour cost per unit, m is material cost per unit, b is the manufacturing overhead, D is a lump sum for development, J is a special product investment, M is a lump sum for marketing, s is selling cost per unit, g is general and administrative costs, P is anticipated profit and p is unit price (so np is total sales volume).

Given a certain unit price it is possible to solve the equation to determine what quantity the company must sell to achieve a normal profit. Conversely, if the market is known, the equation can be solved to determine unit price.

Dr. Peisl has also noted that in his company, which is already strongly oriented towards change, with a well-established structure difficult to alter, the practical approach to planning has been through procedures not through reorganization (see Chapter 11). He stresses too the importance of discounting future values to present values when computing cash flows (DCF, see Chapter 9); and of value analysis (the systematic study of proposed or existing products to realize their necessary functions at minimum cost). But whatever the product and whatever techniques may be employed, the most difficult part of product planning is to assemble cost and market data.

Market Research

Once a limited number of product ideas have emerged from the screening process, it will usually be necessary to evaluate them in depth, using market research. It is a subject that has been amply documented, and it is enough to say here that the purpose of a market survey in this context would be to establish such facts as:

(1) The total size of market and its projected growth.
(2) Competitors, the nature and strength of competition.
(3) The share of the market that the company might reasonably expect to capture.

(4) Preferred product specification and features.
(5) Types and sizes to be introduced—initially and later.
(6) The markets and sometimes individual customers on which effort should be concentrated at first and in the longer term.
(7) Prices, price elasticity and discount structure.
(8) Channels, methods and conditions of sale.
(9) Factors affecting customer preference and why.
(10) Cash flow, profitability and recommended course of action.

The profitability of a market, or even of a product, is meaningless when taken outside the total planning context. As emphasized throughout this book, the product links company and market, and profitability involves all three. What is profitable to one company may be a dead loss to another, which does not have the technical or marketing assets to exploit it properly.

With an innovative product, where competing prices do not exist as a basis for comparison, projecting profits is particularly difficult. As Wolf Mankowitz observes, nothing is worth anything until you sell it and then only what you can get for it.

Essentially different approaches are required for consumer and industrial research and a practitioner in one tends to look on the other somewhat sceptically. The consumer specialist may consider industrial research as statistically questionable and too dependent on informed opinion. Whereas the industrial specialist sees consumer research as a means of employing resting actresses in a procedure whereby statistics take the place of intelligent interpretation. "Of a hundred people interviewed, nine-nine had never heard of the Westmorland resonant deburring system; one wondered how it worked."

In fact consumer research calls for subtlety of questionnaire, sampling, interpretation and analysis, where the informant is essentially an innocent. Industrial research depends more on the subtlety of interviewing and the knowledge of the informant, where the consultant uses a matrix approach to the appreciation of a market situation, filling gaps in a pattern of information and reconciling all data gathered to give an internally consistent picture, compatible with known fact and reasonable conjecture. It is not enough to ask how many? But also: why?

Again, the industrial interviewer must be someone of sufficient stature to talk on equal terms with senior managers, at the same time able to redirect his questioning as the interview proceeds, exploring the knowledge of informants and progressively interpreting their answers, not simply depending on a rigid questionnaire.

But like the consumer research agency, the industrial research company has to interpret past action to project future action, appraising underlying attitudes by indirect questioning plus the weighting and ranking of alternatives, so as to uncover genuine response in a real or active situation.

My colleague Barry Weedon illuminated the importance of market research in an article for *Engineering* by noting that a barrow boy is close to his customers, but a boardroom is not, even if every director is a hard-headed one-time barrow boy. If a housewife does not like what she finds on a barrow, she says so and she says why, and the barrow boy can take the necessary action to put things right. For example, he may lower his prices, take more care in choosing and laying out his stock, or alter the selection of goods he offers. Again, he can easily learn from his competitors, simply by looking at their barrows. Industrial companies are not in such a happy position, but they still must obtain similar kinds of information and take similar kinds of action. Instinct alone is not enough; it must be supplemented or, failing that, replaced by market research.

Selling might be cynically described as the measured use of truth. To present the underlying truth of an ability to a prospective customer who cannot possibly possess the historical knowledge and experience that makes this ability self-evident, it is necessary to present a case that will offset his prejudice. In the same way the magnification of a microscope reveals reality, though no one would believe that a tissue cell is half an inch across. Sometimes genuine reality can only be revealed through magnification or distortion.

Barry remarked on one occasion that in selling my company's services I would no doubt shortly be referring to our "worldwide data retrieval system". I asked him what he had in mind. He said "the public telephone". Market research, on the other hand, should be the significant interpretation of reality and calls for a different attitude of mind from that required in sales.

It Can't Be Done

Unfortunately, in product planning, objective appraisal is too often coupled with a negative reaction, perhaps supported by some spuriously sophisticated argument. Resistance to new products can only be overcome using at least a certain element of selling. Figure 7.17 and Fig. 7.18, borrowed from US Steel, illustrate the traditional answer to any fresh idea.

There was this man talking to his disciples. One day he remarked: "I think I have found the key to human happiness and harmony."

"What is it?" they all cried.

He answered: "Love thy neighbour."

The first said: "Huh?"

The second: "It's been done; it's in the ten commandments."

The third said: "What do you mean by 'neighbour'?"

The fourth: "Disgusting!"

The fifth: "My dear chap, it's against the laws of human nature."

Six others noted that they went along with the idea and suggested that they form a club: "But how do we keep out undesirables?"

And the last: "We shall have to look after our interests and protect ourselves. If anyone gets difficult, I'll cut off his ear."

New ideas and innovation can be resisted in so many ways. Sometimes the decision makers simply do not get the point. Either it is suppressed without a hearing, on the grounds that someone must have thought of it before; put in the pending tray; turned down for some private emotional reason; logically condemned using a sophisticated argument based on the conven-

FIG. 7.17. "Do you realize, sir, that if your invention should gain popular acceptance—which I do not for one moment believe it will—we should have to provide paved roads, throughout the length and breadth of the country, thousands of pumping stations to supply ready access to fuel, and innumerable vacant lots in every city in which to park the vehicles? Take my advice and forget this folly, Henry." (US Steel—*Dilemma: People in Motion*).

tional wisdom of the time; transformed to fit a preconceived opinion, in the process becoming utterly disfigured; or taken up simply as a weapon in political debate.

There is certainly no substitute for fact and the processes of information gathering are examined in Chapter 8. But interpreting the information may be much more difficult. The following cases may illustrate the point.

A company introduced projection television, which was technically ideal and gave an excellent large picture. It sold well at first, then sales almost vanished. It turned out that the ordinary retailer was ill-equipped to service the more complex units, being

FIG. 7.18. "As a matter of fact, one of our tribe conceived the idea of the wheel quite some time ago, but we reasoned that the speed of the outer circumference would be so much greater than the speed of the inner circumference that the whole thing would fly apart, so we abandoned it." (US Steel—*Dilemma: People in Motion.*)

only acquainted with conventional television sets. A row had developed between the company's service and maintenance departments and virtually all its retailers, who ceased to promote the system and, indeed, discouraged customers from buying it.

Xerox developed their excellent copying system but realized that, notwithstanding far greater convenience and much lower running costs, with net gain over a period, few customers would be prepared to buy a machine costing many times as much as conventional equipment. The company therefore decided to hire the machines and sell copies as a service.

A Norwegian company decided to introduce a new form of condensed milk in a new kind of can. Part way through the project someone asked had the market been properly investigated. There was a measure of panic and a leading market research company was asked to carry out a study. Their conclusions were that for this kind of milk, in this kind of can, there was very little hope. By this time the company had a warehouse full. The managing director, a determined man, said: "we've got it, go out and sell it." And they did. It proved one of their most profitable lines.

A company in France developed a portable tree-saw with a neatly modelled grip. They had been successful in their sales to southern Europe but encountered strong resistance when attempting to sell the tool in Scandinavia. They discovered that in northern winters it was essential for lumberjacks to wear very bulky gloves, making the existing grip impractical.

The same facts, unfortunately, may be interpreted by different people in as many different ways. Professor Arnold Corbin tells a story of a no doubt fictitious friend who had a performing flea. He put the flea on a table and said "Jump". The flea jumped. He then cut off two of its legs, said "Jump" again and the flea repeated its performance. Finally he cut off the last two legs, said "Jump" and the flea stayed where it was. "There you are," said Professor Corbin's friend, "cut off their legs and they go deaf."

I understand he used the story on one occasion when addressing a company's sales force. "In this company," came a voice from the back, "cut off their legs and they still jump."

Recently I was addressing a group of scientists and thought I would illustrate my point with the same story. This time, the voice from the back was a little more elegant: "Surely you are mistaken, Mr. Ward, it is the cricket, not the flea, which has ears in its legs."

CHAPTER 8

THE INFORMATION BASE

RUNNING a business involves keeping in balance the various pressures, both internal and external, that are imposed upon it, while achieving its dynamic purpose. To embrace the more important of these pressures in a general statement, we may say that the function of a company is to exploit its present and potential assets in the context of existing and emerging markets by converting an input into a competitive output of greater value, buying and supplying at competitive prices, with competitive rewards to employees and competitive returns to shareholders, or competitive capital growth.

No doubt all the contributory functions could be embraced in the single phrase "competitive returns to shareholders", but over what period are these returns considered? It does not help to speak of net cash flow in the context of anything so complex as a business, since few companies are expected at the outset to have a limited life. To write off a company over, say, 20 years, would be possible but not popular.

It follows that return on investment does not alone provide an adequate measure of managerial performance, particularly since it would be difficult to agree an acceptable combination of risk, level of return and payback period, without reference to the investment market. Once more it is necessary to collapse the future into the present, and my complex definition of corporate function has this in view. It reduces to a dynamic present situation the desirable ends of profit, survival and growth, extending far into the future.

It also allows for special situations, as where a company is financially controlled and managed by a man who sets out, for instance, to impose his own moral standards on the business; or where, for tax reasons, executive shareholders prefer to take their returns in the form of increased salaries.

Emphasis on the word "competitive" shows the purposeful nature of the definition. A company's aim in paying high salaries would presumably be to motivate its staff or to increase their quality or numbers, and it would not wish to pay more than necessary to achieve these ends. Similarly, "competitive prices" does not mean "minimum prices", and Rolls-Royce, for example, could afford to charge a premium on acknowledged quality.

No more should a company seek to maximize returns or pay a dividend far higher than is needed to retain the confidence of present shareholders or to raise fresh capital. The company is, indeed, its members and its members are its shareholders. But their long-term interests lie both in profit and survival, and survival requires that all the functional demands be kept in equilibrium, like a closed polygon of forces. The directed drive towards corporate development may be regarded as the closing vector.

Again, we find that a company has the nature of an organism. An organism comprises organs that have separate functions to perform, but it is also essential that they remain in balance with each other.

If there were only a single yardstick, management's task would be relatively easy. But management is at the nerve centre of a complicated cybernetic system, both as energizing source and controlling agency. Its decisions are critical but cannot be soundly based without the proper input data. Management therefore depends on the collection, selection, analysis and assimilation of information.

A little while ago my colleague Balint Bodroghy prepared a paper on information as a base for planning with particular reference to decision making, and in this chapter I shall draw heavily on what he wrote.

Decision Making

Planning is only meaningful if it leads to practical decisions, and good decisions depend on information. A decision implies action and the action will have consequences falling broadly into two categories: financial consequences and others which might be social, personal, national and so on, as broadly shown in Fig. 8.1. These consequences lead in turn to new decisions.

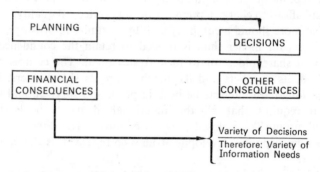

FIG. 8.1. Effective planning leads to decisions which may have financial or other consequences, leading in turn to new decisions. Each class of decision calls for certain kinds of information.

For the purposes of formal business planning, the financial consequences are of paramount importance and other consequences are either intermediate or simply follow from the common decency of the decision makers. Only the financial consequences will be considered here.

Successful management requires continuous decision making at several levels and the information requirements for these levels or classes of decision vary accordingly.

To explain the relationships between planning, decision making and information needs, the argument will be developed in four stages:

(1) Classification of decisions by time cycle and character, showing the corresponding information needs.
(2) An outline of the structure or hierarchy whereby the various classes of decision are linked to make up the active management of a company, noting how transitional or corporate planning decisions fit into the scheme.
(3) A discussion of information, its nature, sources, cost and the methods by which it is collected and processed.
(4) An examination of the decision-making mechanism, particularly where the element of uncertainty is relatively high as encountered typically in long-range decisions.

The planning process is essentially continuous and arbitrary subdivision of the time scale may not be helpful in itself—unless the subdivisions can be defined in a qualitative way leading to different modes of action.

Subdivision of the Planning Process

It has become a commonplace to talk about short, medium and longer-term decisions, as if the differences were clear and the time cycle or progression were universally accepted. In practice these distinctions are not very meaningful, and a more useful approach is to classify decision by their nature rather than the time spans to which they very roughly correspond, as follows:

Short term	Operating decisions
Medium term	Budgeting decisions
Long term	Transitional decisions

Such a descriptive classification is more significant than simple subdivision and avoids the confusing distinction, often loosely made, between corporate and long-range planning. I prefer to speak of transitional decisions, since corporate planning could be taken to cover the whole planning process, but they certainly fall within the province of corporate planning in that they are concerned with major changes in business policy and programmes.

Each decision category spans a broad spectrum, capable of successive subdivision, and Figs. 8.2, 8.3 and 8.4 show their general coverage. Items listed are for illustration and not intended to be comprehensive.

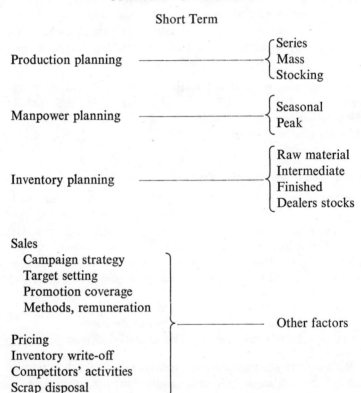

OPERATING DECISIONS

Short Term

Production planning ——————— {
Series
Mass
Stocking
}

Manpower planning ——————— {
Seasonal
Peak
}

Inventory planning ——————— {
Raw material
Intermediate
Finished
Dealers stocks
}

Sales
    Campaign strategy
    Target setting
    Promotion coverage
    Methods, remuneration

Pricing
Inventory write-off
Competitors' activities
Scrap disposal
} ——————— Other factors

Fig. 8.2. Operating decisions cover a broad spectrum of day-to-day requirements and involve most levels of management, though more frequently junior and intermediate management. They assume the existence of an operating framework.

There is no need to dwell on operating decisions (Fig. 8.2), since they will be familiar to anyone concerned with management.

Budgeting or medium-term decisions (Fig. 8.3) are taken periodically, usually on a regular cycle, and are normally concerned with a company's existing products and services. The function of decisions in this class is adaptation, but only in the

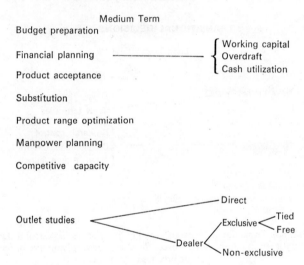

FIG. 8.3. Budgeting or medium-term decisions. Their purpose is adaptation to immediate environmental pressures on a periodic or cyclic basis, normally achieved through the creation of a framework (or targets) for operational control.

sense that an individual adapts, not a species. It is the conscious mechanism that management substitutes for the adaptive capacity of biological systems. In contrast, operating decisions are based on the assumption that a framework already exists and are designed to achieve a measure of optimization within that framework.

If we regard budgeting as management's substitute for immediate adaptation, then transitional or strategic or corporate planning decisions (Fig. 8.4) concern mutation. Successful mutation is, of course, a means of adaptation to major environmental change or a step improvement in the relationship between a species and its environment.

The analogy is complete if it is noted that a mutation will survive only if the mutant strain retains many of the parents' biological advantages. In the same sense, corporate mutations caused by transitional decisions will only survive if the competitive

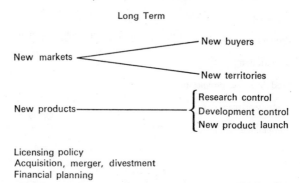

TRANSITIONAL DECISIONS

Long Term

New markets
— New buyers
— New territories

New products
{ Research control
Development control
New product launch

Licensing policy
Acquisition, merger, divestment
Financial planning

FIG. 8.4. Transitional decisions are only likely to be successful if the mutant strain retains or reinforces the competitive advantages of the parent or precursor company.

advantages of the previous structure are retained, and preferably reinforced, by the mutation.

As shown in Fig. 8.4, transitional decisions concern the invasion of new markets, possibly involving new kinds of customer, new territories or both; the development of new products, embracing the control of research spending and research activity, development programmes and the problems of product launching; licensing policy, both as licensor and licensee; the currently fashionable pursuit of acquisition, merger and divestment; and, finally, financial planning.

It will be noted that financial planning appears both among budgetary and transitional decisions. In the case of corporate planning it might involve major company reorganization to alter the company's financial gearing, to achieve tax minimization, or to make better use of available funds.

Information Needs

It is evident that management decisions cover an enormous range, from small adjustments in daily routine all the way to major, single decisions on which a company's prosperity or survival may critically depend. There is a corresponding spectrum of information needs and the next few charts (see Figs. 8.5, 8.6 and 8.7) illustrate the principal features.

In general, operating decisions relate to a familiar pattern of activity. The main problem is to recognize deviations from the pattern and distinguish between noise (used here in the control-system sense) caused by random events over which management has no control, from trends that management must detect and correct or exploit.

To make decisions under these conditions, a steady or continuous flow of information is required. Also the flow must be sufficiently rapid that control by management may have a stabilizing rather than a hunting or yawing effect. It is only necessary to think of the inept driver, with a slow reaction time, who would have a tendency to over-correct and who will in consequence weave an irregular path down the High Street to the consternation of pedestrians and other motorists.

The sources of information on the basis of which operating decisions are made are predominantly internal and, in a well-organized company, there is automatic discrimination between signal and noise, so management is not overwhelmed by trivial material, but important deviations from the pattern are seldom overlooked. Typical information sources for this purpose, as shown in Fig. 8.5, are call reports from salesmen and dealers, stock reports, lost-sale analyses and many others on the marketing

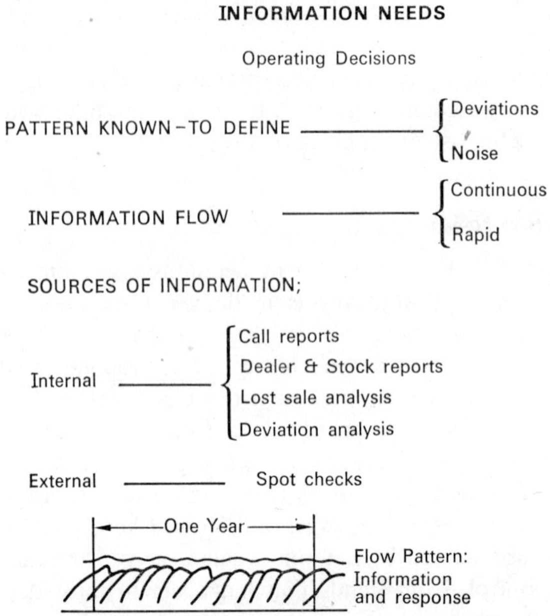

INFORMATION NEEDS

Operating Decisions

PATTERN KNOWN – TO DEFINE ——————— $\begin{cases} \text{Deviations} \\ \text{Noise} \end{cases}$

INFORMATION FLOW ——————— $\begin{cases} \text{Continuous} \\ \text{Rapid} \end{cases}$

SOURCES OF INFORMATION;

Internal ———— $\begin{cases} \text{Call reports} \\ \text{Dealer \& Stock reports} \\ \text{Lost sale analysis} \\ \text{Deviation analysis} \end{cases}$

External ————— Spot checks

|←———One Year———→|

Flow Pattern:
Information
and response

FIG. 8.5. It is necessary for management to distinguish genuine deviations in the normal pattern of activity from irrelevant noise, when making operating decisions. Although information flow is continuous and rapid, human response is essentially discontinuous.

side. There is a similar abundance of material relating to production, manpower, absenteeism and so on, again collected automatically.

External sources of information are useful to provide spot checks on such matters as market share, product acceptance and dealers' stocks. These checks can be carried out through multiclient research studies or specially commissioned surveys, costing usually between £200 and £2,000.

Management's most important responsibility in respect of information for operating decisions is to establish a desired flow process, so that all necessary information may be extracted and recorded, but only significant data is drawn to the attention of decision makers.

It may be illuminating to think of operating decisions as the actions of a controller sitting before the instrument panel of a large chemical plant. Information, particularly on older control panels, is continuously displayed; but the controller himself can only absorb information from time to time. It follows that while the flow is continuous its absorption is discontinuous and therefore the reaction also discontinuous.

Operation therefore differs, and in a very important way, from the operation of an automatic process-control system designed to sense and react continuously to changing conditions. This distinguishing feature of human control tends to be overlooked by management advisers groomed in cybernetics, who consequently tend to build over-ambitious and often impractical corporate models.

The small diagram at the bottom of Fig. 8.5 is intended to show that, although information is generated continuously (represented by the rippling line across the time span), it is absorbed discontinuously through the mechanism of reports, which have to be prepared, circulated, analysed, acted upon and finally filed, as indicated by the pattern of rising and falling curves.

While operating decisions concern deviations from an established pattern, budgeting or medium-term decisions relate to the deliberate alteration of an activity pattern or the setting of standards to which the pattern must conform. But they are still involved with familiar activities or services. The information flow is required in regular cyclic form, as illustrated in Fig. 8.6, and is generated and again absorbed in discrete bits or segments.

Sources of information tend to be predominantly external. For budgeting or medium-term decisions, internal events are relatively unimportant. Exceptions might be in the mining or extractive industries, where the depletion of mineral reserves or the discovery of a new deposit may call for a budgeting decision. Even in this case, however, it is likely that the problem would require a transitional or corporate-planning decision for satisfactory solution.

INFORMATION NEEDS

Budgeting Decisions

TO ESTABLISH AND TO INFLUENCE THE PATTERN

INFORMATION FLOW - Regular (cyclical)
                            Pattern - discrete bits or units (lumps)

SOURCES OF INFORMATION:

Market surveys

Dealer (agent) (division) reports

Econometric studies ————— { credit, investment
                            growth
                            prices, employment

Leading econometric indicators

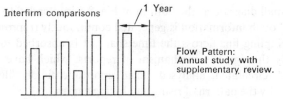

Interfirm comparisons   1 Year

Flow Pattern:
Annual study with
supplementary review.

FIG. 8.6. The purpose of budgeting or medium-term decisions is to define or influence the pattern of a business.

Typical information sources for budgeting decisions are periodic market surveys; dealer, agent or divisional reports; econometric studies of such factors as consumer credit or levels of investment in given industries; forecasts of trends and growth; and studies revealing the movement of wholesale or retail prices, or possibly employment.

As in the case of operating decisions, it is important to distinguish between background noise and signals and to block as much irrelevant information as possible.

The development of leading econometric indicators is very

helpful in highlighting what is likely to be significant. A historical example of such an indicator was the study of railway-truck loadings in the United States; in the nineteenth century, reports of truck-loadings were studied with as much care as is devoted to the pop charts today by people concerned with the entertainment industry.

Interfirm comparisons are another valuable discipline, providing information (in particular, operating ratios) on which to base budgeting decisions. The figures are useful whether the company itself is included in the study or not and, if intelligently interpreted, yield significant conclusions, though data is normally only made available to participating companies.

The flow of information is more segmented or lumpier than for operating decisions and might be based on a major annual study plus occasional minor revision in some companies and quarterly studies in others.

While the information flow for operating decisions in very small companies is usually non-existent or confined to the activities of a sales department, consultants are frequently engaged for this purpose in medium-sized companies, and in really large companies it is the domain of management services. For budgeting decisions there is now a tendency even for the smaller company to employ consultants, while medium and large-sized companies will either utilize the special experience of an individual director or senior manager or have their own management services section.

Since the information is lumpy, preparation of reports puts a strain on the resources of even the largest management services unit, and consultants are therefore often called in as extra capacity or for supporting work. Sometimes consultants use members of the management services team as their own subcontractors.

The purpose of transitional, strategic, corporate or long-range decisions is to create an entirely new business pattern as distinct from budgeting decisions where the aim is to define or modify an accepted pattern and operating decisions which serve to correct any deviations from the established pattern. Although the information flow for transitional or corporate-planning decisions is

INFORMATION NEEDS

Transitional Decisions

TO CREATE A NEW PATTERN

INFORMATION FLOW - Irregular
                   Regularly gathered

SOURCES OF INFORMATION:

Intelligence reports   commercial
                                        technical
                                        scientific

                                        population
                                        resource
Trend studies   spending
                                        travel
                                        energy uses

Product planning studies

Financial analysis (acquisition, merger, divestment)

Risk   analysis

Corporate planning exercise

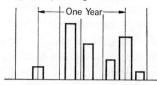

Flow Pattern :
Irregular, determined
largely by external factors

FIG. 8.7. Corporate or long-range planning leads to a fundamental
change in the pattern of a business.

necessarily irregular, the information itself must be regularly
gathered and analysed as illustrated in Fig. 8.7.

Sources of information for transitional decisions are long-range
intelligence reports, dealing with commercial, technical, scientific
or other developments that can be anticipated or foreseen. It
may also be necessary to conduct studies of population trends,

resources, spending habits, energy production and utilization, and particular inquiries related to a company's own business area. A vehicle manufacturer might, for example, commission research on changing travel patterns, as influenced by new modes of transportation or communication. Much of the relevant data is available, either in the literature or from published statistics. Product planning studies are likewise essential to maintain a healthy product portfolio.

It is equally important to carry out financial analysis on a periodic basis. For large companies, whose shares are quoted on lively stock markets, this service is performed by the financial analysts employed by stockbrokers and the insurance companies themselves. Though necessarily superficial and of short-term interest, the conventional stockbroker's letter or circular may be very helpful, though the more detailed studies are unlikely to be published. Nevertheless, it is useful to have a financial analyst's view of the company on record, since the institutional investor is nowadays the most important source of funds for financing expansion and will turn to such reports for guidance in portfolio selection.

The information flow is again shown in the diagram (Fig. 8.7). The flow is irregular to the point of confusion, as might be expected. There is no regularity, since the timing of major corporate decisions depends very strongly on external circumstances such as dramatic changes in trading conditions, variations in interest rates or taxation, important political events, or technical advances made inside or outside the company. Some bits of information will be historical and reasonably certain; others will come from short or long-term projections and hence will be only more or less reliable.

The initiative for corporate-planning studies must always come from general management, who might depend for information on the company's own management services or consultants specializing in the field.

Figure 8.8 reviews diagrammatically the different information needs and flow patterns for operating, budgeting and transitional decisions, with sources, typical costs and the relevant external services.

Operating decisions are designed to control operations so that they conform to an established pattern; budgeting decisions to alter or influence the pattern in a desired direction; and strategic or transitional decisions to change the pattern fundamentally or establish an entirely new one.

The information flow is steady for operating decisions and should be virtually automatic, with high discrimination against irrelevant background information; for budgeting decisions it is cyclic; and for transitional decisions random, with each unit or lump of information calling for a major effort, possibly involving specialized assistance.

Sources of information are generally internal and automatic for operating decisions and largely external for budgetary and transitional decisions. The miniature figures illustrate the flow of information in the larger corporations where for budgetary work general management is fed data by management services, who may rely on outside aid for gathering environmental or published information. For transitional decisions, general management may seek information directly from consultants in parallel with the company's own services.

Typical costs of procuring information are often (though misleadingly) regarded as nil for operating decisions, since the process of information gathering and analysis is an innate part of running a business. Also the flow is essentially continuous, so individual bits of data have negligible cost, though checks may be made, costing say £200 or, rarely, as much as £2000. Single studies carried out in support of budgetary decisions are typically in the range of £1000–£5000, and major corporate planning studies may cost from £5000 to £50,000.

External services are required from time to time. For operating decisions, typical services include the setting up of information systems within an organization or conducting spot checks on the flow of information with reference to external sources. For budgetary decisions, use is made of market research, econometrics

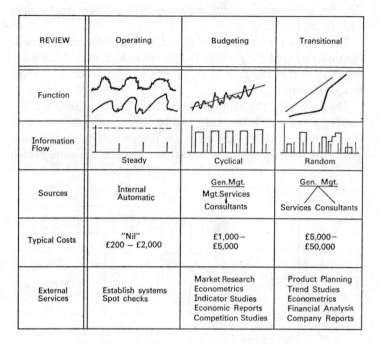

REVIEW	Operating	Budgeting	Transitional
Function			
Information Flow	Steady	Cyclical	Random
Sources	Internal Automatic	Gen.Mgt. Mgt.Services ↓ Consultants	Gen. Mgt. ⟨ ⟩ Services Consultants
Typical Costs	"Nil" £200 – £2,000	£1,000– £5,000	£5,000– £50,000
External Services	Establish systems Spot checks	Market Research Econometrics Indicator Studies Economic Reports Competition Studies	Product Planning Trend Studies Econometrics Financial Analysis Company Reports

FIG. 8.8. Summary of information needs and flow patterns.

and indicator studies, with analyses of competitor activities. In the case of transitional decisions, there are product-planning and trend studies, econometric forecasting again, financial analysis and major company profiles.

Decision Structure

The three levels of decision making naturally interlock and indeed they are, essentially, different sectors of the same continuous spectrum. In consequence, the information base for each level also contributes to decision making at adjacent levels, as shown schematically in Fig. 8.9. As will be seen, too, each decision level requires additional information sources independent of adjacent levels.

The arrows are not intended to suggest that information flow is continuous; as already noted, the nature of human decision making is such that the flow of information must proceed in units, lumps or quanta.

The reason for this lumpiness lies in the nature of the decision-making process and there may also be other direct and secondary causes. One is clearly the need to absorb and retain a multiplicity of data in order to make an effective decision, which

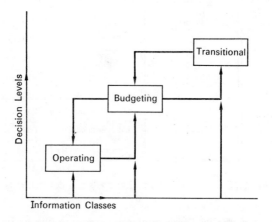

FIG. 8.9. Decision structure, showing the interdependence of different levels in decision making and the need to gather information from sources independent of the decision hierarchy.

therefore requires a single major effort greatly compressed in time. Another lies in the difficulty of information gathering, involving the cooperation of several or many individuals, though the decision itself may be made by one individual, or perhaps an entirely different group of people.

At the same time, management is concerned with a number of problems simultaneously, and must turn its attention from one to the next.

The factor of mental stress may have a bearing on the problem too. The work of Hans Selye in the Neurological Institute of Montreal suggests that the capacity of a human being to sustain mental stress is limited and fixed at birth. Each successive pressure depletes this human reserve and, if depletion proceeds at a rate leaving no opportunity for recovery, mental breakdown may follow. The natural reluctance to take decisions and the perhaps subconscious wish to husband the available resources for sustaining stress, may again lead to lumpiness in information flow.

In general a decision is a discrete step or change in direction and therefore discontinuous, tending to lump information into concentrations.

Although the decision structure, typical of corporate management, has been shown simply in Fig. 8.9, there are special problems that arise in the case of transitional decisions. We have seen that the lumpiness and uncertainty of information increases as the time scale is extended. Also it will be evident that corporate planning decisions call for information not limited to a company's immediate environment or field of operations. For this reason it will be necessary to examine in rather greater detail the relevant sources of information in considering the processes by which non-routine, long-range or transitional decisions are made.

Environmental Insulation

An important problem in seeking, absorbing and interpreting information for management decision making lies in the insulating effect of a company's trade environment, shown diagrammatically in Fig. 8.10.

There is a natural flow of information from the trade environment to a company by way of the sales force, membership of trade associations and the specialized trade and technical Press. This flow is to some extent reinforced in certain industries by the movement of personnel from company to company, though this mobility tends to be strictly limited by speciality and company activity. Among the employees of companies making chemical

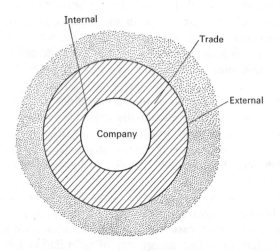

FIG. 8.10. Although familiarity with a company's immediate trade environment can be of great value in making operating and budgeting decisions, it may actually insulate the company from the information it requires for making transitional or corporate-planning decisions.

process plant, there will usually be people who have worked for two or more of the major competitors in succession. Similarly in cryogenic, nuclear, construction, automobile, aircraft, instrumentation or almost any other branch of engineering, it is a commonplace to encounter, at conferences and exhibitions, the same groups of people who reappear under different company names and with different titles.

Every segment of trade is a small self-contained world, largely isolated from other worlds. It is the very strength of these multiple internal links within groups which reduces intercommunication between groups, leading to an insulating or blanketing effect.

The closeness of a company to its trade environment is a great advantage in exercising operating and budgetary control. The intentions of competitors are generally known, even their expan-

THE INFORMATION BASE 205

sion plans, as are their internal problems. Also, most companies are conscious of major commercial opportunities within their prescribed areas of business.

But for transitional or corporate-planning decisions, the information needed is generally alien to the company's immediate business context and does not originate from its trade environment. It follows that the company has few if any automatic channels for gathering such vital data.

It is for this reason that my own company, for example, in promoting its services, notes that it could never hope to equal a client's deep knowledge of his own particular business, but has inevitably accumulated in its work a broad, if less intense, understanding of many industries and markets. It is because of this wide experience we believe we can contribute to the corporate planning of individual companies. For similar reasons, the Stanford Research Institute and similar bodies offer multi-client studies covering wide spectra of industry.

Publishers have also recognized the need for intercommunication between disciplines and specialities and the journal *Engineering* in the United Kingdom deliberately set out to serve this requirement, as did *Scientific American* and several other publications in the United States.

Another method of encouraging a natural flow of information across industrial barriers is to hire staff whose experience in other companies has been widely spread, as in marketing or planning, rather than closely oriented towards a given activity, industry or market. There are in addition bodies such as the recently established Centres for Industrial Innovation, part of whose responsibility is to highlight opportunities over a broad cross-section of industry, covering established or emerging sectors of commerce and technology.

Internal and External Data

Although external information is of predominant importance in corporate planning decisions, some internal information is also needed. It is described as internal, but also embraces the immediate business environment and covers such financial factors as the likely availability of funds, either from internal cash generation or from the market, the cost of funds, cash requirements of competing projects and so on.

It will also be necessary to make periodic reviews of research and development activities within the company. Frequently the flow of information from research to general management is pitifully poor, and in one instance at least a major American concern seriously considered commissioning a study from an outside consultant to report on the work of its various research departments.

Periodic examination of the company's identity and image, and a rapid and highly condensed flow of information on the company's current operations, is naturally assumed. Sources of trade information have been discussed, but also include technical intelligence reports, input–output studies, and projections of materials displacement, for example. Materials displacement does, of course, relate to the substitution in existing applications of new or newly competitive materials in place of those previously employed.

Although I am at present considering the part played by this information in corporate planning, much of it also contributes to operating and budgeting decisions. In the case of corporate planning, the fundamental difference lies in the way in which such information is interpreted and used.

Figure 8.11 shows schematically how a company's internal and external information field changes over time. At the base of the diagram is the present view of a company's internal information field (Fig. 8.10), surrounded by the trade environment, which is itself immersed in all the external sources of information.

Time Effect

When dealing with corporate-planning problems, the decision maker is not only required to penetrate the insulating effect of

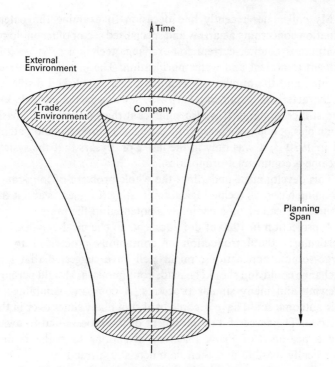

FIG. 8.11. Time–information space effect in medium- and long-range planning. Growth in the volume of data available—from internal sources, from the insulating trade environment and from the outside world—will almost certainly continue to expand during any period over which plans are formulated, leading to serious uncertainties.

the trade environment but also to project the information forward to cover the entire planning span. It follows that he must consider a future situation when the quantity of information available is likely to have grown very substantially. Most people are only too aware of the information explosion and, though I would question whether even the clearest trend will continue indefinitely, it is certainly probable that in reviewing any problem in 10 years' time there will be more data to take into account.

My colleagues recently had occasion to examine the patent situation concerning a narrow and specialized sector of technology: continuous counter-current ion-exchange techniques, as used in effluent treatment and water purification. The history of patents granted and the number of scientific papers published displayed a characteristic exponential growth, starting in the early 1930's and still continuing. It is also significant that, although the basic principles of counter-current processing were invented and patented in 1930-3, it was only in the last 2 or 3 years that the system became a commercial proposition.

This development underlines the whole problem of long-range planning based on technological forecasting (or guesses about the future), instead of on a company's potential in the present.

A projection in 1930 of developments in chemical engineering, particularly the introduction of continuous processing to all large-volume applications, might well have suggested that ion-exchange could and should be made continuous, as should perhaps brewing and many similar processes. A company gambling on this outcome could have become bankrupt many times over in the interval. The successful development of the process had to await the appearance of many ancillary inventions to make it first technically feasible and then commercially attractive.

In the next pages and in the following chapter on forecasting, I shall mention some of the techniques for tackling the problem of information space and time. Although obscure and sometimes misleading names are used by specialists, the subject itself is short on technique and therefore needs to be long on common sense.

Aids to Decision Making

Much of the information used in planning is collected and verified through some form of market research. The term is employed here in its broadest sense, though originally, as applied to the consumer product industries, it normally meant periodic audits of consumer behaviour. Nowadays, it covers much more and is often taken to embrace all fundamental information work concerned with business.

The scope of modern market research makes it particularly important to establish a clear and universally accepted terminology. Assessment of demand is a field in which some confusion has arisen and it may be useful to distinguish between demand and what we may conveniently call "needs" and "wants", bearing in mind that fundamental, undifferentiated, needs do not alter.

The distinction between the three terms may be illustrated by an example from dentistry which clearly refers to a country where there is no public health service. If I have a cavity in my tooth but am not aware of it, I am perhaps in need of dental care. If the tooth begins to ache, the need soon becomes converted to a conscious desire for treatment or a want. Now if the tooth hurts very badly and I have sufficient money to obtain the services of a dentist, then my want will contribute to overall demand. Demand is thus a want backed by adequate purchasing power.

It is failure to recognize these differences that has led to some misunderstandings and even false conclusions from studies of the market. A notable instance has been the failure to predict demand for fertilizers in the subcontinent of India. Most studies have been confined to a forecast of the want, calculated on the basis of expanding population and expectations of improving living standards. In practice, the necessary purchasing power has never so far materialized owing to the runaway growth of population and internal or external disorder.

Exclusive concentration on demand, in other words wants plus purchasing power, can also lead to error if it is forgotten that advertising and other forms of promotion designed to influence consumer behaviour may be used to convert needs into wants. Indeed, in advertising circles it is often claimed that such techniques are able to create new needs. The role of advertising, I have heard it said, is to devise a cure for a non-existent ill and then promote them both.

Consumer versus Industrial

Market research tends to be more concerned with demand than needs or wants, and purchasing power must therefore be borne in mind. Perhaps the principal distinction between the markets for consumer and industrial products lies in the distribution of purchasing power.

As a general rule, purchasing power for consumer products is widely dispersed, with relatively small individual variations, as indicated in the upper diagram of Fig. 8.12. One consumer will account for only an insignificant fraction of demand and, normally, a very large number of consumers make up the total. Consequently, demand can usually be assessed on the basis of

CONSUMER
PRODUCTS

INDUSTRIAL
PRODUCTS

FIG. 8.12. The upright triangle represents the distribution of companies by size and the horizontal dimensions of the inverted triangle the aggregate purchasing power for companies of given size.

statistical sampling, and it is sometimes surprising how small a properly structured and representative sample may be sufficient to ascertain the pattern of demand. In most consumer surveys, the sample of consumers interviewed is well below 1 per cent of the consuming population.

In contrast, demand for industrial products is highly concentrated. It is a familiar observation that "20 per cent of the companies in a given industry account for 80 per cent of the demand for a particular industrial product". Known as the 80:20 rule, it is frequently encountered in industrial market research. In fact it is very rarely true and important deviations on either side frequently occur.

For instance, in the United Kingdom chemical industry, ICI

alone account for perhaps half the demand for new capital equipment. Another extreme example might be the demand of the nationalized coal industry in Britain for mining equipment or the demand of the National Health Service for drugs sold on prescription.

In the lower diagram of Fig. 8.12, the two interlocking triangles are designed to illustrate the 80:20 rule, where the upright triangle represents the distribution of companies by size and the horizontal dimensions of the inverted triangle the aggregate purchasing power for companies of given size.

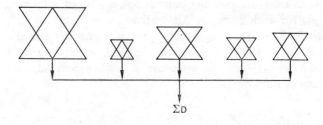

ΣD

FIG. 8.13. Owing to the wide range of applications for industrial intermediates (such as steel pipe, sheet or section, adhesives, insulation or chemical intermediates), the overall market cannot readily be sampled and aggregate demand has to be built up from individual elements.

The diagram is, of course, a gross over-simplification, and for most industrial intermediates the situation is much more complicated. Steel pipe, sheet or section, for example, find application in a multitude of industries. Customers for steel pipe include almost every conceivable form of engineering concern plus most producers of consumer durables such as motor-cars and domestic white goods. It follows that the market comprises a whole series of interlocking pyramids, which have to be summed in order to produce a representation of the aggregate demand, as suggested in Fig. 8.13.

In these conditions, the statistical sampling methods appropriate to consumer products are totally inadequate. Normally in industrial market research, the sample size is far larger as a percentage than in consumer research. A complete census is not uncommon, involving a detailed account of every customer's requirements. If such an approach is not feasible, for reasons of cost or time, or because it is impossible to secure the co-operation of certain companies, sampling of some kind then becomes necessary.

A sample is drawn, correctly stratified by size of customer, and, in grossing up demand, the variations in purchasing power for different companies must be considered. One approach is to divide total demand into a convenient number of segments, establish the corresponding populations, and draw off a random sample for each segment. Alternatively, a total census may be taken for the largest or most important customers and the remainder represented by a random sample, which is grossed up using a sensible ratio or indicator of relative demand, such as number of employees.

Derivative Demand

Since most commercial activity is aimed, directly or indirectly, at the ultimate consumer, it may be useful to examine the relationship between the demand for consumer products and the demand for capital goods.

Apart from government spending, the only fundamental source of demand is the consumer, though government action can influence trading conditions, causing periodic fluctuations in the level of demand.

The demand for consumer–product manufacturing facilities is derived from consumer–product demand. It is thus the first derivative of consumer demand, while the demand for plant required to manufacture production facilities for the consumer industries is the second derivative of consumer demand, as illustrated in Fig. 8.14.

This situation may be compared with equations showing distance, velocity and acceleration as functions of time. The greater the remoteness from ultimate consumer demand, the more severe become the fluctuations. In mechanics there might be negative acceleration. A corresponding recession in demand results in premature scrapping, moth-balling and the retention of under-utilized plant.

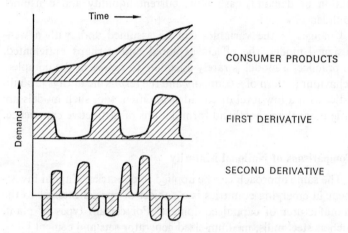

FIG. 8.14. Demand for consumer products (for example cars), with first and second derivatives, representing industrial demand for, say, steel and steelmaking plant respectively.

Econometrics

Attempts have been made for many years to represent aggregate purchasing power by means of mathematical expressions. The problem is extremely complex and the usefulness of the results somewhat limited. Given a suitable mathematical model it is feasible to explore the likely outcome of various actions or influences upon the market.

Hopes have even been expressed that we may be able to dispense with experimental government, from which most countries have been suffering, and replace it with more sophisticated forms of national planning. Unfortunately, none of the models have as yet succeeded in reflecting in a satisfactory way such psychological

influences as consumer confidence, which so often have a dispro-
portionate effect on the propensity to purchase. An alternative
approach, catalytic planning, is considered in a later chapter.

A model describing the propensity of a manufacturing concern
to purchase or invest is likely to include such factors as a sum-
mation of demand, cash flow, current liquidity and consumer
confidence.

Changes in the variables can be assumed and, with a well-
designed model, the effects explored and perhaps anticipated.
In practice, a model is rarely adequate to represent the complete
behaviour pattern of a company and the results are always probablistic, with a low level of confidence. Often, too, such models are
little more than shorthand formulations of instinctive experience.

Comparisons of National Maturity

The same approach can be applied to countries. Capital investment in emerging countries is a subject of special interest to the
manufacturer of capital equipment. For certain types of plant,
such as steel mills, medium-sized generator sets and cement kilns,
emerging nations provide an unexpectedly high fraction of total
demand. Consequently, skill in spotting countries on the threshold
of economic take-off is of considerable importance in current
planning.

A somewhat crude model has been devised for the process
whereby traditional society transforms itself into a mature
industrial society as illustrated simply in Fig. 8.15. I am no economist and would prefer to think of this view as descriptive rather
than econometric. Transition has occurred in this way in some
instances, but its form in practice no doubt depends on a variety
of conditions.

There seem to be two stable modes of existence for societies,
and the transition from one to the other occurs suddenly and
perhaps irreversibly. The closest analogy is that of hydraulic
jump in engineering. Water emerging from a sluice gate under a
high head will travel in the sluice with high velocity and shallow

depth. If some obstruction is placed in its path, a hydraulic jump occurs and the flow pattern is converted into one of low velocity and much greater depth. The jump is irreversible.

In society, a technology-free existence appears to be stable over long periods of time. A nodding acquaintance with the results or benefits of technology need not perceptibly affect the way of life. Then a combination of circumstances causes a relatively sudden change and the society is transformed.

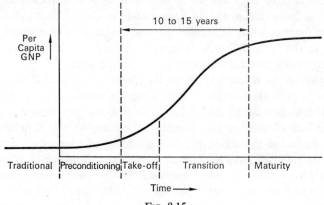

FIG. 8.15.

The transition is usually turbulent and is frequently accompanied by widespread changes, affecting not only the means of production, but also the entire fabric of society. This turbulence is unconsciously reflected in the descriptive terms applied to the phenomenon. We talk of an industrial revolution or an economic miracle.

Typically the transition takes 10–15 years to accomplish from the point of take-off. This time interval as applied to such widely different countries as the United States, the Soviet Union, Italy, Mexico, the Philippines and Formosa, seem to indicate that there are fundamental common underlying causes.

The preconditions of take-off in the economic sense have been extensively analysed. Apparently there has to be a minimum technological infrastructure in terms of capital goods, including a communications network, with roads and other forms of transport. At the same time, there must be a basic inventory of skills and some secondary manufacture to provide a rudimentary industrial context and social attitude.

Next, there must be a sudden accumulation of capital, particularly available or "hot" capital. In the Soviet Union, capital was accumulated by enforced saving from internal consumption. In the case of Italy and to some extent in post-war Germany, it came from foreign aid. In Britain and the United States saving came from commercially enforced postponement of consumption and in the United States, foreign investment and the discovery of important natural resources also played a part.

Spain is an interesting example, where take-off in the early sixties was made possible by military and commercial investment by the United States and other countries, leading indirectly to an influx of foreign investment, particularly by the American petrochemical industries, plus the spending of tourists in Spain and the remittances of Spanish workers dispersed through Europe.

In North Africa, which may well be the next geographical region to reach maturity, it has been the discovery of oil and the associated heavy investment in extraction facilities which provided the basis for transformation.

There is a final important precondition, namely confidence. It calls for a stable currency, a stable political system, international stability and some mysterious optimism which is needed to liberate the creative energies of businessmen.

Theories of economic transformation involve a vast range of factors, and the predictions derived from available models are so uncertain as to be useless for purposes of business planning, except in special cases where, for instance, capital products are to be exported to emerging countries. A slightly more practical tool is based on the assumption that a given standard of living at a particular time will generate a calculable demand for a certain type of product; and that development in different countries passes through the same stages, but staggered in time.

Scatter Diagrams

The method is illustrated in Fig. 8.16, in which a measure of living standards is plotted against consumption of a chosen commodity in the country concerned. The standard of living is normally measured by *per capita* gross national product (GNP), preferably expressed in terms of constant value (i.e. irrespective of currency

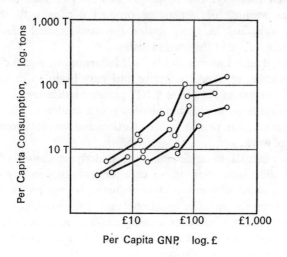

FIG. 8.16. Each line joining two points represents the change in consumption over a specific period (say from 1950 to 1960) and a succession of lines the time series for a single country.

fluctuations and inflation). Against *per capita* GNP, *per capita* consumption of the commodity can be plotted. The typical appearance of such diagrams may be seen in Fig. 8.16. There is a scatter of points on a logarithmic grid which exhibits a linear relationship initially and possibly shows saturation of demand in the later stages.

The usefulness of the diagram can be increased if in addition to plotting a scatter of production–consumption figures, a time series is included. The diagram might characteristically represent the scatter of production–consumption figures for a number of countries at two points in time, separated by say a ten-year interval. Points for a particular country can be connected by straight lines.

As might be expected, this form of analysis generally reveals a rising trend for new products and a falling trend for products past their maturity. The technique may thus be used to obtain advance warning of impending product decline with shadow curves staggered in time, unlike the conventional life cycle, which stops dead at the present instant.

Rising demand affects and is itself influenced by social change. For instance, demand for motor fuel may begin to exceed the rate of increase in *per capita* GNP, possibly indicating growth of leisure time spent in pleasure motoring, or a tendency, with urban development, for people to live further and further from their places of work.

It is essential to understand the underlying causes of such trends, since increasing use of cars for travelling to city offices may lead eventually to a decline in fuel consumption when congestion becomes excessive or attempts are made to improve public transportation. Conclusions would be still more difficult to draw if the outcome were that the Government took action to control the distribution of population.

Apart from commodities and consumer products, it is possible to draw scatter diagrams for the production of primary materials and the output of secondary manufacturing industries. The econometric model is gradually built up from the elements listed before, and attempts can be made to establish the availability of credit, cash flow and other relevant factors.

It is sometimes useful to replace *per capita* GNP by some other indicator of well being. Gross investment, for instance, has a characteristic relationship to GNP that reflects the country's position on the evolutionary scale. During the preconditioning period gross investment is typically small. During take-off it rises to 22 or 25 per cent of GNP and is an essential feature of this period. In a mature society it settles down to 15 or as little as 8 per cent of GNP. In some countries statistical information is also available on industrial investment as a whole, which tends to bear a fixed relationship to gross investment.

The method by which a model of demand is built up for a particular commodity can be illustrated by reference to a study concerning the demand for seamless steel pipe in the chemical industry of a recently developed country. Pipe is, of course, a basic component of chemical plant. The quantity of pipe used in a plant will depend on a variety of factors, some of which can be regarded as significant. The quantity of pipe will obviously depend on the size of the plant, on its complexity, and on the type of plant or its design.

As a first step, it is possible to establish a meaningful relationship, such as the following:

$$T_p = K\,[(\text{size})^x\,(\text{complexity})^y\,(\text{type})^z],$$

where T_p is pipe tonnage and other symbols are constants or exponents to be determined. It is then necessary to choose measures of size, complexity and type in accordance with this relationship, and then obtain a sufficient scatter of relevant data to determine the unknown coefficients and exponents.

Throughputs of products in tonnages per day were taken as a suitable measure of plant size. Such figures are frequently published, and it was thought that differences in pressure and specific weight would be accommodated by choosing an appropriate measure for plant type.

It was rather more difficult to select an indicator for complexity, but added value appeared likely to give the best result. It seemed logical to assume that the added value of the product would increase if the product were passed through several processing stages and would also be reflected in the price. Again, added value for the entire chemical process industry could be aggregated and projected forward, providing a link with overall industrial development in the country concerned. Plant types were classified (though unsatisfactorily) by the phase in which products were predominantly handled, namely in solid, liquid or gaseous form.

Having reduced the problem to a manageable simplicity (though at what cost in accuracy it was difficult to say) information was gathered on a large number of projects recently completed in a variety of countries and the coefficients and exponents determined by a multiple curvilinear regression, virtually a method of curve fitting and successive approximation (analogous to successive focusing).

The results proved reasonably consistent with other information available, both for the particular country and other countries which had passed through a similar period of development.

Necessities and Luxuries

The behaviour of communities displaced in space (geographically) or time (historically) may therefore help to guide us in projecting trends or transitions in demand. Data may be made meaningful in any number of different ways, but one further example may be sufficient to illustrate how information can be usefully interpreted, drawing on studies carried out by Törnqvist on family expenditure and budgeting in Sweden and Finland.

The price elasticity of demand is a well known concept in economics, relating to the effect of a small change in price on the quantity demanded. It is evident that demand for necessities is less affected by price changes than demand for goods considered to be luxuries. Analogous concepts appear in other disciplines: thus in feedback control theory, sensitivity corresponds to elasticity.

As formulated originally by the economist Marshall, the elasticity of demand at any price is the percentage increase (a) in the quantity demanded resulting from a certain percentage reduction, (b) in that price, or a/b, where b is small. If the change in volume is such that the volume times the price, or the total outlay, remains constant, the elasticity of demand between the two prices is said to equal unity; and demand is inelastic when it remains substantially the same however prices fluctuate. Elasticity in the case of any product will clearly depend on the scope for disposing of income on alternative goods or services, and consequently involves an expression of preference (indifference maps).

Törnqvist observed certain patterns in family expenditure and budgeting represented by the four curves reproduced in Fig. 8.17.

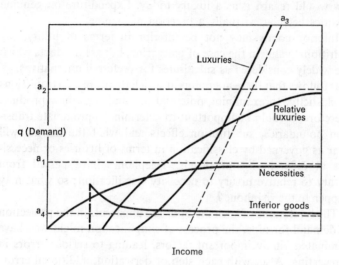

FIG. 8.17. Curves based by Törnqvist on studies of family purchasing and budgeting in Sweden and Finland. The dotted lines are asymptotes. (Reprinted from *A Methodology for Systems Engineering* by Hall, Copyright 1962 by Litton Educational Publishing Inc.)

The values *q* represent penetration of households as percentages and the dotted lines are simply asymptotes to which the curves tend at higher income levels. These characteristics were discussed in a chapter on "Needs research" in *A Methodology for Systems Engineering* by A. D. Hall of Bell Telephone Laboratories (D. Van Nostrand).

At low incomes, most expenditure goes for food, clothing and shelter. As income increases, more is available for luxuries. There is some correspondence with the allocation of investment discussed in Chapter 9.

Relative luxuries are goods which are regarded as luxuries by the lowest income groups, but are no doubt thought to be necessities in higher brackets. Farmers in remote country areas have managed without the motor-car from time immemorial, but few would regard it as a luxury today. Expenditure on genuine luxuries becomes virtually a function of income.

Inferior goods may not be inferior in terms of utility, say nutritional value in the case of margarine, but are products which are widely considered as substitutes for preferred alternatives.

It follows that there are points at which there are step transitions in elasticity. In examining potential demand for a new product, therefore, it could be important to determine approximate transition boundaries, substitution effects and what the market will bear as governed by classification in terms of luxuries or necessities at different income levels. Telephones have passed from luxury to relative luxury to necessity classification; so what may happen to the visiphone?

The limitations of such methods are apparent. In the projection of demand for pipe, the process of simplification might well have eliminated vitally important factors, leading to serious errors in forecasting. Also, with each step of derivation, additional errors may be introduced and inaccuracy may well increase in a cumulative way.

On the other hand, notwithstanding their pitfalls and limitations, such methods are better than no methods at all. Similarly, careful use of information is a better guide than guessing. In planning there is certainly no substitute for fact inasmuch as it can be gathered and properly interpreted. Processed data may be expensive—what Nelson Rockefeller has called "the high cost of finding out"—but the cost of not finding out can be considerably higher.

CHAPTER 9

FORECASTING AND RISK

PROPERLY interpreted and processed information increases our appreciation of reality, but the future remains uncertain. I have tried to suggest that in planning the anticipation of alternative outcomes is a more modest and more practicable guide to future action than forecasting, but attempts to forecast provide much of the material on which anticipation has to work. At the same time, it is desirable that the risk involved in any venture is understood, even if it cannot be measured.

I have also stated that no approach to forecasting, econometric, technological or otherwise, could hope to map the future. The best that can be done is to extend our vision along selected lines, branching and recombining them, as may seem appropriate; or locate a few isolated areas of greater probability within the future and determine how they may affect the fulfilment of our purpose.

I have also questioned why we should imagine that the configuration of the future is likely to be any less complex and surprising than unexplored terrain. Descend in parts of Colorado or the Gobi Desert from another planet and the visitor might justifiably suppose the earth were dead.

All I intend here is to sketch some of the more credible methods of forecasting currently employed, both economic and technological; endeavour to structure risk so that its extent may be perceived; and show how forecasting itself changes the situation of the forecasters. We shall never know how many elections have been won by courtesy of Dr. Gallup and his colleagues.

Through a Glass Darkly

In the chapter on working methods I have suggested how in the exploration stage of a single product-planning project, some effort is made to evaluate long-term requirements by investigation of emerging opportunities. But to forecast future product needs over the next 10, 15 or 20 years, is far more difficult. Nevertheless, to keep abreast of change, a company must attempt to do so, bearing in mind that it is easy to be mistaken.

I have stressed the problems of prediction in the early chapters, but some examples in the field of product forecasting may help to underline the hazard.

Had we known of Fermi's experiments with uranium and graphite piles 20 or 30 years ago, most of us would have predicted that by now our power generating industry would have been transformed. So far, changes have come from the growth in unit size of plant rather than from the development of nuclear power. More pessimistically, the pioneer nuclear physicist, Lord Rutherford, dismissed the possibility of extracting useful energy from the atomic nucleus by comparing the task with hitting a fly in the Albert Hall with a peashooter.

It is not only the scientist who sometimes fails to see the wood for trees. Even the most imaginative prophets sometimes go astray. I gather from a recent Barclays Bank advertisement that H. G. Wells once wrote (*Anticipations*, 1901): "I do not think . . . aeronautics will ever come into play as a serious modification of transport and communication."

A blinkered view along a single track may lead us to overlook developments in parallel. Most research on the peaceful application of thermonuclear reactions (the fusion of hydrogen nuclei to form helium, as in the hydrogen bomb) seems to be directed towards confining a plasma at many million degrees (C. or K.) by electromagnetic fields so that the hot, ionized gas may not vapourize the walls of the material container. At high temperatures, the velocity of the ions is sufficient to overcome the resistance to fusion by what may be figuratively called a battering-ram effect.

In 1956 I read of some modest experiments of the universities of California and Liverpool, where fusion had been achieved in liquid hydrogen and therefore at very low temperatures. By simple mechanics, as illustrated in Fig. 9.1, it can be seen that if a negative μ-meson (a) of roughly 200 times the mass were substituted for the orbiting electron (b), the orbit would be substantially reduced in size.

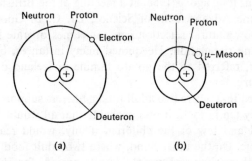

(a)   (b)

FIG. 9.1. Although experiments on the control of nuclear fusion seem to be directed predominantly at containing ultra high-temperature plasmas by electromagnetic fields, the fusion of heavy hydrogen nuclei (deuterons) to form helium has been achieved in liquid hydrogen and therefore at very low temperatures. (Reproduced from *Engineering*, 11 January 1957.)

Resistance to fusion becomes intense when the orbits of neighbouring atoms overlap, and the smaller the orbit the lower the battering-ram energies needed to achieve fusion.

It may be that the short life of μ-mesons or other factors preclude a net yield of useful power, but the experiments show that there is more than one way to skin a cat. Most scientific problems are in fact open-ended, calling for divergent thinking, and we shall rarely solve them if we treat them simply as an exercise in logic.

Population Explosion?

Even our most cherished predictions may prove unfounded.

The population explosion is today so taken for granted that journalists and scientists alike are prepared to be categorical in forecasting the worst. Typical of these statements was one that appeared in a Sunday paper colour supplement: "By the end of this century the world's inhabitants will have doubled to 7,000 million: well over half of them will be living in cities. Certainty is absolute"; the writer admits neither doubt nor qualification.

In fact as long ago as 1956, at a meeting of the British Association for the Advancement of Science, Dr. C. B. Goodhart explained how natural selection can sometimes operate in favour of declining population. He quoted many instances, but one, I remember, referred to the potato famine in Ireland during the last century.

He noted that where two adult food gatherers supported a large family, say ten in total, it was probable that all would be under-nourished and few of the children, if any, would reach child-bearing age. On the other hand, where two adult food gatherers had only themselves and two children to provide for, there was a good chance that the children would live to have offspring. In these circumstances, therefore, there would be natural selection against high fecundity. I read, too, that a single vessel of GB (a material developed for military purposes) could destroy the population of the world. My present weariness must be due to seepage. Although increasing life expectancy may have immediate and critical effects on population, it is not impossible that a falling birth rate (for natural and unnatural reasons) may lead eventually to a declining population.

Change Sectors

The projection or extrapolation of current trends has little value in the context of longer-term prediction, since a technical innovation or a change in fashion can critically fault the straight-line progress of development, corresponding, for example, to the comfortably rising profits recorded in a company's last three balance sheets.

Improved methods of metal forming could lead to some decline in the wasteful processes of metal cutting, which may now be only capable of marginal refinement. The closing of the Suez Canal precipitated or accelerated overnight the construction of large sea-going oil tankers. The advent of North Sea gas knocked the bottom out of the market for coal-gasification plants.

Trends in demand, as recorded in statistics, are often manifestations of unknown circumstances—the visible portion of an iceberg which beneath the surface is melting away and may capsize at any moment. Indeed, the very existence of a trend in demand means that the demand is, to some extent, already being satisfied, and is certainly no guide to innovation. If extrapolation is the only way to make a forecast, then the basis for projection should be—not the superficial consequences—but their underlying causes.

These basic patterns of evolution are not easy to discern and still more difficult to project, but perhaps the problem can be broken down into more manageable components.

Change springs in many cases from an interaction between resources and requirements, triggered perhaps by invention or discovery and channelled by purchasing power. Conditions for change are particularly favourable where it tends to resolve some conflict or reduce some tension. Spotting these areas of pressure may therefore be helpful in projection. Thus growing requirements for transport and communication, imposed on limited metropolitan resources in amenities and space, lead to congestion. Congestion, in turn, may prompt the wider introduction of vertical automatic car parks, parking meters, auxiliary crab drives for retrieving parked vehicles, double-tier roads, battery-powered mini-cars, high-speed monorail links and pipe-line urban supply systems.

Requirements are ultimately a function of population and may be compounded far beyond the basic rate of population growth. For example, in order to communicate by line, two people only require one two-way channel; five people ten channels; and seven people twenty-one. Also, the need for multi-channel visual communication in business condemns people to concentrate in cities, further multiplying service relationships and introducing an even greater requirement for communication.

Likewise, with growing organization and prosperity, each person requires more and more accommodation, not only in his home, but in his place of work and places of relaxation and entertainment. Whatever recessions may from time to time occur, the building industry in one form or another is likely to survive.

Good long-term prospects for the capital equipment industries may arise from a conflict between optimization and versatility in the production process. Optimum economy of manufacture may call for automatic flow-line methods, which tend to be inflexible; while at the same time, versatile facilities are needed to cope with the increasing rate of product obsolescence, particularly since with market saturation, many industries are passing from the initial-sale to the replacement phase.

One solution might be to introduce a three-factory system, corresponding to the three-field system. Each factory would be optimized for a particular range of products and scrapped when the products were no longer in demand—planned obsolescence of the factory rather than the product. Such a development would certainly encourage the manufacturer of capital goods.

Taken more seriously, this line of reasoning can often be effective in conceiving future products. Requirements may, of course, be inflated by fashion, advertising, legislation, standard of living and invention. Conversely, resources may be released by a technical breakthrough, discoveries of raw materials, or simply an operating surplus. It follows that, with increasing affluence, a greater margin of national income can be spared for leisure, education, safety precautions, welfare and insurance.

The principle is not concerned simply with needs and raw materials, supply and demand, but is a means of focusing the creative process, which depends on the recognition of new relationships. It should be possible to promote innovative thinking in this way if a suitable routine can be developed. Once again, use can be made of the dynamic product area, with the assistance of another concept—the "change sector". The method follows from the systematic application of the question "What's in it for us?" introduced in Chapter 5.

Change sectors are those mainstreams of social and industrial change which are flowing fastest. Typical sectors are production, territorial development, energy conversion, building, communications and production processes. The dynamic area is peculiar to the company; the change sector to the company's environment. Thus, corresponding to dynamic areas, which represent the company's field of operations, are change sectors, which represent the company's field of opportunity. By matching one against the other, a company may discover product opportunities, as suggested in Chapter 7 (see Figs. 7.2–7.5).

For example, a company having "separation plant" as a dynamic area might discover, in reviewing the change sector of "energy conversion", that power stations caused atmospheric pollution. The company might then consider whether the problem could be solved by a separation process, say the removal of sulphur from fuels or sulphur dioxide from flue gases, and if so whether they were well equipped to solve it and exploit the process.

The practical implementation of this method involves maintaining files of material drawn from the technical and daily Press under dynamic area and change sector headings, and making comparisons at regular intervals.

Synthesized and Keyed Projection

Another technique, which I have called "synthesized projection", recognizes that the application of new technology is often triggered by cross-fertilization or parallel breakthrough in fields which, superficially, are unrelated. Like the Delphi method, to be mentioned later, it requires the interrogation of specialists, but covers far more widely scattered specialities and depends much more on the interpretive faculty of the interrogator. His task is to follow clues like a detective, leading perhaps into unexpected areas, and eventually to construct a unified projection from the most compatible selection of individual forecasts.

In other words, the purpose of synthesized projection is to reconcile the isolated insights of individual specialists, whose knowledge may have a direct or tentative bearing on a chosen field. These insights are assembled through large numbers of depth interviews, with particular reference to points of conflict or reinforcement, and then integrated into a single consistent pattern.

If, for example, I wish to project the future of illumination, I may need to explore such widely separated areas as architecture, interior design, the domestic and working environment, road and vehicle construction, reaction times, optics, colour, luminescence and fluorescence, the rare gases, transparent and transluscent materials, selective energy conversion, photo-response and the economics of existing light sources and systems.

It may also be useful to identify what may be described as "fixed conditions" or (with fingers crossed) "persisting points of certainty", and to use them as a framework for conjecture. Little can be certain about the future, but some things are more permanent than others. Thus, Cromarty Firth and Milford Haven are two deep-water harbours, of which there are very few in Europe, a distinction they are likely to retain.

Other reference frames to which projection may be keyed include impending legislation, five-year plans (which are often modified before their course is run), construction programmes and overseas investment schemes.

Patterns in Events

Once when seeking staff I designed an advertisement in the form of a stark black and white chequer board, calculated to catch the attention of casual Sunday-paper scanners. In each white square I put a question, the first of which was: "Are you quick to see a pattern in events?" I hopefully believed that pattern recognition was the key to forecasting and to an understanding of the way in which historical processes occur.

I note that most current attempts at forecasting are based on pattern recognition of one kind or another. Patterns may be found by plotting points, and if coordinates can be found (logarithmic or otherwise) such that points are seen to lie sensibly on a straight line, then a mathematical relationship may be assumed. Through long experience, engineers and even physicists have grown wary of jumping to linear conclusions.

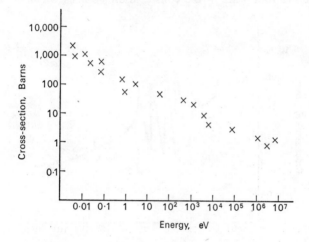

FIG. 9.2. There appears to be an approximately linear relationship.

Figure 9.2 shows a series of points which might have been plotted by a physicist studying reaction cross-section for fission of uranium 235 at different neutron approach energies (effectively velocities). Cross-section (in barns) is really a measure of the probability that a reaction will occur and may be visualized in terms of two cars approaching one another: the likelihood of collision depends on the frontal area that each car presents to the other. It may also be a function of the relative speeds.

The points in Fig. 9.2 seem nicely arranged. Naturally, the coordinates are logarithmic, and to give a good effect I chose a mixture of inches and centimetres for the scales in preparing the original drawing.

More detailed plotting will reveal that between about 1 and 1000 electron volts (eV) there are violent departures from simple linearity, as seen in Fig. 9.3. The cause is known as resonance, a phenomenon that frequently occurs, sometimes through impurities in materials, but often through the basic nature of a system.

It is not only extrapolation, therefore, that can be misleading. There are four stars in the constellation Pegasus which lie in a

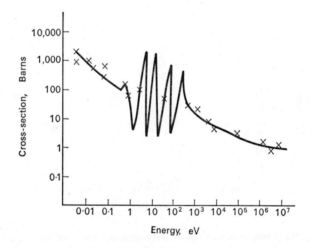

Fig. 9.3. Detailed plotting of neutron cross-section against energy for fission of uranium 235 reveals marked resonance in the band 1 eV to 1 keV.

straight line, but no one would forecast the appearance of other stars on an extension of this line or even within its length. Again, few would argue whether the three stars in Orion's belt lie on a straight line or logistic. But I have seen linear plots of lumens per watt against calendar year for forms of lighting, starting with a paraffin candle and spanning the period 1850–1990. The sloping line is shown perfectly straight and intersecting the vertical axis, notwithstanding that before 1850 (logarithmic scale or not) the line would lie parallel to the horizontal axis for a very long time indeed. Lack of homogeneity between candles, filament lamps and fluorescent tubes would raise most people's suspicions. But worse, the line is projected straight through the point where the efficiency of converting watts to lumens is 100 per cent and it appears that by 1990 lamps will be available approaching 200 per cent efficiency.

In view of the pitfalls in pattern recognition, it may be helpful to classify some of the patterns that we encounter:

(1) A pattern that appears in nature because it has a genuine underlying cause, for example a trajectory, the double helix of DNA, the gas laws and the motion of the planets (planet does, of course, mean wanderer and before Copernicus, the essentially simple pattern of planetary movement was by no means clear).

(2) A pattern that is imposed on nature for purely subjective reasons, say as a mnemonic; thus a constellation has no reality in astronomy, except as an aid in recognition (to me Cassiopeia looks like a W lying on its wide—the man who saw it as a woman no doubt had women on his mind).

(3) A pattern that is purely man-made for purpose of design, such as a jug, which is part functional and part aesthetic (if the first men on the moon discover a perfectly geometrical piece of stone, they will probably conclude that some other living thing has been there first).

(4) A pattern that appears by chance; if a coin is tossed a sufficient number of times, we can expect eventually a sequence of, say, ten heads, and if someone enters the room at the beginning of the sequence he may wrongly infer that it is a double-headed coin.

(5) A pattern that is tautological or a mathematical identity; thus rainfall on an island would no doubt show a close relationship with total river discharge to the sea (also we should not be surprised to discover that plotting the values on two sides of a metric–English conversion table, say kilowatts against horse-power would give us a perfectly straight line).

In practice, the patterns we observe tend to embrace many overlapping and interlocking component patterns of both subjective and fundamental kinds.

Econometric Forecasting

Now that I have questioned some of the assumptions that we take for granted when attempting to foresee the future, I feel I may more safely examine the techniques which are currently in use. First I will discuss briefly econometric forecasting, based on the construction of mathematical models.

I have already drawn the distinction between a projection based entirely on extrapolation of historic trends and one where extrapolation is qualified by an understanding of the underlying causes. As far as possible, extrapolation should be limited to those values which in principle or practice cannot be built up from individual cases or where inquiry into cause and effect would be prohibitively expensive or time-consuming.

For example, in sales forecasting, long-term turnover might be influenced by population growth, increase in discretionary expenditure or changes in the average distance of consumers' homes from retail outlets. Values for each of these factors would probably have to be obtained by extrapolation from past records. Nevertheless, if they are seen to have causal links with sales volume, genuine predictions can be made, treating the extrapolated quantities as accepted premises.

In projection, mathematical methods can sometimes give better results than intuitive interpretation of figures plotted on a chart. Such methods include exponential smoothing, where a running average is weighted in favour of more recent values. In some cases, a cyclic term is introduced to account for seasonal (or shorter-term) variations. Techniques of this kind are best suited to short- or medium-term sales forecasting for items having a rapid numerical turnover.

Longer-term forecasting is normally based on either (1) selection of the simplest mathematical expression which can be made to fit the known data, or (2) assumption of a simple law by analogy with some known pattern of growth and decay. Meaningful results can often be achieved by a combination of the two.

The most common curves used in forecasting are the exponential and logistic. The exponential assumes a cumulative growth rate and is derived from the expression

$$P = Ae^{kt},$$

where P is the dependent variable (in this case population), A, e

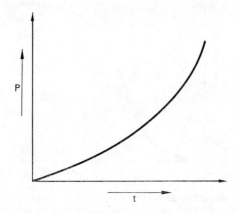

FIG. 9.4. One of the most common curves used in forecasting is the exponential, which assumes a cumulative growth rate and in most situations can only be true for a limited period.

and k are constants, and t is time. The curve is shown in Fig. 9.4. (Population need not, of course, mean human population.)

Population is said to be increasing at an exponential rate and, for some unaccountable reason, is expected to do so for ever. Following the war, similar predictions were made concerning power consumption and have already proved grievously mistaken. After a certain stage, any exponential curve proceeds rapidly towards infinity and cannot therefore represent any real situation for very long—even a nuclear explosion has to stop.

In a logistic it is assumed that growth rate begins in a cumulative way but cannot continue at this rate indefinitely. It therefore takes the form of an S-shaped curve, as illustrated typically in Fig. 9.5, which tails off on approaching a maximum value. A logistic can be written in the form

$$P = \frac{A}{1 + e^{-kt}} \text{ or } \frac{dP}{dt} = KP\,(A - P),$$

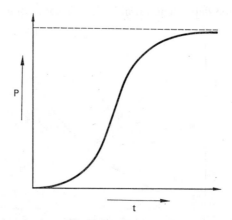

FIG. 9.5. Another curve used in forecasting is the logistic, where it is assumed that growth begins in a cumulative way but then falls off, approaching a maximum value asymptotically.

where the symbols are as before, but A in this case is taken as the maximum level possible (so $A - P$ is the residual "capacity" at time t) and K is another constant.

It follows that the growth rate at any time t is proportional to P and to the residual capacity $(A - P)$ for absorbing any increase. Thus when P equals A or zero, the slope of the line is also zero. In sales $A - P$ might be the unsatisfied demand and A the saturation level.

Both the exponential and logistic can be applied to the introduction of new products, but each only shows a fraction of the truth, as will be seen by reference to the product life-cycle curves in

Chapter 5. In other words each represents only a portion of the complete lifecycle.

Use of the logistic is based on the assumption that a new product can achieve a certain share of the market after a certain time. The share may, but is unlikely to be, 100 per cent of the total. During the period immediately following introduction, sales build up slowly against resistance, but as the product becomes more widely known its share of the market rises more and more steeply until a time is reached when proportional saturation is approaching and the rate of increase begins to slacken off, as illustrated in Fig. 9.5.

According to the logistic, sales will now remain steady at this level, but in practice never do. Competition, obsolescence or simply loss of interest will sooner or later result in a decline.

It may be argued that there has never yet been a sustained decline in the demand for ships, for example, but business is concerned with particular kinds of ship, not with ships in general. I do not think it is incautious to suppose that every class of ship must eventually be superseded—and one day even ships in general. Companies who had manufactured steam locomotives for 100 years made the discovery of ultimate decline, and railroad operators likewise experienced decreasing profits whatever the form of traction they employed. Figures for workable reserves of minerals initially followed the logistic, but no one would consider them inexhaustible.

Technological Forecasting

Over the past 10 years attempts have been made to develop means of forecasting technical innovation and I should like to refer briefly to the methods of technological forecasting that I have seen described. Perhaps the best detailed account of these methods is given by Jantsch in his book *Technological Forecasting in Perspective*. Essentially there are two basic classes of approach—the exploratory and normative.

Exploratory methods revolve round the extension of present thinking and development. In normative techniques, a desirable situation is postulated a given period ahead, and it is necessary to work back to the present showing what steps need to be taken and what alternative routes followed in order to reach that destination. In other words, the normative approach looks backward from the future and the exploratory approach looks forward on the basis of historical and present knowledge.

The most common exploratory technique is similar to the methods of econometric forecasting already discussed. Key functional parameters, such as cruising speed and a specific fuel consumption for an aircraft, are plotted in order to determine the growth characteristic, whether linear, exponential, logistic or otherwise; an attempt is made to fit the characteristic to all the known data; and the resulting curve is then projected forward. As will be realized, it is a very unreliable method, particularly since the impact of what may seem a quite alien technology may have dramatic consequences. Nevertheless, the act of performing this analysis sometimes provides useful qualitative information.

In the method known as Delphi, a concensus of expert opinion is collected, then progressively refined and reconciled by returning the results of successive stages (recorded without identifying sources) to the same experts for further comment. Precautions are taken to minimize collusion, prejudice and any artificial weighting. Delphi is in fact a focused reiterative brainstorm.

The Scenario method involves the imaginative description of as many different credible futures for a given technology as the scenarist can conceive and might be described as "an essay in the techno-economic history of the future." Like science fiction, it has the virtue of revealing the scope of the possible. Again, Morphological Analysis takes the key parameters of an existing product, say a jet engine, and projects their development forward in an interrelated way.

Under the normative heading, fall relevance trees, based on the setting of objectives and examination of the many interrelated paths for reaching them, using network and critical path techniques. Another method is to pose a series of future problems and see what is required to solve them, while a third seeks to study the impact likely to be made by some probable technical development.

In most cases, the fascination of the method far exceeds its fruitfulness and many a forecaster has fallen for the attraction of a pretty curve. Still, as Professor A. N. Whitehead once observed, "It is the business of the future to be dangerous".

The dynamic area, because of its essentially enduring character, is neither normative nor exploratory, but in a sense embraces both approaches. Of possible value in the planning of research, technological forecasting has yet to demonstrate its usefulness in business planning.

Risk and Return

In an earlier chapter I have suggested that one aim of dynamic planning is to collapse the future back into the present. The now familiar method of discounted cash flow (DCF) has a similar function and is an aid to choosing between projects, bearing in mind the present value of future expenditure under the influence of such factors as interest and taxation. In other words, alternative projects are reduced to a common base for present comparison.

The net present value (NPV) of a project can be evaluated by discounting the cash flow at a predetermined rate. The difficulty of choosing the rate of return is avoided in DCF by calculating the rate of return which will reduce the net present value to nil. The rates for different projects can then be compared.

There is, however, no question that decreasing weight attached to more distant cash flows in any way balances the greater risk and uncertainty of the remoter future. I shall be discussing the relationship between risk and the corresponding expectation of return later in this chapter. It is, of course, the cost of capital, not any artificial factor, that is set against the rapidly increasing risk associated with the hope of longer-term reward.

Strictly, DCF analyses are only applicable in comparing projects where the risk is equal, but where there may be differences in scheduling or overall duration. Figure 9.6 shows expenditure (negative cash flow only), on two plants for acid manufacture. The first is built in mild steel and costs half as much as the second, which is built in stainless steel. After 5 years the mild steel plant has to be replaced at the same capital cost as before. The stainless steel plant lasts a full 10 years.

It might be supposed that there is nothing to choose between the two and the stainless steel plant may even be preferred since the trouble of construction is confined to a single occasion and once-for-all has a particular appeal.

In fact, the mild steel plant is economically the more attractive,

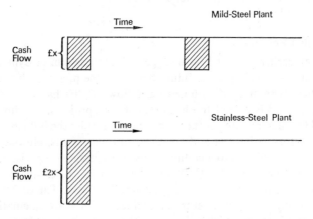

FIG. 9.6. The diagrams show only cash flow relating to expenditure, without discounting.

since only half the capital is committed from the start and the notional remaining half could in theory be invested, yielding a return. Neglecting inflation and other factors which in practice would have to be considered, when the second mild-steel plant is constructed, the accrued interest up to that time on the sum then expended is a net gain. Also, the second mild-steel plant could embody any technical advances in the five-year interval.

DCF analysis, which allows for the time effect on cash value, may also, by extension, be applied in situations where the risk is similar though not precisely equal. Companies tend to operate in areas of homogeneous risk and on roughly corresponding time scales. A company geared to long-term capital projects would be out of its depth if it tried to cope with the hit-and-run requirements of some consumer markets, and conversely.

It is just conceivable, therefore, that a company might consider investing in an acid plant or in a tube mill, and have to choose between the two. Using DCF analysis, the present equivalents of both cash flows could be compared.

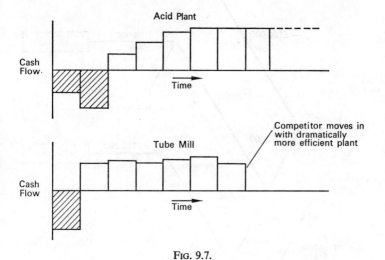

Fig. 9.7.

Figure 9.7 shows simplified cash-flow diagrams for both projects, suggesting the kind of risk incurred, as when a competitor moves in and perhaps, because in the interval a more efficient plant has been developed, takes over the complete market. The process of discounting is not shown, but simply involves adjustment to future cash flows in relation to their remoteness. Tables of figures for this purpose are available.

Given a cash-flow approach to accounting, it is possible to structure a sequence of decisions and the resulting outcomes so that the pattern of risk may be understood more clearly. Risk, as has already been amply emphasized, is difficult to calculate, but

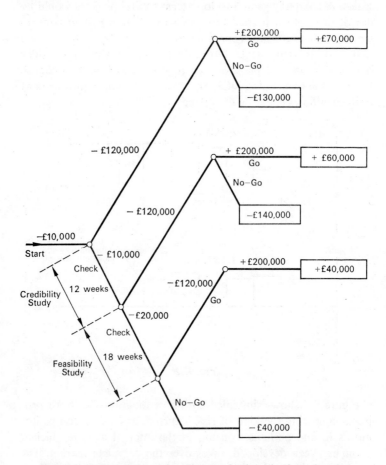

FIG. 9.8. Rudimentary option diagram for introduction of capital product shown in terms of cash flows. Each node represents a point at which a choice must be made. Steps have been simplified and any consequent misinterpretation of the underlying principles (developed at the Harvard Business School) are the author's responsibility alone.

the scope for error is reduced if the options can be systematically defined. Fig. 9.8 may be described as an option diagram for introduction of a capital product, shown in terms of cash flows. Each node represents a point at which a decision must be made (here reduced to simple alternatives). At the start, it is assumed that a requirement has been identified from examination of the market, with critical performance parameters, and already £10,000 has been spent on these preliminary studies.

The first decision is whether to spend money on further market research (taking 12 weeks to complete and costing £10,000) or to go ahead with technical development at rather greater cost (£120,000). After this development has been completed, the company will know broadly whether they have a product adequately suited to the market need and can then take the decision whether to sell and instal it (go or no-go). Assuming that the go decision is in all cases backed by correct technical and market information, it will result in a positive cash flow (£200,000) which is offset against cash already spent to produce a net positive return. Net cash flows are shown in boxes after the product has been sold or the project abandoned.

Eventually there will come a point at which the cost of any further market and technical research will not be justified by the possible benefit, as where the gain on a go decision is comparable with the loss on a no-go decision. In other words, the net positive cash flow resulting from a successful sale has fallen to a level where neither option is attractive. It is clear that a decision to proceed or abandon the project would normally be taken long before this point.

Decision Trees

The diagram shown here is a drastic simplification (if not an oversimplification) of techniques developed at the Harvard Business School and elsewhere for risk analysis, in which "decision trees" show, not only alternative decisions (two or more), but also the range of possible outcomes following a decision (represented as a fan), with notation indicating uncertainty or the probabilities involved, particularly with reference to the impact of external factors, such as the judgment in a patent suit.

It will be evident that the decisions taken at the various nodes will depend on a great number of objective and subjective factors. The situation of a company or individual at the time a decision is taken will have a very considerable bearing on the choice, as illustrated by the following example.

Two men are in a bar. One says to the other: "I am feeling very generous tonight, having won a fortune on the pools, and am prepared to give you £10 if you will toss a coin and it happens to turn up heads."

At this point a bystander joins in the conversation and says to the man who has received this somewhat surprising offer: "I would like to buy the opportunity from you; what will you sell it for?"

If a sale is negotiated, the sum is likely to be less than £5, but the actual figure will depend on the seller's situation. If he is far from home, has missed his last bus, spent all his money and knows that the taxi fare is just £2, he may agree to sacrifice the opportunity for this low figure. If there is no such pressure on him, he may prefer to take the chance of winning the more substantial sum.

The weakness of any branching approach is that the number of alternatives increases geometrically at each node, as I attempted to show in relation to doubling effect in Chapter 2.

Hot and Cold Money

The development of market research and the proliferation of other techniques for gathering and analysing data may have reduced to some extent the risks inherent in decision making, but they have brought new dangers of their own.

Quite rightly we believe in information, but are becoming ever more reluctant to take decisions without a fully comprehensive and convincing case. But the facts can never all be known, and over-dependence on processed information may lead to indecisiveness and eventually to the atrophy of our decision-making faculty. There are signs of it already.

Not only are decisions inhibited but, in addition, the cost of decision making progressively increases. Time spent in seeking and reviewing information expands and diffuses like a gas to fill the space available.

In financial terms, therefore, forecasting can be self-defeating, with time and expenditure building up in a cumulative way, such that the benefit will be marginal for any single company, as foreshortening defeats us when we endeavour to exceed the speed of light. In other words it may eventually cost more than it is worth. Competitive forecasting is like giving trading stamps: we may have to do it in order to remain abreast, but in the longer term it is only an additional drain on our resources.

This situation has been examined by my colleague, Balint Bodroghy, and I would like to record his views, particularly with reference to the risk value of money.

It is difficult to put a value on executive time. Expressed in terms of opportunity cost, the value of a middle or senior executive in industry must be somewhere between £100 and £1000 a day. In other words, on a good day, and it is assumed that most days are good, a capable company executive should be able to undertake actions that will ultimately yield an incremental profit in that range for every day of his working life.

It is disturbing to think that members of top management from dozens of small, medium and large companies should sit together at seminars and courses, in Europe and America, discussing management methods, corporate planning, the impact of innovation and technology on business, and how to benefit. Although the cost to industry cannot be known, it must run well into seven or eight figures per annum.

Since companies act, or are expected to act, in a rational manner, we must suppose that there are sound reasons for the obvious preoccupation with management and innovation. What are the reasons and the motivation?

On a human level, there is clearly an element of beauty and excitement in invention and its embodiment in practice. Indeed, there is something beautiful in doing anything for the first time, whether it is sailing round the world single-handed, climbing a mountain, or falling in love, and with certain notable exceptions, the also-ran is heavily discounted in the private and the public eye. The first men to climb Mount Everest will be remembered; but who followed in their tracks? The name of the first man to swim the English Channel is recorded in the *Guinness Book of Records*, but though it takes much the same effort to perform the feat today, no one is very interested.

Undoubtedly, we attribute certain intrinsic values to primogeniture, but there must be more to it than that, and it seems probable that the key consideration is the element of risk. The second time round everybody knows that the feat can be accomplished; it may be difficult, but certainly not impossible. The reduction in risk leads to a heavy discounting in esteem.

The intellectual beauty of innovation attracts most human beings. They like to be associated with it and enjoy the experience. But the sensation is personal, and on the commercial level it would be surprising if industry consented to support such whims without good business reasons.

Innovation is more fashionable today than it has ever been. Annual reports, which become ever more image-conscious and elaborate are no longer limited to the obligatory denunciation of national economic measures and expressions of appreciation for the loyalty of staff, but are full of fascinating facts. Certain kinds of phrase appear with growing frequency: "Your company were pioneers in the development of left-handed screw threads in the United Kingdom", or even more often: "More than 80 per cent of what we sell today did not exist ten years ago"—doubtless a reference—not to innovation—but to better stock control.

Fashion alone is not a sufficient explanation. Perhaps innovation has become a weapon in the battles of corporate politics. Innovation means change and change means opportunity for junior executives not yet near the top. Those at the top no longer have ambitions to achieve and welcome a fluid situation immediately below, since it diminishes the threat to their authority.

At the same time, without innovation, competition between companies becomes ever more sterile, like trench warfare in the years 1914–18. The only weapons are more and better advertising, more and better packaging, more and better promotion, and more and better brand managers, succeeding their fallen predecessors ever more rapidly, but with diminishing returns. In such static warfare, attrition continues until the only escape is a tacit truce or accommodation.

Where innovation rules and ideas proliferate, business conditions resemble those of desert warfare. Battles are fought over ground which is precious one moment and valueless the next. The situation is fluid and exciting because it is a war of movement and the unexpected is part of the game. As a consequence of flanking manœuvres, entrenched positions are lost overnight, almost without a struggle.

Similarly, the advent of efficient air conditioning and structural gaskets, whereby glass windows can be set directly into concrete, coupled with the need in city offices to keep out noise and dirt, may sharply cut demand for opening windows and hence for window frames. The steady progression from wooden frames to metal frames to plastics frames is outflanked and loses its meaning. Again, an air-supported bearing, a solid-state device, welded fabrication, powder metallurgy or a plastics film on a stainless razor blade can change the whole perspective of an industry, suddenly and with very little warning.

Are we therefore to visualize the captains of modern innovative industries in dark goggles and peaked caps, standing upright in open tank turrets, like generals in a desert war? Hardly. While embracing the freedom of desert warfare, they are clearly determined to impose on it all the stability of static trenches. The programmes of management training schemes and seminars show that the prime concern today is how to avoid risk while retaining the benefits of innovation.

Under competitive and public pressure, we have adopted

innovation, but not the mobility that goes with it. Rather than exploit it through adaptive management, we attempt to plot it in advance and write it in a programme. We seek stability and compromise with change by regarding it as predetermined and hence foreseeable and static.

It may be possible in some degree to underwrite the future by management research and forecasting, but the premiums are likely to be high.

Though we may be driven to innovate by force of circumstances, I am not suggesting that innovation has any virtue in itself. Indeed many successful companies have in the past, consciously or unconsciously, deliberately or accidentally, been consistently second in the field and made substantial profits. Some of them have recently seen fit to apologize for such conservative behaviour and are now maintaining large-scale research programmes. At the same time, they are finding it necessary to explain to shareholders why pretax profits have fallen so dramatically.

The problem of innovation and security is one of the great dilemmas facing modern management. It bears closely on our attitude to risk and return in capital commitment and provides one more reason for management's concern with innovation.

The point may be made clearer by considering money in terms of dimensional analysis—a method familiar in engineering. We think of money as having a single dimension, namely its face value, but this is only true in isolation from an owner. In fact, the value of money only assumes meaning when related to an owner, as purpose is meaningless divorced from personal or corporate identity.

As soon as a quantity of money comes under the control of somebody, be he an individual, a board of directors or a government, it acquires a second dimension, which may be conveniently called its "temperature". As a consequence of currency crises, the phrase "hot money" has passed into the public vocabulary. We may usefully extend the idea to embrace warm, cool and cold money, in addition.

If a quantity of money is controlled by a body, it will have the two dimensions of value and temperature distributed as shown in Fig. 9.9, where value is given as percentages of the total sum controlled. These percentages are plotted on the vertical axis and temperature on the horizontal axis. Temperature is a measure of both risk and return in combination, when any fraction of the total sum is committed or invested.

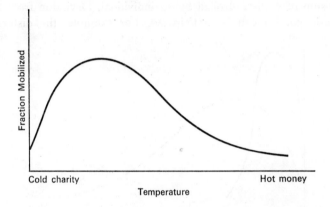

FIG. 9.9. Attitude to risk and return can be illustrated by plotting the fraction of a fund that becomes mobilized if presented with a given opportunity for spending. The opportunities range from the hot money of gambling to cold charity, and represent extremes in risk and return.

A body or individual will normally be prepared to invest a fraction of the total sum, generally quite small, in an opportunity combining very high risk with very high return. Another fraction, usually even smaller, would be available for opportunities where risk and return are minimal, such as donations to charities of unimpeachable reputation. Slightly higher up the scale might come donations for a political cause, where both risk and return are somewhat higher. The bulk of funds would be mobilized only when opportunities offer modest returns with a relatively high measure of security.

This kind of distribution is typical of aggregate funds available on a free capital market, funds held by private individuals, funds

controlled by corporations, or the budget of a nation. It is unlikely that the precise shape of such a curve has ever been defined,
but its existence and approximate form seem consistent with
experience. Even without numerical values, examination of the
curve yields some useful and interesting conclusions.

For purposes of argument it is assumed that the curve refers to
a sum of cash controlled by an individual. Deviation from the
basic pattern can be anticipated. For example, the distorted

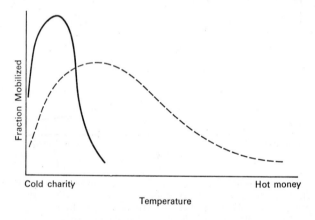

FIG. 9.10. Distortion of the pattern under the miser syndrome.

curve shown in Fig. 9.10 seems entirely feasible and would indicate the miser syndrome. Such a distribution would be typical of
the pauper who dies with a few thousand pounds hidden under the
newspapers and tins that litter his lodgings.

In an individual, such behaviour would be tolerated as a mild
eccentricity, but in a company it would be entirely unacceptable.
A company exhibiting a distribution of this kind has under-
utilized financial assets and will either be overtaken by inflation
or taken over by a Slater or a Weinstock.

A similar anomaly at the opposite end of the scale would
describe the behaviour of a compulsive gambler, as suggested in
Fig. 9.11. There is no corporate equivalent, since no company

could survive reckless gambling over any period of time. On the other hand, it may be that individual entrepreneurs have founded their fortunes on a comparable pattern of investment.

It will be evident that if all money controlled by a single body is governed by a temperature distribution such as that in Fig. 9.9, then the sum total of all money in a national economy would show a similar distribution. The pattern will therefore represent the behaviour of the investing public, offering a small proportion of its funds for low yield quasi-charitable investments, a small

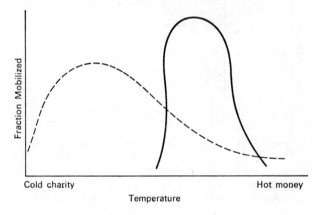

FIG. 9.11. Distortion of the pattern by compulsive gambling.

proportion for a flutter on speculative investment, but the bulk being mobilized only for investments offering the normal combination of risk and return. For convenience, the large volume investment can be considered as falling in the "6 to 9 per cent category".

In summary, money—with reference to the body controlling it—has a quality in addition to its face value which can be described as temperature ranging, in accordance with the distribution shown, from hot money to cold charity.

So far the vertical scale has represented percentage of the total fund examined. If instead of a percentage an absolute scale is used, it is possible to speculate on the way in which the distribution changes as the absolute size of the fund increases. It could be assumed that the relative proportions remain unaltered, with the line assembly shifting up and down the vertical scale, as suggested in Fig. 9.12.

It is suspected, however, on the basis of personal observation,

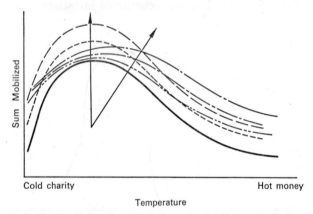

FIG. 9.12. The influence of growth in the fund on behaviour: the pattern could move vertically but a lateral shift is more likely. The curves are all hypothetical.

that, instead of a straight up-and-down movement, the distribution becomes gradually distorted, increasing the proportion of funds available, both at the hot and cold ends of the scale, as the absolute sum expands. Certainly on an individual level this is so. As the more immediate human needs are satisfied, extra marginal satisfaction is derived from acts of charity and from the milder forms of gambling. In other words, the attitude to risk changes as more money becomes available.

It is likely that a similar development is taking place in companies. Since the war, companies have been growing bigger and richer overall. The slowly distorting distribution of hot and cold money places additional pressures on those controlling it to find suitable investments in the hot-money region. It is submitted that it is the increasing size of the hot-money portfolio which accounts in large measure for the concern, the universal concern, with innovation. This money is available and crying to be utilized in ventures offering a high return at risks in excess of those normally accepted.

Unfortunately, this phenomenon is not sufficiently understood either by corporate investors or by the decision makers. The pressure is unconscious and the mental adjustment to accept the risk has not yet been accomplished. In consequence, the approach of companies to hot-money investment is based on the techniques and attitudes assimilated in dealing with the 6 per cent portion of the portfolio. There is a constant search for certainty.

Every attempt is therefore made, using the power of modern information gathering, economic manipulation, statistical forecasting and electronic data processing, to eliminate the risk from risk investment. It is a contradiction both in terms and fact, and poses a great dilemma for the 6 per cent mentality.

The attempt to eliminate the risk from risk money is inherently self-defeating. The first result of any determined effort is a dramatic reduction in returns. The effort itself involves a heavy expenditure, since, in seeking certainty, a company may insist on running through the full range of management techniques. First, there may be extensive product development, followed by evaluation, using prototypes, consumer panels and elaborate physical testing programmes. Next, there will be market research on a local, national or global scale, followed by an appraisal of purchasing motivation and the decision-making process.

By this time the quantitative information is so enormous and the number of variables so large that, short of commissioning a major computer simulation, useful decisions cannot be based on the results. The outcome of the computer simulation will be predictably indecisive and a test marketing programme may then be launched. Finally, buried by information, the management may resort to probablistic decision making, the virtually mechanistic application of hunch, to help make up its mind.

The application of these techniques costs large sums of money and in fact there are now computer programmes available such as Demon 1 and Demon 2, developed by the agency BBDO, which attempt to optimize the amount of money spent on seeking information and making decisions in relation to other variables involved in a project. A situation has now been reached in certain industries where the cost of information, not the cost of development, production or distribution, is the single major dominating factor governing the profitability of projects.

But other consequences of these frantic attempts to remove risk from risk capital are much more far reaching and equally self-defeating. Assume that the attempts to eliminate uncertainty succeed beyond the wildest hopes of the decision maker; also that the cost of these attempts has not completely eradicated any hope of profitable exploitation.

Then the mere fact of converting a risk situation into one of relative certainty will suddenly shift the project from the hot end of the curve to the 6 per cent section. Here the funds available are much more generous within the company, but at the same time, the opportunity will now attract a far larger segment of the investing public, including competitors and their financial backers. Funds from these sources will not only be available, but will be positively chasing prospects of this kind.

It is, of course, the hope of all managers to eliminate risk and to be in a unique position when they do so. Unfortunately, information spreads very rapidly today and is universally available. Techniques for eliminating risk are known to all, discussed in public meetings, and the subject of extensive experiments in industry and the academic world. Any advantage will therefore be temporary, and a pioneer deciding to exploit an innovation, believing he has eliminated risk, may find himself in competition with a vast investing public whose reactions could not have been anticipated in the computer programmes.

Unlike the self-fulfilling prophesies of certain forecasters (such,

I suppose, as the spring or autumn fashions predicted by *Vogue*), eliminating risk from risk investment is entirely self-defeating; the risk has vanished, but so has the return.

The picture is less gloomy than it seems. The point is not that the body of management techniques designed to minimize risk in decision making is a waste of time, only that it is often misapplied. When the full resources of information collection and analysis are devoted to an innovative project (and few worthwhile projects involve no innovation) it will tend to move from the hot-money to the 6 per cent region. In other words, the stakes have been raised all round and the new situation must be accepted as a fact of life.

But the pressure resulting from the temperature distribution of money, in particular the increasing size of the hot-money region, still remains. It will therefore become necessary to look for satisfaction further and further afield, to projects where the resources of modern management techniques cannot be applied.

There is still room for intelligent action. It is first of all important to be acquainted with all techniques at the disposal of the decision makers, with a good working understanding of their limitations. It is then essential to consider which of the techniques should be applied in any particular case, and at what cost, so as not to erode unduly the potential profitability.

Finally, the project should not be considered in isolation but in its own particular environment. In other words, it is desirable to take up projects which, in relation to the differentiated assets of the business, provide advantages which no competitor can equal, no matter what techniques are used and at whatever cost.

In the end, when all the available techniques are seen in perspective and used with discretion, the benefits will be real, leading to better utilization of the available resources.

Uncertainty Remains

For purposes of argument it has been assumed that risk can be eliminated, but in practice this is very far from true. Uncertainty remains and business problems are much more complex than we habitually suppose. Perhaps the environment is not entirely un-predictable, but the unforeseeable so dominates the planning situation that rapid adaptation is basic to survival. Because some events are forecast easily and with precision, such as an eclipse, we fail to recognize the overwhelming uncertainty which character-izes the commercial context.

As a measure of the extent to which business operations call for constant adaptation and replanning, I would refer to the rela-tively simple game of chess. There are only thirty-two pieces (many identical), only sixty-four squares on a board, and only two independent players. But what master could plan his whole game with another from the outset? It is enough to note that in chess problems, where usually only a few pieces remain in play, the requirement is generally to mate in two. Even then, contingent moves are sometimes numerous.

So how many moves ahead can we reasonably plan in business where players and pieces are legion and of infinite variety; their disposition uncertain or unknown; the field limitless, ill-defined and fluid; and the rules complex, largely unwritten and often unobserved?

In such circumstances it is very easy to be wrong. Scientists are often encouraged to prophesy where current discoveries may lead us, so it seems rather ungenerous to quote them when they prove to be mistaken. Yet to do so may sometimes help us to realize how capricious events can be and to recognize that what seems fanciful today may tomorrow be a commonplace. A book by a great scientist of worldwide reputation, published in 1940, con-tains the following passage:

> A few years ago we used to read sensational stories about what would happen when atoms were split. The coalminers were to be put out of work by atomic power. A single bomb would liberate enough energy to destroy a whole city. And so on. Unfortunately the prophets had for-gotten to do a few little calculations. The sun turns out energy at 60 horse-power per square inch which sounds very impressive. But if we make the calculation in a rather different way, we find that it is only producing 1 horse-power for every 3,000 tons of its weight. I am an optimist, and I hope that within a century it will be possible on earth to construct a motor using atomic energy as efficient as the sun. If so, it

will probably weigh a ton and develop several mouse-power. It is true that it will not need refuelling for a good many thousand million years, but it will not earn a thousandth of a percent interest per year on its cost. That figure will perhaps be exceeded later on, but the universe is pretty solidly constructed, and atoms are remarkably tough, so I think many generations will elapse before atomic power is of practical importance.

It is easy to be mistaken. I have been wrong myself so often that I am conscious of the hazard.

Having been brought up within earshot of Britten, Bach and Brahms, I find I have a flair for spotting potentially successful pop records—or tracks from the latest Beatles LP likely to be taken up by other groups. (Bach, in one form or another, has made the charts quite frequently.) In the days of the pirate radio stations, which tended to be more outspoken than Radio One, it was also possible to conduct a statistical study of disc jockeys in terms of their success in recommending "climbers."

It seemed to me that I might capture some editorial space for my company in the popular dailies (it is unprofessional—and expensive—to advertise) by writing a piece called "Picking pop records before they reach the charts". My job is after all concerned with forecasting and picking winners from lists of product opportunities.

Unfortunately on the occasion that I put it in writing, necessarily choosing an unknown (American) group (otherwise it would not have been particularly clever), and sent a release to several newspapers, my record not only failed to reach the charts, it didn't even reach the country.

The future is certainly a risky business to a degree of magnitude that, perhaps deliberately, we tend to overlook. But having said that, I would not preach paralysis or the degree of caution said to have been shown by a well-known diplomat, noted for his unwillingness to commit himself on any issue. One day he was travelling by train with a colleague, who observed from the carriage window a field of sheep and remarked that they had recently been sheared.

"So it appears," replied the over-cautious diplomat, "at least on this side."

Some improvement in our understanding of events is always possible; the future is not totally intractable. By discerning patterns in the past we may be able to see some structure in the future. Even in the case of my geographical analogy in Chapter 2 (Figs. 2.2), had there been a chain of hills running west to east north of the River Thames, we could say with reasonable certainty that the Thames would be unlikely to turn in their direction.

We can never be certain, but must nevertheless decide—and act. In making decisions we should be irresponsible not to use all the appropriate techniques of forecasting at our disposal, bearing in mind the scope for error. And when we prove mistaken we should be ready to change our plans. I am not rejecting these techniques, simply advocating an approach to planning in which purpose and adaptation play a greater part.

CHAPTER 10

IMPLEMENTATION AND ACQUISITION

PLANNING I have defined earlier as the purposeful programming of action. In Chapter 6, Action was listed as the final stage of a product planning study. Indeed, if any planning study does not lead to action or to a decision, then it has been a waste of time.

Sometimes I wonder if requests for further market information and the commissioning of planning studies are simply means for putting off the evil day when a decision must be taken. It has already been suggested that planning decisions involve more risk and greater capital commitment than any other act of management, and it is not surprising that managers become reluctant when the moment of decision arrives.

I recall a project for a marine engineering company who made large ("cathedral") diesels under licence, developing up to and beyond 20,000 shaft horse-power. They were typical of many such concerns, and I have therefore been able to disguise their identity. Similar licences had been granted to most of their competitors and, in consequence, with a depression in the shipbuilding industry, too many companies were chasing too little work, prices had fallen to break-even point and shops were operating seriously below capacity. We were asked if we could find new products compatible with their experience.

The problems were several. As marine engineers building under licence, the company had minimal design resources. Well known to every shipbuilder, they had no sales facilities as such and their senior management were responsible for negotiating with their customers. Their manufacturing plant and skills, though capable of high-quality precision work, were optimized for very heavy engineering and, as might be expected from the normal distribution curve, extremely large alternative products were likely to be few and specialized.

The search was completed and a number of opportunities discovered. In particular a North American company noted that they were prepared to license a range of heavy metallurgical plant well within the manufacturing competence of the company concerned. At the same time the prospective licensor had a network of agencies in Europe, the proposed franchise territory. Also, the managing director of the American concern had just completed a European sales tour and secured £1 million of orders. The cost of shipping large items of equipment across the Atlantic was high, and manufacture under licence in Britain seemed an attractive alternative.

With a certain saintly air of a job well done, we reported our findings and presented our recommendations. The problems arising from the design, manufacturing and marketing constraints appeared to have been solved. To our dismay, on reporting (and it is now some 5 or 6 years ago), we learned that the company had just in the past few weeks secured three orders for cathedral diesels and had no capacity to spare. For some months afterwards, I was able to conclude talks on product planning with the words "So if anyone would like a million pounds of orders. . . ."

The story has been modified to emphasize my point. In fact I do not know the outcome and believe that the British and North American companies came to an agreement. I certainly hope so, since the marine-diesel market has suffered further vicissitudes since then. But if the occurrence of large diesel orders did in fact lead the company to postpone yet again its long-term planning problem, then the hazard is apparent. In any planning study it is necessary that a date be set on which action becomes due.

Active Sequence

Taking action is always simplified by precedent, properly processed information and a sequence of stages. The Ministry of

Defence were kind enough to send me their own current simple headings for an operational order, which are as follows:

1. Situation.
   (a) Enemy forces.
   (b) Friendly forces.
2. Mission.
3. Execution.
   (a) General outline.
   (b) Grouping and tasks.
   (c) Co-ordinating instructions.
4. Administration and logistics.
5. Command and signal.

Broken down in this way, the task is seen to be less amorphous and formidable, and thought can proceed more rapidly. In other words, the headings provide a framework for thinking usefully about future action. It is noted that in the Army, too, the final step is to issue an instruction; in other words to make a decision effective.

Later in this chapter I shall discuss particular sequences for putting product-planning decisions into effect, but I should first like to draw attention to the analogy between the Army's headings for an operational order and the process of successive focusing described in Chapter 6. In the first instance it is necessary to understand a situation in terms of enemy and friendly forces, before a mission can be usefully defined. Similarly, I believe that corporate objectives cannot be stated except in terms of the dynamic relationship between a company and its environment. Also, this relationship has little meaning until the company's identity is known. It follows, as I have suggested earlier, that a clear definition of corporate identity is a prerequisite of continuing effective action.

Real statements of corporate identity could usefully illustrate the point, but statements known to me are confidential documents and, with one exception, I cannot reproduce them. The exception is one I have prepared for our own company.

Own Medicine

First, I should like to summarize the history that led to our corporate philosophy. When I was thrown in at the deep end on my first product planning study it seemed that there were many miscellaneous methods and ideas, but no unifying view. Emphasis was on the product life cycle and on screening processes. The life cycle showed there was a problem but went no way to solving it; screening was accumulated common sense, but presupposed a reasonably focused product–search procedure.

In "Marketing Myopia", Theodore Levitt referred to the American railroad business and noted that the "reason they defined their industry wrong was because they were railroad-oriented instead of transportation-oriented; they were product-oriented instead of customer-oriented". This was certainly illuminating, but, for reasons I have tried to explain, it seemed to me a swing of the pendulum, even a much needed correction, but still unbalanced, still a partial view. The problem of planning surely had to be seen as an integrated whole, as the complete and continuous reconciliation of corporate resources with environmental change. Customers were certainly important, but so was a company's potential for serving them competitively.

At the same time, I was conscious that planning, whether on a corporate or national scale, was frequently defeated by events that no one could foresee however good his forecasting. What, therefore, seemed to be needed, was an approach to planning which was essentially corrective or adaptive. I understand there are two kinds of lifeboat: one that turns over quite easily, but immediately turns back; and another which is very stable but once turned over, sinks. Plans corresponding to the first type would seem to have the better chance. The convenor of a conference on technological forecasting opened the meeting by saying he could not guarantee that nothing would go wrong, but if it did he would do his best to put it right. I took his word as the theme for my contribution, beginning by noting that dynamic planning was an approach to planning where everything went wrong.

Also, when I began my consultancy career, I discovered that I had been recruited to advise companies on the organization of a product-planning function, not to conduct product-planning studies. I soon realized that I could convey all I knew on the subject in a very short time and, since our work was charged on a time basis, an advisory activity could never yield much turnover. So, instead, I decided to concentrate on building up a planning information service, based on a combination of marketing and technical experience.

Later, on looking at consultancy in general, I saw that companies were either specialized or comprehensive. The small specialized consulting company could be vulnerable to changes in its market; the large concern, particularly if it had a bureaucratic structure, might lose the personal touch and find it increasingly difficult to recruit men of the necessary calibre.

To avoid these pitfalls I conceived our company as a commando operation, designed to exploit the skills of a relatively small but multi-discipline team, with a capacity for taking pains, rather than focus attention on a single narrow speciality or try to cover the whole consulting range. By seeking to identify specific emerging problems and selecting those problems germane to different combinations of our several skills, a succession of services could be provided, consistent with current market needs. As existing services became no longer saleable, or were adopted by competitors, others could be conceived to take their place, providing the flexibility necessary to dynamic planning.

It was thus the application of our own philosophy to a consulting operation. Whereas for clients we explored markets in order to identify emerging product needs, for ourselves we sought to recognize emerging problems, common to many companies or situations. The outline solutions to these problems could constitute a sequence of specialities, a succession of new activities. Thus, although in a sense we specialized, we sought to avoid the weaknesses of specialization, particularly obsolescence. Dynamic planning was itself a dynamic area, within which there should be continuing scope for devising new services based on the collection and analysis of planning information.

Generally, our company's strength lies in its unusual blend of technical and commercial knowledge over a broad industrial front and its skill in relating a client's existing assets and experience to present and potential markets in order to discover new opportunities for growth. Also, aware that much market research tends to be negative and hedged around by ifs and buts, we set out to provide the necessary nerve for innovation by presenting fact and argument in a substantial, systematic and convincing way—giving the innovator the courage of his convictions.

The second section of our company statement, as at 31 December 1967, appears in Fig. 10.1. It is essentially a document

FIG. 10.1. Extract from statement of identity for Peter Ward Associates (Interplan) Limited, showing how the philosophy of dynamic planning has been applied to a consulting company.

IDENTITY AND AIMS

---

1. Peter Ward Associates (Interplan) Limited was set up to undertake planning studies for business and government, calling for a combination of technical and marketing experience over a broad cross-section of industry.
2. To a client's deep knowledge of his own activities, Interplan adds a much wider (if less concentrated) understanding of the overall scientific and commercial context in which he operates, serving for example to uncover opportunities in unfamiliar markets or to reveal the impact on his own markets of technical developments elsewhere.
3. Taking this comprehensive view of industry as the company's main differentiated asset, and applying to itself the principles of planning evolved for clients, Interplan is able to define its own long-term identity and role. On the one hand, Interplan is concerned with the changing relationship between a company or other corporate body and its environment and how this interaction may be usefully exploited (dynamic planning); and on the other, with the introduction of self-sustaining active elements into a complex economy in order to induce desired changes or results (catalytic planning).
4. Both are instances of organic planning, which recognizes the limitations of forecasting and target setting, and provides a framework within which

a company (or other organism) can work out its purpose progressively, by taking advantage of opportunities as they arise (planned opportunism).

5. Within the two activity areas (dynamic and catalytic planning), any number of specific services may be conceived. Thus Interplan conducts market research in relation to a client's present and potential assets, in order: to improve their exploitation; to determine the most promising directions of development; or to prepare an optimum programme of investment. Conversely, the resources and structure of a group can be examined in the light of changing markets with a view to reorganization, acquisition, concentration or divestment. On a national scale, Interplan is able to devise commercial criteria for the selection of research projects or the promotion of mergers; or to assess the assets of a region as a basis for industrial development.

6. In performing its work, Interplan has also acquired skills in the gathering, analysis and interpretation of information, and in formulating plans of action, leading to various complementary services, including: product seeking and evaluation; technical market research and exploration; project conception and appraisal; and techno-economic, feasibility and applications studies.

7. Although Interplan will provide conventional consultancy whenever it can profitably and usefully do so, the company's aim will be to identify new or emerging problems common to many companies or situations (emerging market needs) which at any time it is well equipped to solve using different combinations of the skills available, so developing a succession of unique services in which it has exclusive competence, at least for a period.

8. At present, for example, national statistics in many fields are inadequate or incomplete. Interplan is therefore currently presented as a multi-discipline commando unit able to carry out short research tasks with speed and precision. Interplan proposes to become a research institute of international standing, when it will tackle many-faceted operational studies embracing several industries, and perhaps involving, not only field inquiries, but also technical experiment.

9. This outlook represents a new approach to consultancy, distinguished from orthodox consultancy in a number of significant respects:

   (1) Interplan works predominantly within the environments of companies, rather than inside the companies themselves.

   (2) Interplan is essentially concerned with change and with the future, so its services are associated with the high returns of innovation, rather than the diminishing returns of marginal improvement.

   (3) Interplan specializes in solving new and emerging problems within the corporate and national planning areas, developing fresh services as the older ones are adopted by competitors.

   (4) Interplan sets out to bridge the gap between conventional management consultancy and traditional engineering consultancy by employing engineers, scientists and mathematicians with commercial awareness, plus economists, lawyers and accountants who have worked in industry.

(5) Interplan conducts specific studies that can be estimated in advance and normally submits a firm quotation for work defined in detailed terms of reference; the client therefore knows the maximum expenditure to which he is committed, including all expenses, and the probable completion date, fees being calculated exclusively in terms of time expended.

(6) Interplan does not offer a blanket service, but acts only where its special skills may be appropriate, working in close collaboration with the client and accepting the authority of management.

Generally, Interplan's strength lies in its unusual blend of technical and commercial knowledge over a broad industrial panorama and its skill in relating a client's existing assets and experience to present and potential markets in order to discover new opportunities for growth.

10. With this in mind, Interplan bases its recruitment policy on the view that its staff and their personal resources are its key assets and therefore does not impose any speciality constraint in selecting consultants. It concentrates rather on creating a team of exceptional quality, developing the business in directions that their individual experience and interests may determine, consistent with the company's identity.

11. The market environment is not limited by national boundaries, and consultants are recruited whenever possible with a knowledge of at least one foreign language. A world-wide network of associates adds to the company's resources for operating overseas.

12. In order to attract, and retain, staff of the necessary calibre, a policy of growth has been adopted, making opportunity self-evident and providing scope for individual progress within a flexible company structure.

13. Given this definition of corporate intention and identity, financial objectives can be established. Growth and return on investment are both functions of performance, but to some extent relate inversely. Return has been taken as the basic variable and the profitability of ICFC's present customers as an arbitrary yardstick. Interplan proposes to expand at the maximum rate compatible with a yield to shareholders in the upper quartile of ICFC's other customers, and consistent with reasonable security.

14. A detailed budget based on these assumptions has been prepared and is available. Interplan's first profitable month was in August 1967, four months ahead of schedule, and the company has continued profitably ever since.

---

prepared for shareholders and gives a candid view of our identity and aims.

It must have been a reasonably attractive concept since a leading city institution, a millionaire professor from the Harvard Business School, a director of a major merchant bank and the managing director of an international electronics company decided to invest in us—at a time when we had no profit history, no clients, no order book, no premises and virtually no staff.

"So you're so clever, why aren't you rich?" is a question frequently implied. We may not be particularly clever, but our company is in fact yielding a comfortable return. Could we not be even richer if, when we identified a product opportunity promising several million pounds of profitable turnover, we took it up ourselves? I doubt it. That is not our thing. It is our role to add a broad if less intense experience of many industries and markets to clients' far deeper and concentrated knowledge. In innovation such interaction may be useful.

We believe that our own peculiar assets are best exploited in this way and not in pursuing single opportunities, for which we have few skills. Many people claim to have invented cats-eyes for roads to facilitate night driving, but to the best of my knowledge only one man made his fortune by supplying them. The concept, or even the fully developed product, is only a beginning; from there the way through to a profitable business is fraught with hardship and hazard, calling for the persistence, inspiration and courage of Bunyan's Pilgrim.

Networks

Implementing product opportunities involves the whole portfolio of management resources. Company appraisal, industrial group analysis, financial planning, investment programming, DCF comparison, value engineering, product specification, feasibility studies, licence negotiation, productionizing, factory planning, the direction of research, marketing and budgeting are some.

Once the decision has been taken to proceed, a detailed programme is prepared. Imposing something new on an existing structure is seldom easy. Entirely different costing, scheduling, inspection and marketing procedures may be necessary, as, for example, when aircraft pneumatic components were adapted for industrial applications.

There is also a natural human resistance to any departure from established practice. Busy men tend to resist change, not because they are opposed to it in principle but because they already feel fully extended and are afraid that any diversion from their customary routine will introduce an intolerable extra burden. Such resistance can be overcome with care and wisdom.

First, it is important to decide whether a project manager should be appointed to take the project through from beginning to end, from development or licensing to marketing; whether a new division of the company needs to be set up, with separate premises and staff; or whether the new product should be assimilated within the existing manufacturing and sales framework. However the project is handled, it is only likely to be successful if one individual is charged with its success and freed from other day-to-day responsibilities.

Circumstances may vary, but generally a project manager would be appointed during the approval stage and will take part in the decision to proceed. He then prepares a time-table and ideally a network diagram, particularly where several individuals or departments are involved. He will normally require the help and participation of managers over whom he has no line authority and will therefore have to sell his project to them, securing their co-operation and agreement for stages in the network outside his sovereignty.

In a sense, his duties correspond to those of a product manager in a consumer company, who is essentially a marketing man in the full sense defined in Chapter 4. In other words, the project manager is a self-contained business, or at least its chief executive, though subcontracting manufacture. Before designs are finalized he will ascertain the structure of requirements with a view to revising the most apt specification and the optimum range of types and sizes. Often he will build up a sales and design staff in accordance with his findings, though if the product can be readily designed and sold using existing facilities, again he may decide to sub-contract this work.

Nevertheless, for any manager to succeed, he must have an

adequate degree of freedom and options should be open to him. Indeed, in the extreme case, he should be at liberty to obtain tenders from outside the company, have the product made or sold by other companies or even license it if his own colleagues are unable or reluctant to assist him—in order to create a competitive situation. Also, the project must be protected while it is

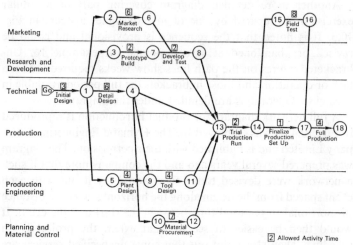

FIG. 10.2. Typical network for introducing new products, as used for illustration by Eric K. Ford, managing director of Serck Jamesbury, at a conference on Marketing Industrial Products organized by the Production Engineering Research Association. The diagram, which was reproduced in the *Financial Times* (5 April 1968), is considerably simplified, in that all elements are not included, and shows main events with anticipated timing (in weeks or months) from authorization to full production.

still delicate and an organizational structure to provide a suitable nursery is discussed in Chapter 11.

The content of his task is best illustrated by reference to actual network diagrams. Figure 10.2 shows an admirably simple and precise PERT network for introducing a new product used for illustration by Eric K. Ford of Serck Jamesbury, from authorization (go) to full production.

The diagram is typical and gives the time scale and logical order for project development. Monitoring the line stages permits checking of progress and expenditure against forward plans. The purpose of such a diagram is that interdependent tasks are completed in proper sequence and to ensure minimum time between inception and profitable working.

Another more detailed diagram covering part of a similar exercise and prepared by one of my colleagues appears in Fig. 10.3. It is noted that the sequence is provisional and could be revised or abandoned at several points, for example 16. Unbracketed figures on the path lines show weeks required for each task or operation and those in brackets the full period available in each case. Operations are detailed under the diagram.

A full network diagram for product introduction is reproduced in Fig. 10.4. It was employed by The Hymatic Engineering Company Limited and is published with their permission. The diagram was prepared several years ago and the company note that if such a network were devised today they would lay it out with each event spaced from the origin along the horizontal axis at a distance proportional to the total time between the start and the event. It would then be easier to see to what extent the project is on schedule. They also point out that some unspecified services are assumed to be available at the required times and that some of the intervals are a little optimistic. Fig. 10.5 is another detailed diagram, devised by the product management department of a major electronics company, indicating the added complexity in the case of a large multi-department organization.

Complementary Assets

As suggested in the section relating to the work of project managers, a company may have some, but not all, of the assets necessary to exploit a new product successfully. Occasionally these missing assets may be obtained through acquisition.

One product planning study conducted for a manufacturer of small arms seemed to involve particularly unpromising material. Production facilities were highly specialized and his sales resources

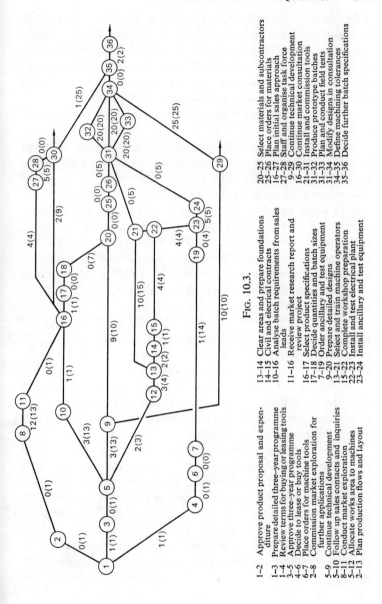

FIG. 10.3.

1–2   Approve product proposal and expenditure
1–3   Prepare detailed three–year programme
1–4   Review terms for buying or leasing tools
3–5   Approve three–year programme
4–6   Decide to lease or buy tools
6–7   Place orders for machine tools
2–8   Commission market exploration for further applications
5–9   Continue technical development
5–10 Follow up sales contacts and inquiries
8–11 Conduct market exploration
5–12 Allocate works area to machines
2–13 Plan production flows and layout

13–14 Clear areas and prepare foundations
14–15 Civil and elecrical contracts
10–16 Analyse batch requirements from sales leads
11–16 Receive market research report and review project
16–17 Select product specifications
17–18 Decide quantities and batch sizes
7–19   Order ancillary and test equipment
9–20   Prepare detailed designs
13–21 Select and train machine operators
15–22 Complete workshop preparation
22–23 Install and test electrical plant
23–24 Install ancillary and test equipment

20–25 Select materials and subcontractors
25–26 Place orders for materials
16–27 Plan initial sales approach
27–28 Staff and organise task force
9–29   Continue technical development
16–30 Continue market consultation
21–31 Install and commission tools
31–32 Produce prototype batches
31–33 Plan and conduct field tests
31–34 Modify designs in consultation
34–35 Define machining tolerances
35–36 Decide further batch specifications

were almost non-existent, since selling guns to governments calls for top-level discussions between directors of the company and the Ministry concerned, without the intervention of a conventional sales force. At the same time the rifle was made under licence, so the design staff was very small. Conscious that the rifle was approaching obsolescence and that contracts were likely to expire within the next few years, the company began to seek new products.

We defined dynamic areas based very tenuously on their specialized experience both in manufacture (such as drilling long holes) and on function. The containment and direction of explosive force did not seem very fruitful, but it led to the consideration of other cartridge actuated devices, as suggested earlier—humane killers (for cattle), girder punches, cable cutters, fixing tools, rock breakers and explosive-forming—but it was very apparent that numbers off for such devices differed by an order of magnitude from the requirement for small arms. Humane slaughter would never equal human slaughter in volume of demand.

Next we put in hand a market exploration, to identify, not emerging needs, but agencies importing products of the right general engineering character and size who might be available for acquisition. It so happened that we came across an agency selling fixing devices, in particular anchor bolts for cartridge-actuated fixing tools. Volume was of the right order and manufacture was within the competence of the small-arms company, provided they installed some automatic lathes.

Market research was completed and the recommendation was put forward. The company's new marketing manager was satisfied with our conclusions and his board took the very sensible decision to make him responsible for the success of the operation. They were, however, rather more cautious in following other recommendations and bought only a minority holding in the agency, with an option to buy more if the project was successful; also, they installed only two of the six automatic lathes we recommended.

A year or so later I met the marketing manager again and asked him how the project was developing. "Like a bomb," he said, "we have an order book as long as your arm, but we cannot meet the agency's requirement and they are threatening to return to their Continental supplier." It also turned out that he had been made a director of the company. Several more years passed and I encountered him again, this time in a smart white Jaguar. He offered me a lift and again I questioned him. "Oh," he replied, "I am now in business on my own."

"What kind of business?" I inquired.

"I run an agency selling fixing devices to the building industry including bolts for cartridge-actuated tools."

It had evidently been a successful exercise and the original agency had provided one of the missing assets, notably a ready-made sales force. As in the case of the marine engineer mentioned earlier in this chapter, I have changed some aspects of the history, but the substance is broadly in accordance with the facts.

Interleaving Acquisition

An association in terms of complementary assets is often desirable, particularly if we accept the view that a successful company is one that exploits its present and potential assets in the most effective way consistent with its purpose. In that the ideal product is one that serves to reconcile a company with its environment, a successful merger is one where the two companies combined are better adapted to the environment than either company alone.

The favoured route to diversification has traditionally been through the acquisition of companies. Though it is often thought that acquisition provides turnover more rapidly than independent development of products and with less trouble, in practice, acquisition calls for a surplus of management resources that few companies possess, and today acquisition is sometimes looked upon as buying trouble.

In theory it should be possible to find a going concern with good current profits and potential that can be purchased and, apart from establishing financial control, left to continue as it is. By successive acquisitions, a holding company could assemble a satisfactory spread of interests. In fact, a first-generation conglomerate is seldom a conglomerate at all, but the working materials of an entrepreneur who is simply seeking capital growth by improving the utilization of multiple corporate assets through the combination, restructuring and partial divestment of acquired concerns.

Groups of both kinds have long existed in the United Kingdom and excited reference to conglomerates in the United States puzzled the managements of long-established holding companies elsewhere; results subsequently led to a waning of enthusiasm. Some five years ago I addressed a meeting on the way in which holding companies would change, containing as they did the seeds of transformation, and I will endeavour to reproduce my argument. British conglomerates had passed through stages in their evolution which Litton, Textron, Ling-Temco-Vought and certain others had still to reach, so I was able to draw on cases conveniently advanced in time.

There were certainly differences in structure, but arising rather from origins and personalities than differences in function. In the United Kingdom the decline of certain industries, which were not yet bankrupt, prompted some companies to band together and invest in miscellaneous subsidiaries selected on performance and potential. In the United States, no doubt, the anti-trust laws limited the growth of companies confined to single industries and led to expansion by diversity. Whatever their provenance, such groups fell between the two stools of banking and a positively managed industrial operation.

Also, the basic conditions in which these companies operated were gradually changing. While abundance still existed in the United States (even after the closing of the frontier), particular resources were becoming scarce in Britain and had to be conserved, leading to new competitive pressures. The holding company, in its free form, offered little scope for achieving a more than marginal collaborators' surplus and efficient use of the limiting resources was therefore inhibited. It therefore became necessary to streamline the conglomerate and adopt a new philosophy.

While the original entrepreneur existed, these weaknesses could be overcome. He was usually an exceptional man, able to run his business with more than normal energy, recognizing companies with underutilized assets, reconstructing them and acting fast in accordance with his personal concept of the business. Without him, the operation would lack its meaning and essential force.

Few entrepreneurs attract like-minded men and are consequently weak on management succession. Once when I was interviewed by a particularly aggressive and successful Cash McCall, who was considering the purchase of my own company, I was taken to the door by one of his colleagues who in a friendly but enthusiastic way told me that the group was really dynamic and that the managing directors of companies acquired usually burnt themselves out in a couple of years and had to be replaced. As managing director of a potential acquisition, I decided to retain my independence.

When, therefore, the founder of the holding group has retired to the Bahamas, a group has necessarily to change its character, base its further development on effective management through reinforcement of its strengths and disposal of its liabilities.

The industrial holding companies which grew up following the war found their competitive position increasingly vulnerable. There were, I think, two basic reasons: firstly, their activities were miscellaneous and did not reinforce each other; and second, so as to avoid having too many eggs in one basket, they tended to acquire small to medium sized concerns, in fields of business which, as industry evolved, called for operation on a larger scale.

Control was usually effected by allotting holding board directors to the boards of member companies, but when a conglomerate had expanded to embrace several hundred subsidiaries, no holding board could possibly encompass the range of commercial and technical experience essential to make the necessary judgments, and finance for expansion tended to go to the subsidiaries whose managing directors shouted loudest.

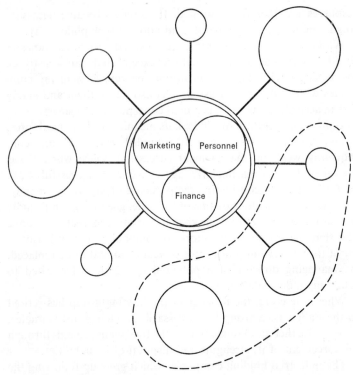

Fig. 10.6. Theoretical structure and organs of control for a conglomerate or holding group. In practice this formula is becoming decreasingly competitive.

For example, a subsidiary making power-generating plant for the electricity authorities after the Second World War was required to supply sets in the region of 30–60 MW capacity. Now the Central Electricity Generating Board calls for sets of 500 MW or even 1000 MW, and any company not equipped to build units of this size would almost inevitably be out of business. If the company had been unable to persuade its source of capital that an evolution of this kind was taking place and had therefore failed to keep up with its market, it would now be seeking jobbing work.

As suggested in Fig. 10.6, a miscellaneous group of companies could in theory be controlled given three basic services: an accountancy department to measure financial performance; a market research department to check if performance could be better; and a personnel selection department to replace the managing directors of companies not performing in accordance with their targets. This simple structure, though attractive, must increasingly prove inadequate, and operating relationships between member companies are becoming necessary in order to maximize return on capital or net cash flow.

In other words, a group can be greater than the sum of its parts, not only through the flexible and economic use of finance, but also by optimum exploitation of all available assets, irrespective of their location within the member companies. Thus some measure of inter-company trading could help to retain a greater proportion of available profit within a group, provided that it did not lead to commercial relaxation. But conflicts are likely to arise where operating companies are accustomed to autonomy. At the same time, since autonomy and drive are often found together, it is difficult to strike a proper balance between centrally co-ordinated planning and a healthy operational independence. One company may make nuts and bolts and a sister company may produce equipment incorporating nuts and bolts. Says the chief executive of the second company: "Their nuts and bolts are of poor quality, the price is high and I can purchase more economically outside. If you want us to buy their nuts and bolts, please do not expect us to make a profit." No management should be subject to over many or too rigorous constraints.

Human and organizational factors make it undesirable in general to submerge the identities of individual companies. I have heard mergers described as games of executive musical chairs in which one or more executives are left standing. But conditions can be created by a holding company such that inter-relations are self-optimizing so as to maximize return. It is through detailed study of differentiated and undifferentiated assets that such relationships can be discovered and exploited. Size alone is no longer enough; sometimes its only property is unwieldiness

When a conglomerate has been built up totally at random, with a completely miscellaneous collection of subsidiaries, the prospect for exploiting internal relationships is minimal. I knew one group which contained a switchgear company, a heating and ventilating service, a foundation-garment business and a zoo. The opportunity for collaborators' surplus or any synergistic benefit in such a situation is likely to be small.

At the same time, few companies are acquirable unless they are deficient in some way. One or more key assets is likely to be missing. It may be that a company is short of liquid capital, senior or middle management, adequate sales resources, modern equipment or even a marketable product. On the other hand, it may be simply that the assets are not being utilized in the most profitable way. Thus one company, because of its particular function, may see the assets of another company in a new light, and thereby be in a position to increase their value.

This synergy, or symbiosis to use an organic metaphor more consistent with the thesis of this book, is illustrated in Fig. 10.7. On the left of the diagram is an ancient inn surrounded by a large car park. On the right of the dividing fence is a petrol station rather pressed for space. Before the advent of breathalyser tests, the park adjacent to the public house was full of cars almost every evening, particularly on Fridays and the weekend. Once the tests were introduced, the cars evaporated overnight (at least for a time). Acquisition of the petrol station by the public house or the pub by the petrol station could increase the overall benefit by simple transfer of the fence as shown by the dotted line. The inn no longer needed its large yard and the petrol station could develop its business by simplifying entry and exit, increasing the number of pumps, installing a car wash and setting up a shop to sell those chromium plated accessories which many motorists adore.

Figure 10.8 illustrates the principle of interleaving acquisition in a more general way. The large squares represent companies, the smaller dotted squares the basic subdivision of their assets—it is a consequence of geometry not of business that a large square contains nine smaller squares. Company X has been created and built up by its chairman and managing director, who also has a controlling interest. He wishes to retire, but his only issue are daughters, all of whom are planning to be models, so there is no management succession. Being the company's owner, he has also devoted more time to it than might otherwise have been the case and he is also its one and only salesman. It follows that when he goes the company will lack top management and sales facilities.

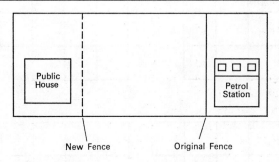

FIG. 10.7. A synergistic merger is one in which the union is greater than the sum of the separate parts.

Companies A, B and C are seeking to acquire company X and are making bids. The sales force of company A has spare capacity and sells in the same markets as company X; for example, it might be selling bottles to the wine industry when company X is selling corks. Company B has a surplus of good senior management—it recruited large numbers of business graduates when it was fashionable to do so in the hope that some good would come of it at last and now has rather too many ambitious potential managing directors. Company C has both an appropriate sales force and top-management capacity. It is clear that, all things being equal, companies C plus X provide a more viable union than either companies A plus X or companies B plus X, so company C can justify the most competitive bid.

A real example, quoted in *Management Today* was the acquisition by the Reed Paper Group of, first, Wall Paper Manufacturers, to provide an outlet for paper with vertical integration, and, second, Polycell to secure a complementary modern marketing organization, oriented towards the do-it-yourself business.

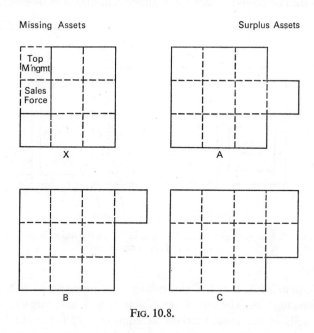

FIG. 10.8.

The ideal acquisition is one in which the acquired and acquiring companies supply each other's missing assets. Lack of finance is unlikely to be the only weakness, since, given promising human and material resources, capital can usually be raised. Conversely, money must have other assets to work upon if it is to yield an increase.

It is for this reason that acquisition, like any other commercial activity, becomes increasingly competitive as its exponents grow more skilled. It follows that if holding groups are to remain viable, then a new structure is necessary, involving a major thickening of holding management. Leading holding companies, both in Britain and elsewhere, embarked on such a course several years ago. Figure 10.9 shows a typical checklist for examining an acquisition prospect and Figure 10.10 a more comprehensive list for investment proposals generally. Both checklists are used by several large concerns, but their ultimate provenance is unknown.

Restructuring of holding groups has mainly been approached by the formation of divisions, as suggested by the dotted line in Fig. 10.6. In this way markets can be exploited more effectively and economically and a greater proportion of the profits earned by member companies retained within the outer envelope. Inevitably, the creation of divisions has led occasionally to conflicts and human problems, and some divisions are divisions only in name, since member companies refuse to work together, cherishing their independence. In fact, autonomy is energy creating and, as far as possible, should not be withdrawn. Cost and profit centres, meaningful titles, prospects for advancement and sympathy, all play a part in making the most of any holding group. Even then, problems will remain.

Take a hypothetical group which has been subdivided into divisions. Companies making rolling mills, heavy presses and plastics extruders are conveniently located together in a heavy-engineering division; instrument, telephone and telemetry companies could usefully come together in an electronics division; and bituminous products, plastics raw materials, laboratory chemicals, with dyes and paints form a chemicals division. Unfortunately the group is left with a mixed collection of activities fitting no intelligible pattern including: a printer producing directories of nightclubs, a pharmaceutical concern whose only profitable line is an emollient for ulcers, a constructor of light aircraft and a new company which has introduced a highly successful device for rapid copying.

Seeking a common theme, some wit suggested that the four companies be lumped together and called Executive Services Division.

Fig. 10.9. Table showing checklist for evaluating acquisition prospects. Other factors covered in earlier checklists (see Chapter 7) would also be relevant. (List used by several large industrial and consulting groups, but ultimate source unknown.)

COMPANY FOR ACQUISITION

The following questions are normally put to companies being considered for acquisition:

1. *Accounts*
    1.1. May we have accounts for the past 5 years?
    1.2. Has the company any contingent liabilities not shown in the accounts, e.g. guaranteed loans, guarantees of products, etc.?
    1.3. Who are the main debtors?
    1.4. Who are the main creditors?
    1.5. What are the principal stocks and what is the basis of valuations?
    1.6. On what basis are profits on long-term contracts taken into account?

2. *Fixed Assets*
    2.1. What is the age and condition of the main items of plant?
    2.2. What is the tenure of the premises?
    2.3. What space is available for expansion and is planning consent available?

3. *Personnel*
    3.1. What is the age, qualification, length of service and remuneration of each senior member of the staff?
    3.2. What service agreements are in existence with directors or employees?
    3.3. What bonus payments are made?
    3.4. What benefits in kind are provided?
    3.5. What are the pension arrangements?
    3.6. Is the labour force reliable and adequate?
    3.7. Is more labour obtainable if required?

4. *Suppliers*
    4.1. What are the main raw materials and other supplies purchased by the company, and from whom?
    4.2. In what cases are there no suitable alternative suppliers?
    4.3. What agreements are in existence for suppliers?

5. *Customers*
    5.1. Who are the main customers?
    5.2. What agreements exist with any of them?
    5.3. What business is done with overseas customers, in what countries, at what prices relative to home, and how vulnerable is it to import and currency restrictions?

6. *Competition*
  6.1. Who are the main competitors?
  6.2. Which competitors are bigger than the company, and how big are they?
  6.3. What approximate share has the company of its industry in the UK?

7. *Orders*
  7.1. What is the current outstanding order book?
  7.2. Are these orders all firm?

FIG. 10.10. Table showing checklist for examining investment proposals generally. Again, it should be used in conjunction with earlier lists (used by several companies, but source unknown).

INVESTMENT PROPOSALS

---

1. *Markets*
Does the market justify entry or further penetration?
Relevant factors:

Growth of the market	Duration of growth, past and forecast. Sectors of growth—fringe basic? Reasons for growth—technological, consumer?
Size of the market	Suitable scale of operation, pre-emption of market—if underdeveloped. Size compared with other countries.
Competition (firms)	Number of competitors. Growth rate of competitors. Competitors' plans for expansion; effect on market distribution; shares; competitors' possible reactions.
Competition (products)	Number, type of competing products. Developments liable to affect market division. Effect of imports—exports guaranteed outlets, protection.
Prices	Stability. Price history, mechanism, expectations. Make-up of cost prices—materials, labour process—and area of greatest dependence. Inflation. Effect of price changes on profit margins.
Stability	Possible impact of technological change, changes in taste; dependence on national factors—e.g. defence—beyond control/prediction, single outlets; guaranteed outlets, breakdown of price mechanism, e.g. RPM.

2. *Technology*
   What technological considerations affect or may affect the project?
   Factors:

Rate of change of technology	Obsolescence of processes or products. Fluctuation of competition. Cost of R & D product improvement.
Technological content of the firm	State of acquaintance with the technology. Acquisition of know-how, mergers, take-overs, joint venture. Cost of know-how acquisition. Cost of pioneering products. Prestige considerations. Size and technological ability of competitors.
Technical staffing	Training. Availability of graduates. Apprentices. Location effects on staff.

3. *Resources*
   What resources will be necessary?
   Factors:

Finance	Cost of borrowing; criteria of return on capital employed; liquidity; government loans, tariffs, subsidies, tax allowances, depressed area policies, purchase tax changes.
Services	Distribution networks, supply structures; service departments—technical, personnel, etc.—buildings, plant.
Goodwill	Possible bad effects on customers, suppliers, retailers, "contacts", reciprocal arrangements.
Management	Availability; technical, administrative and supervisory know-how; control structures.

4. *Policy*
   Does the project conform to policy or the aims of policy?
   Factors:

Diversification, Concentration, Consolidation.	Integration, vertical or horizontal; effect on costs. Reduction or increase of dependence on outsiders; quality control; know-how factors; management satisfaction and influence of market factors (prices, size etc.)
Organization	Trends to centralization or decentralization.

5. *Items Relevant to Individual Projects*
   What issues are raised by this proposal, which have not been defined in the framework above?

If the division is to have a recognizable identity, some rationalization is clearly necessary. Perhaps, for example, it would be sensible to sell the light-aircraft company, which is a tricky business for an inexperienced outsider to manage, and use the resulting cash to augment the copying business, with complementary lines in office equipment or office data processing. In other words, the object is to discard their weaknesses and reinforce their strengths.

In summary, before any business can clearly distinguish its objectives, it is necessary to define a corporate identity. Otherwise, all companies would tend to have the same objectives. Identity should be dynamic in the sense that, though maintaining an essential continuity, it must be adaptable to the changing environment in which the company or division operates. Again, in conceiving a suitable identity, it is necessary to be outward looking, in other words to construct it in terms of opportunities.

No concept of identity could be sharply bounded, and overlap with other divisions will inevitably occur. At the same time, to forbid competition within a group would prevent the organic evolution of the most effective companies. It follows that divisional identity, which might comprise a number of dynamic areas, is simply the first stage in a process of successive focusing, as described in Chapters 5 and 6. These areas would not be fully occupied, but simply fields from which to select the most promising business opportunities.

It should be possible for any group with growth in mind to identify industrial sectors which, though currently fragmented or dispersed, are, through changes in the technical, commercial or economic situation, on the point of precipitation into larger operating units. Within such an industry, an ideal combination of companies could be associated to give collaborative benefits, without undue loss of management or enterprise. The catalytic effect of such activity is reviewed in Chapter 12, but in the next chapter I wish to propose a corporate structure promoting the dynamic or organic changes which have already been envisaged.

CHAPTER 11

ORGANIZING FOR INNOVATION

IN ANY company, established and emerging policies tend to be in conflict. My purpose in this chapter is to suggest a corporate structure in which the two opposing forces are adequately represented, redressing the balance of decision making in favour of the future. Here "the necessary nerve for innovation" could mean a modification to the corporate nervous system so that it reacts more readily to environmental change. Essential to such a system or structure is a formal link between technical research and market planning, aiming at an overall improvement in research and marketing effectiveness.

In Chapter 5 I discussed the relationship between technology and marketing and now propose to consider its organizational implications. Figure 11.1 is a simple version of the familiar diagram showing the two main axes of activity development. Marketing effort may result in greater penetration of an existing market or the exploitation of an entirely new market. Similarly, technological effort may lead to an improved product or an entirely new product.

In practice, movement along one axis is often associated with change along the other. Thus an improved product with better price-performance characteristics could give increased market penetration or permit a breakthrough into new applications, serving different customers. It follows that most developments will fall within the areas contained by dotted lines, though total diversification, where an alien product is sold in unfamiliar markets, would seldom be attempted in a single step.

Communication between the technical and marketing departments would therefore seem essential, particularly since both are critically concerned with innovation and with the future.

Strictly, there are only two sources of new products: the possession or discovery of some property or concept for which demand might be created; and the identification of some market requirement which could be embodied in a saleable device. In one case the property or concept precedes identification or creation of the market need; in the other, the market need is recognized before the means by which it can be met. Either way, a product is a market plus technology.

FIG. 11.1

The first source includes access to identification of a new material, come upon by chance without any potential application in view.

Marketing men may argue that "potty putty" has very interesting properties but its only commercial value has been as a novelty; therefore products arising independently of market needs have little virtue. But if we consider nickel, the picture is quite different. A company found itself embarrassingly rich in this material, mined in association with other deposits, but had no use for it. Research staff were set to work and the results of their studies have given us such invaluable alloys as 18/8 stainless steels and the Nimonics that made the jet engine a practical proposition.

No marketing man conceived the gas turbine in terms of market needs—"What the customer wants is a prime mover with no recip-rocating parts, capable of burning a wide variety of fuels and operating efficiently at great heights." It was in fact the conse-quence of intuitive technical thinking, followed by a deep involvement in the absorbing problems which emerged and a breakthrough in knowledge of materials. Yet no one would deny that it has been commercially successful.

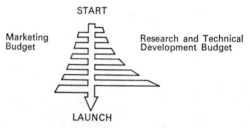

FIG. 11.2. Research-marketing dialogue: budgeting for the develop-ment of an innovative product from idea to launch, showing alternate expenditure on the two sides of the pivot.

Much the same is true of television and, no doubt eventually, the hovercraft, as suggested in Chapter 5. Perhaps the market (or military) need for radar, on the other hand, was established before the system was developed, though the necessary technical and scientific elements were to a great extent available.

In engineering (and no doubt also most consumer) companies, a concept will normally emerge from the technical research or R & D department, while a market need will be uncovered by the marketing department. Each proposal could be evaluated by the other through a dialogue on the lines of Fig. 11.2.

It will thus be necessary to demonstrate the marketability of an ingenious invention or to show that a practical machine to meet a market need can be developed at a reasonable price. Ideally, a succession of tests or development phases, usually involving progressive increase in expenditure up to pre-production prototype, will be undertaken on alternate sides of the technical and marketing pivot.

The new Pharaoh decides to build a pyramid in honour of his father recently deceased. He calls in the directors of his research and marketing departments and notes that the main problem will be moving massive stones.

The marketing director conducts some field inquiries and discovers that the slaves find hauling stones on the traditional skids very arduous. He communicates this news to the research director, who announces a few days later that one of his lads has had a bright idea. Instead of skids he proposes that tree trunks be introduced as rollers. The marketing director conducts some preliminary research and notes that although most of the taskmasters are opposed to change, some of the slaves would be interested to try. He also mentions that abundant tree trunks can be obtained from Lebanon.

The first prototype rollers are produced and a further market check is put in hand. The main problems seem to be the need to retrieve rollers left behind the stones and return them to the front; this task tends to offset any advantage in the speed of movement.

The research director returns to his laboratory and begins to think about the roller-circulation problem. A colleague suggests: "Could we not cut discs from large tree trunks and place them in pairs on smaller trunks as shafts, which could then support the heavy stones?" Back on the marketing side, the idea gains enthusiastic interest, but a number of taskmasters and slaves interviewed point out that if the shafts turn they will move along the stones just like rollers, and if they do not there will be frictional resistance to rotation, wear and tear, and the probability that discs will work their way along the shafts until they slip off the ends. Also, the great stones can easily be lifted on to skids but the shafts will presumably be some way off the ground.

By this time the interest of the research department is fully absorbed and they start to resolve these problems. They decide on a static shaft, inserting pegs to prevent the discs moving along shafts, and use grease to aid rotation. A subsection is charged with developing a tipping trolley to simplify the task of lifting.

Eventually a prototype is ready and the marketing department carry out a full evaluation suggesting a few revised dimensions, and finally the trolleys are put into production.

As will be apparent, the expenditure on marketing and on research gradually increases as the project goes forward, the most costly being the final stages. In other words the lateral arms in Fig. 11.2 depict successive increases in the cost of time expended as the project moves towards the launching stage.

Research Effectiveness

Market-oriented planning has been examined at some length, but technically oriented planning or the planning of research has not so far been considered. Since my own research experience is marginal, I will draw on the knowledge of others better equipped to comment, but will first examine what I see to be the basic problems and indicate how dynamic planning could play a useful part.

Research can only be justified in industry if it yields commercial benefit. Conversely, it may be argued that all research leads to practical consequences, sooner or later, and that no one can predict which field of study, however esoteric, will bring the best return. "There's no research so pure it hasn't any progeny", the head of a United States Naval research establishment pointed out to me on one occasion.

How then can companies increase their chances of reaping tangible rewards from their research expenditure? Success in industry is judged financially—by return on capital invested or net positive cash flow over a given period. Can research be measured in these terms?

It is to be expected, too, that different industries, at different stages in their development, will call for different levels of research expenditure. But how can the appropriate level be determined? Philips Electrical are reported to devote 8 per cent of annual turnover to technical research (in the proportions 30 per cent fundamental to 70 per cent specific), while the Royal Dutch Steelworks allocates only 1 per cent of turnover. Both are highly successful companies.

Again, the scientist is often motivated as much by curiosity as by hope of economic gain. How then can corporate objectives be reconciled with private purposes? This, in fact, is the task of management: to create a context in which a man serving his own interests, whatever they may be, contributes to the common corporate advantage.

With growing sophistication and complexity of scientific work, general managers become increasingly vulnerable to arguments they do not entirely understand. Awe of science has made it difficult to control the work of scientists, who are often preconditioned by their education to dismiss any presumed limitation on scientific freedom. Can their efforts usefully be focused towards commercial ends?

A closer relationship between marketing and technical research has already been proposed and might provide a framework whereby research effort could be directed towards developments that consolidate and reinforce a company's strengths, at the same time matching opportunities against available resources. In that dynamic planning is concerned with the changing relationship between a company and its environment and the exploitation of differentiated assets in the light of emerging market needs, it would seem to be relevant to the planning of research. At the same time, it is based on a precise and formal statement of corporate identity, without which research might wander at random and become dispersed over too wide an area.

Mr. T. S. McLeod, Research Coordinator of the Plessey Company Limited, notes that new products originate in basic scientific research, which is carried out in universities, institutes and also industrial firms. One of its characteristics is that the results are published and made available in other ways to all who might be interested. The function of an industrial laboratory is not only to contribute to this research but to keep in touch with work going on elsewhere and to recognize anything which may eventually lead to a suitable new product. When such a possibility is seen, work of a different kind is undertaken. It aims at meeting a definite material or technical specification, which can be made the basis of a new product design.

These stages are usually carried out in research laboratories and it is only when they have been completed that product design and engineering start. This work should be performed in close collaboration with the staff who will eventually be responsible for sale and manufacture of the product. In contrast to the original research, which should be conducted with as little restriction as possible, the final stage of product design should be governed within firmly controlled time schedules and expenditures.

In other words, although there is a sense in which all sectors of research and development may be regarded as different wavebands in the same continuous spectrum, Mr. McLeod's company finds it useful to break research and development into three distinct sectors:

(1) Fundamental research.
(2) Applied research.
(3) Product development.

Product development has been discussed at length and need not be considered in this chapter. It is enough to say that the unsuccessful project tends to be more expensive than the successful project since it tends to be continued longer in the hope that outstanding problems will be eventually resolved.

The aim of fundamental research is to advance the frontiers of knowledge and calls for a considerable degree of freedom. It might be thought that there is no place for such research in a commercial operation, but in fact any technically ambitious company must keep in touch with fields related to its interest. It is a sector of research where publication and open conferences are normal, but to gain acceptance in "the club", a scientist must himself be able to make some contribution.

In each selected field of fundamental research, a company should therefore employ the smallest team necessary to gain access to the worldwide findings of fellow scientists.

The purpose of applied research is to see if any result of pure science could have commercial application and to translate the discovery into quantitative data as a basis for design work. Here the largest team that can work efficiently should be employed.

It is worth noting that if there were two possible research projects and ten scientists, and it takes five men 2 years to complete each project, then, neglecting overcrowding or diminishing returns, it is better to load one project with ten men, since both projects will still be completed in 2 years, but the first will be finished in one. Results of the first project will therefore be generating cash one year earlier. There is, however, no record of nine men producing one baby in a month.

Mr. McLeod's calculation for a number of tasks and any size of research unit is reproduced in Fig. 11.3.

Given this condition, the size (and quality) of a research department should be such as to ensure that the numbers of new products coming along just exceed the numbers falling obsolete.

To me, the main problems in controlling technical research seem to be human, concerned as I have suggested with the motivation of the scientist and how his interests can be reconciled with those of general management. Then, too, the nature of research presents unusual problems.

Firstly, research objectives can seldom be defined precisely. It may be thought, for example, that the purpose of a particular inquiry is to develop a bearing material permitting an unlubricated shaft to rotate at high speeds. In fact, the ultimate solution may be to eliminate the shaft entirely and suspend the rotating element in a magnetic field; or simply to rotate a plasma.

Secondly, tangential or unforeseen results may yield far greater commercial benefits than the solution to a predetermined problem.

FIG. 11.3. The more tasks that are undertaken simultaneously by a research department, the longer is the mean time before each is completed. It follows that each product has on average a shorter life and that recoveries are correspondingly lower. (T. S. McLeod, Plessey Company Ltd.)

LOADING OF RESEARCH TEAM

m = men are available

n = tasks are to be carried out

y = man/years are required for each task

x = of the n tasks are undertaken simultaneously

The calculation is simplified by assuming that each task takes the same amount of effort: the conclusions are the same if different amounts of efforts are required, but the mathematics are harder.

We assume that the first lot of x tasks are attacked, they are finished simultaneously and all hands are then turned on to the next x tasks, and so on until all are completed.

Then the first batch are completed after time

$$\frac{y}{m/x}$$

The second batch after time

$$\frac{2y}{m/x},$$

etc.

Then the average time before the task is completed will be

$$\frac{\displaystyle\sum_{w=n/x}^{w=1} \frac{wyx}{m}}{n/x}$$

$$= \frac{y}{2m}\,(n+x)$$

It is said that a research chemist seeking to synthesize a transparent material with the elastic properties of steel produced an unpleasant looking substance which he put in a jar and left on a shelf. Some years later a rival company prepared butadiene (a synthetic rubber) which proved to be the same material.

Peripheral discoveries of this kind must frequently be lost and a mechanism for recovery is clearly desirable.

It may be convenient to envisage a research objective as a dark central shadow (not a point), surrounding which is a penumbra of potential discoveries. To what extent a company can leave scientists free to explore the penumbra or should focus their efforts on a central problem depends on circumstances, and particularly competition. If, for example, a competitor has recently introduced an innovation which is likely to put you out of business and your own research department are on the threshold of a comparable discovery, all effort should be concentrated on bringing the project to a successful conclusion.

Dr. H. M. Finniston, when managing director of the International Research & Development Company Limited, suggested in an address to the Society of Chemistry in Industry in 1966 that technological ideas developed as byproducts of a main research project could be taken as starting points for new programmes. For instance, research into magnetohydrodynamic systems using many special types of material had led to the development of temperature-resistant ceramic technology; laser work had led into medicine and cryogenics; and work for the United Kingdom Atomic Energy Authority on nuclear materials had led to the development of titanium–carbide coated boron–carbide materials suitable for cutting tools.

An exploratory checklist of questions which I prepared some years ago in connection with a proposed study of research effectiveness appears in Fig. 11.4 and includes a question on spin-off opportunities.

Writing in *The Financial Times* (2 October 1968), Mr. E. W. Osmond, Executive Director, Research Division of Courtaulds, listed the ways in which a research programme could go wrong:

(1) The work may have no clear aim in the first place.
(2) Work may be started which it is not within the competence of the research staff to complete due to lack of ability or resources.

Fig. 11.4. Table showing exploratory checklist to generate discussion in connection with a study of research effectiveness, covering attitudes, policy and practice. It is essentially a trigger questionnaire and not designed to elicit predetermined data.

DISCUSSION ON RESEARCH EFFECTIVENESS

---

1. To what extent does control inhibit scientific creativity? Can industry afford to offer scientific freedom?

2. Are fundamental and applied scientists simply distinguished by their motivation, in that one wishes to understand the universe, the other to improve it? Will they work happily in harness? Can a useful distinction be drawn between pure research and practical development?

3. When should research projects, which have their own peculiar momentum, be terminated so as to minimize misapplication of effort and hoarding of manpower?

4. On what basis should decisions as to penumbra limitation or extension be made? How can a company ensure that spin-off opportunities or research byproducts are recognized and properly exploited?

5. Which of the following elements are considered to play a significant part in the successful management and planning of research?
    5.1. Recruitment policy and methods of selection; staff mobility.
    5.2. Academic breadth compared with working field.
    5.3. Staff motives and attitudes, especially on research.
    5.4. Expenditure: budget allocation per head: company turnover.
    5.5. Manpower and cost ratios, materials and equipment.
    5.6. Preparation of budgets and financial control.
    5.7. Organization, incentives and management.
    5.8. Liaison and communication with other departments.
    5.9. Liaison and communication outside the company.
    5.10. Channels of communication: internal and external.
    5.11. Information storage, retrieval and distribution.
    5.12. Selection and planning of research programmes.
    5.13. Review procedure and period of review.
    5.14. Duration of projects and policy on termination.
    5.15. Definition of objectives; freedom to digress.
    5.16. The recognition and exploitation of peripheral discoveries.
    5.17. Routes from concept to commercial product.
    5.18. Follow-up procedures: production and marketing.
    5.19. Policy on licensing and co-operative projects.
    5.20. Effects of taxation and government policy.

6. Distinguish between successful and unsuccessful research projects. What factors, in real cases known to the informant, have contributed to research effectiveness?

7. What form does communication take at present between technical research and marketing departments? How can such communication be improved in practice? How can excessive preoccupation with the present be redressed in favour of the future and the planner be given adequate authority?

8. Can planning be so conducted that a company may benefit at the same time from changes in the environment and from internal innovation? How can the two be constantly related?

---

(3) Successful research may be carried out which the company is not in a position to exploit.

(4) Successful work may be done but the cost of the research is higher than the gain which can possibly result from it.

He also suggests that a member of a research department who has had an idea for a modification to, say, an existing fibre might discuss it with a member of the market development department, considering such points as:

(1) The size of the market if the development is successful.

(2) The amount of R & D which is likely to be required and the time which will be taken.

(3) The capital and marketing costs which will be required to exploit results of the development work.

(4) The probability of success.

Mr. Osmond also recommended the use of DCF in evaluating research projects, since returns might not emerge for several years, noting that it helped to stress the importance of solving problems quickly and enabled all cost factors to be considered, including those relating to research investment, pilot plants, commissioning and marketing.

Again, he underlined the importance of project review as an essential part of research management, checking:

(1) That the product is still required—many research teams have solved a problem only to discover that the need has disappeared.

(2) That the basic assumptions are still valid—costs may have changed or the competitive situation may have altered.
(3) Whether the time scale has changed so that the work ought to be speeded up or slowed down.
(4) That the resources of the company are still adequate to exploit the results of the work.

It is evident from what Mr. Osmond says that he considers the problems of research and marketing to be interrelated. There is little doubt that technology in isolation from marketing and marketing without technology can lose touch with reality.

An aircraft company developed a superbly efficient forage harvester based on aerodynamic principles which did not sell until an agricultural-equipment company acquired it, modified the design and sold it aggressively. Shortly after the war another aircraft company introduced a photocopying machine, only to find that there was insufficient sensitized paper in the whole world to make the machine a practical proposition.

Conversely, the marketing manager who calculates the future market for stainless steel razor blades and mounts a massive campaign to increase his company's market share might be completely foiled by the development of a suitable depilatory in some alien industry. The market need for multi-channel visual communication systems for business conferences, eliminating travel, is probably self-evident, but the technical problems are very great. It would also be useful to have an economic model of a national economy programmed into a computer, but I am told that the limiting speed of light makes the proposal impracticable. Products have occasionally been specified through market research and proved impossible to manufacture economically.

Reporting Structure

From what has been said it becomes increasingly clear that there should be formal channels of communication between technical and marketing staff and that these channels must become well worn. Perhaps the answer is that research and marketing should report to the same director and that the director should carry responsibility for the future of the company.

A typical conventional corporate structure is shown in Fig. 11.5. As new areas of responsibility appear to assume importance,

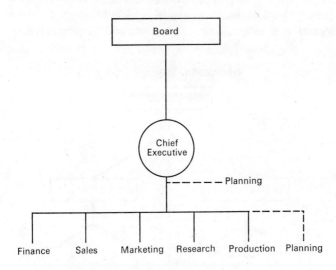

FIG. 11.5. Traditional company structure, showing how the addition of new responsibilities may overload reporting channels. A sales manager may report to a marketing director (line), or a marketing manager may provide a service (staff).

additional branches are added, as shown by dotted lines, often overloading the reporting channels. In some companies a vice-president or manager (planning) takes his place on an equal level with his colleagues; in others he is introduced as a service function reporting personally to the chief executive. Too often lip service is paid to the importance of a company's future, so a planning executive is appointed, given an office and never seen again.

The situation is confused too by variations in the role of marketing: in many consumer companies a marketing manager is a line executive, responsible for the profitability of a product group; while in an industrial group or engineering company, his function may be simply advisory.

Planning is frequently conceived as a committee function since it is noted, rightly, that any innovation will involve most, if not all, of a company's departments. But although involvement and approval by all departments can be achieved through formal and informal committees, the origination and implementation of

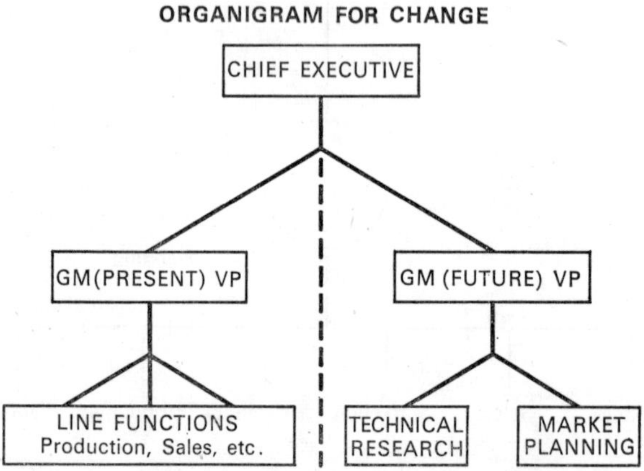

ORGANIGRAM FOR CHANGE

Fig. 11.6. Company organization designed to redress the balance of corporate activity in favour of the future. The dichotomy is strictly between (1) running present activities in the most effective way, and (2) seeing that desirable change is introduced.

change can seldom be effected in this way. There is no question that planning must involve a wide participation, but co-ordination and direction can never be a distributed responsibility.

As I have said, the future of a company is at least as important as its present, and present and future, inevitably in conflict, seem to me the key dichotomy which should be recognized in company structure. A successful organization is one in which the underlying realities are recognized: where a fundamental conflict is made explicit, politics are likely to be less insidious than where it is concealed.

We might therefore envisage the reporting structure shown in Fig. 11.6. Reporting to the chief executive (or possibly to a product manager in a consumer company) are two vice-presidents or general managers of equal status and only two—one for the present, the other for the future. To the vice-president (present) report the normal line functions of a business; to the vice-president (future) report the market planning and technical research departments.

It may be asked: "Where does the future begin?" Performance is usually measured in terms of return on capital employed or net cash flow over a given period. But a corporation (as distinct from an individual project) does not have a predetermined life; indeed, each company expects to be immortal. Do we mean return this year? Or return over the next 5, 10 or 15 years? Where do we draw the line?

No line need in fact be drawn. The VP (present) is responsible for running present operations as efficiently as possible. The VP (future) is responsible for seeing that desirable change is introduced. He does not deprive the present function of freedom to innovate, but provides the pressure towards innovation. Mobility between the functions could be relatively free.

In all divisions of responsibility overlap occurs (who has ever known production and sales departments that lived in constant harmony?), but in the new concept any conflict is explicit rather than latent or submerged.

Also there is now a man of adequate status and authority to represent the future. Status, whether we like it or not, often depends in business on the number of staff an executive controls. The important consideration is not whether the future function is line or staff, but whether it carries sufficient weight, changing the balance of authority in favour of the future.

Admittedly, the VP (future) will normally have fewer people reporting to him than the VP (present), but they will tend to be better informed and able to provide him with convincing arguments. Perhaps his real authority arises from the scale of funds which he controls; in a sense he is a long-term profit centre, concerned with major transitional decisions.

Human experience reveals that a case is only put effectively by a single-minded advocate, hence the party system and the normal pattern of debate. The proposed structure might be likened to a court of law, where the chief executive is judge. Surely the future of a company is sufficiently vital to deserve its own exclusive advocate? In practice I would imagine that the chief executive would seldom be required to arbitrate and direct communication between the two vice presidents would be the rule.

The VP (future) would also be in a position to review penumbral discoveries and decide the basis on which a penumbra limitation or extension should be made, so that spin-off opportunities or research byproducts are recognized and properly exploited. He should also be better equipped than the normal research director to know when projects should be terminated.

Organic Regeneration

As I have said, the future development of the company is no less important than its present performance, but the present inevitably wins more attention: sales must be secured; production schedules met. Also, the future is an abstraction—we cannot see it, touch it, measure it or test it, we can only think about it; and the concrete present, with its urgent demands, tends to appeal more to the practical manager in industry, who is often impatient with abstract ideas.

I believe that this preoccupation can be overcome in the interests of survival and continued growth by a structure similar to the one I have proposed. It enables a company to optimize its current business while making adequate provision for the future.

Planning is the corporate activity concerned with the future evolution of a company and most companies show at least token recognition of its importance. Titles such as "long-range planning manager" and "director of corporate planning" are common-place in today's organization charts, but they are normally located to indicate staff or advisory roles, out on a limb, simply append-ages added to the traditional reporting structure. Consequently, the influence of the executives concerned is often marginal. A retired director or recently recruited graduate is put in charge of planning and then largely ignored.

The consumer industries have been less vulnerable in this respect since the marketing role, which in consumer product companies carries considerable weight, has evolved in many cases to embrace the planning function.

The essential condition of survival is regeneration and only an organism is sufficiently self-maintaining, self-restorative and self-reproducing to refresh itself. A company might therefore usefully be modelled on an organism and the regenerative element in corporate life is innovation. It follows that company policy and structure should be such as to promote and harness innovative effort. Also, an organism is normally constructed in such a way that the parts look after themselves. It might be said that the task of management is not to direct every element towards the corporate advantage but to create a context in which the cor-porate advantage is automatically achieved.

It follows that every key function in a company should be represented by a self-sustaining force, or individual with authority and responsibility commensurate with the importance of his task. The future of a business is surely sufficiently important to require a truly formidable representative. I believe that the balanced binary structure I have shown will give the planner adequate authority and extend the meaning of accountability.

Also, through the closer relationship between technical research and marketing and the concept of dynamic planning, research effort may be directed towards developments that consolidate and reinforce (rather than diffuse) a company's strengths and assets. At the same time, the forward evolution of a company will be organic and self-directing. The company is organized to take advantage of its opportunities. By explictly allocating responsibility for change to an individual with adequate power, the company becomes a self-adapting organism, innovating automatically in response to changing needs.

No doubt analogous structures have already been employed, but I think it important to recognize and emphasize in company structures the eternal conflict between change and efficiency, freedom and order.

The structure is readily adaptable to different situations and mobility between the two arms presents no problem, as when a project manager moves with his project from innovation to assimilation. Again, an explicit conflict is better than undercover politics, and outside the courtroom rival counsels may be the best of friends.

At the same time, the structure is not such as to exclude the emergence of other formal or informal structures. Thus it is consistent with a cost and profit structure based on product– oriented production, market-oriented sales and function-oriented planning, a three-tier example of which is illustrated in Fig. 11.7.

Again, it is a structure which can accommodate the conventional product planning committee, embracing representatives from all sections of a company, so that present line managers may participate in formulating future policy. Communication of this kind is critical to the acceptance of change and innovation by those concerned with day-to-day running of a business; but the onus for ensuring that desirable change is introduced must be placed somewhere and remains squarely on the future management.

The proposed structure also allows for the project, task-force or commando approach to launching new developments. The future management complex provides a womb or nursery for new projects, while they are still delicate. When they have become sufficiently confident and strong to go out into the world, they may be effectively transferred, with the associated project staff where necessary, to the present side—or possibly set up as independent ventures. Indeed, movement of staff occasionally from one side to the other will have the effect of reinforcing both functions and making each more realistic.

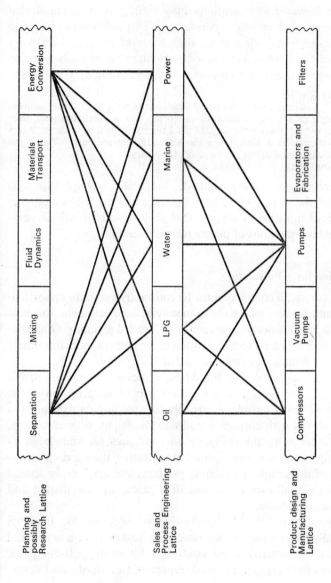

FIG. 11.7. Notional structure in terms of cost and profit centres so that production may be product oriented, sales market oriented and planning function oriented. A variation is the matrix system, where any manager has access to the whole range of company services; it can, however, suffer from a conflict of responsibilities.

But however organizations may evolve, it is essential that marketing and technical people develop the habit of talking to each other—notwithstanding differences of language. I am reminded of a letter, said to have been written by the mathematician Babbage to the poet Tennyson, which went roughly as follows:

> My dear Tennyson,
> I have just seen your poem which includes the lines "Every moment dies a man, Every moment one is born." This is clearly incorrect, since the population is increasing. Might I suggest a slight rewording: "Every moment dies a man, Every moment 1.16 men are born." This is not strictly accurate, but good enough for poetry.
> Yours, etc.,   BABBAGE.

In borrowing this story from Mr. McLeod, I have perhaps misrecalled the facts, and do both Babbage and my fellow engineers a serious injustice to suggest that they would so wilfully misunderstand the aims of poetry (or marketing).

Position for a Polymath

To survive, a company must be constantly awake to opportunities and, ideally, where the company is large enough, someone should be exclusively concerned with forward planning. Otherwise the future may tend to be forgotten in the press of more immediate matters. What sort of man is needed?

A planning executive should be conscious of his company's potential, but must give the greater part of his attention to the changing world outside. Preferably, he should be a man not too encumbered with corporate tradition; he might, with advantage, be a stranger to the company who acquires his knowledge by looking round and asking questions. Rather than a deep knowledge of the company's existing products and markets, he should possess a shallower experience of a much broader market and product panorama.

Although he should be capable of ordering his thoughts logically, he should be an associative rather than a sequential thinker—a butterfly mind controlled by strong self-discipline. Perhaps both types are needed, reporting to a third—an integrative thinker—if associative, sequential and integrative qualities cannot be found in a single individual.

He must be able to maintain a proper balance between the concrete and the abstract, bearing in mind that preoccupation with practical affairs has often inhibited the creative and imaginative thinking necessary for growth; but without practical implementation his work will come to nothing. If we agree with Elliott Jaques that a man's remuneration should be in proportion to the time it takes for his mistakes to be found out, then the future manager should be very highly paid.

Permanence and Change

In business, as in national life, the conflict between freedom and order is critical. Autonomy generates drive, but too much autonomy can lead to chaos.

Organization is shape and interdependence. Without duration shape cannot be recognized; without duration interdependence has no meaning. The essence of organization is that it be understood.

Marriage is the basic form of organization. It is made permanent so that we may stop worrying where the next partner is coming from and get on with the real job of living (loving?).

Without a degree of permanence in organization, nothing can be taken for granted and politics is all. It is surely a mistake to assume that, because rigidity is crippling and sterile, its opposite is ideal. Without some enduring datum, change is meaningless. Growth occurs most readily in an organism whose parts can develop separately within a fixed relationship.

Organization is made enduring (endearing?) so that the mechanics can be forgotten. It is made simple so as to work itself out of a job. Organization is best that requires no organizing and calls for a minimum of arbitration. Organization ideally should organize itself so that vitality may spring from within and energy be generated at all points of the structure. It is failure to utilize this internal energy (compare the tail) not specialization alone (compare the teeth) that leads to extinction.

Once self-developing, organization can be allowed to atrophy, to become organic.

It is perhaps an over-confident assumption that planning is possible in companies and that they can be organized accordingly. But planned opportunism and adaptive planning would seem a reasonable compromise. Certainly it is an oversimplification to formulate business policy exclusively in financial terms, and personal values play a greater part in company development than may sometimes be supposed.

Against the financial view, I would emphasize again that a company sets out to achieve a competitive, not a maximum, growth-returns performance, so that the other pressures which are inevitably imposed on any business may be kept in balance. An effective organization is one that recognizes this reality.

CHAPTER 12

CATALYTIC PLANNING

COMPANIES inevitably plan within the national and world context. I remember a vice-president of a large American corporation complaining many years ago that if only the Government would make up its mind, his company could plan its own affairs with much more confidence. So much of the business environment is created by governmental action that no consideration of business planning could be complete without reference to national planning.

Few measures are ever likely to achieve precisely and exclusively the results a government intends. It is therefore useful, and I believe desirable, to look on governments as acting catalytically. Seen in this way, a government, whatever its colour, introduces a variety of catalysts into a complex of interacting processes, with consequences more or less foreseen.

Given an understanding of the processes and the action of the catalysts, not only governments themselves, but also individual companies, should be better able to conduct their planning.

Uncertainty can never be eliminated, and on a national scale imponderables are legion. Is there, in fact, a credible approach to national planning? Perhaps the business of governments is less to organize than to harness the organic (as distinct from the dynamic) of a nation in the democratically decided common interest. The process of harnessing again involves continuing correction, but based on an appreciation of ecology.

Since forecasting is difficult and unreliable, I have proposed an approach to planning that is essentially organic or adaptive, subdivided into dynamic and catalytic planning. An organism comprises organs which have separate functions to perform, but which

309

ideally remain in balance with each other. If mechanics is concerned with the operation of machines, where predictability is high, then organics might be regarded as the study of more complex entities, where predictability is low.

Organic planning is distinguished from mechanistic, or more correctly didactic, planning in that the desired things happen as natural consequences of conditions introduced, rather than in accordance with precise instructions. Thus on a caravan site, conventional red-ringed signs didactically dictating a speed limit of 10 m.p.h., may or may not be obeyed; but the introduction of vicious ramps or ridges in the road every twenty yards will quickly condition the motorist to an organically effective response.

Business is sometimes regarded as a game and the organic principle can be seen clearly in its application to another game, familiar to scouts and cubs, known as flag raiding. It is played in an open, partly wooded area and the task of each side is to locate and capture their opponents' flag. Normally a half-way line is indicated and a player touched in the enemy half is required to return to his own flag before re-entering the game.

The half-way line is difficult to identify and monitor. A simple change in the rules simplifies the situation, notably that when a player is touched by an opponent, both return to base. Not only is the half-way line eliminated, but players are discouraged from touching each other, so they remain in play for longer periods. Also, a player in defence will more willingly touch an opponent, in that he has a shorter distance to cover before returning to the game. Organic solutions tend to be self-governing and call for a minimum of monitoring or enforcement.

Changing the Environment

Planning is the purposeful programming of action. Dynamic planning considers an organism seeking its own purposes within an environment, through adaptation, while the aim of catalytic planning is to alter the environment itself.

The first is concerned with the dynamic relationship between a company and its surroundings, both of which are in a constant state of change, and acting on each other. In other words, dynamic planning is a means of redeploying business assets to maintain a competitive position in changing markets, through selective innovation and product succession. It depends on a clear statement of identity, defining what business a company is in, based on a study of its technical and commercial strengths, or differentiated assets. A company should certainly do what it is able to do well, but present assets can frequently be redeployed in complementary new activities. Also, the interaction between company and environment may itself be used to promote and focus the innovative process, so that innovative energy may be channelled in commercially desirable directions.

It follows that corporate identity should also be dynamic, evolving in response to changing markets and requirements. Awareness of identity in relation to the external environment enables a company to recognize those innovative opportunities which it is best able to exploit: looking at the world and asking, as each pertinent development emerges, "What's in it for us?"

Catalytic planning, on the other hand, is applied to complex and amorphous situations, where boundaries are ill defined. Like dynamic planning, it is adaptive in the sense that when a particular direction proves to be mistaken, the course can be changed, and changed as often as may prove desirable.

Catalytic planning may be defined as the introduction of self-sustaining motor elements into a complex economy in order to induce desired changes or results, and where necessary their subsequent withdrawal. In Chapter 2 I noted that the limited liability laws were a typical catalytic element in that, perhaps more than any other single factor, they had contributed to the development of business and the growth of wealth. Even as an engineer, I put them well before the steam-engine or any other technical device. It is an approach to planning with some hope of realizing a satisfactory outcome, bearing in mind the real world in which we live.

Implication Studies

For companies engaged in dynamic or adaptive planning, catalytic planning may also be of value as a way of understanding the environment. For example, it is possible to examine the potential of a novel product by studying the interacting implications of its introduction; or the impact on a company's business of a new material. Seeing developments or situations catalytically can often illuminate the way in which change is likely to occur.

Had we simply thought of radio or television as a substitute for the piano (in the home-entertainment business), we should have missed their real significance. It is the feedback or the repercussions from an innovation that reveal its character, and experience of many innovative situations helps us to foresee the pitfalls in conventional projection.

A thoughtful speaker at the Symposium on Plastics Towards 2000 in 1968 pointed out that wood was a very good material for trees and wool for sheep, but that men required materials (or molecules) tailored to their purposes. The next great task in the study of materials is to classify them by their properties in a multi-dimensional lattice, relate the lattice to human requirements and fill the gaps where needs are concentrated. The catalytic consequences of this achievement will surely be profound.

Students have protested, understandably, that nowadays, democracy is not sufficiently distributed for individuals to influence the circumstances governing their lives. On the other hand, many of the same students would reject the price mechanism or the profit motive in favour of a planned society. Here lies the most conspicuous conflict of our times, between two similar indignities. On the one hand, it is not dignified to be ruled or manipulated by other men; but it is no more dignified to accept the domination of economic or other natural forces.

I imagine it was rejection of the two indignities that led to the philosophy of public ownership. To be tossed about by economic forces was unacceptable, so planning was essential, but planning seemed impossible unless the key resources were controlled.

Control (perhaps through subconscious acceptance of mercantile principles) was associated with ownership, so nationalization was regarded as the answer.

But in practice, the prime element in any country's national resources (or differentiated assets) is human energy, which, unlike a mineral, is not found lying idle, waiting to be used. It tends to be generated in greater or lesser quantities and directed by mysterious impulses that as yet are not completely understood. Successful planning, therefore, will depend to a great extent on the means chosen for generating and directing human energy.

When I was a journalist, I was sent to Moscow in 1957, where I sought and succeeded in obtaining an interview with the Russian physicist, Peter Kapitsa, who studied at Cambridge. He said that the development of data-processing techniques in the West had made the centrally planned economy of the Soviet Union a practical possibility. I think he had his reservations, but his argument is even more questionable today, with the current unwillingness of students at the super-universities to be processed like punched cards or perforated tape. Surely the contention that the mature man determines his own purpose, makes, to the best of his ability, his own world, not pursuing some predetermined pattern, some supernaturally-ordained objective, is a noble concept. A human being, a company or a society is only fully grown when it accepts responsibility for deciding its own destiny.

To control our social destiny calls for planning on a national scale. But so we may control our individual destinies, we are unwilling to be planned. How can we reconcile these two conditions of vitality?

No longer is it a simple conflict between freedom and order (as in conglomerates) since even the most powerful leaders do not seem able to generate the kind of order they desire. The organism of our world is showing signs of an independence we seem scarcely able to control. A new view of the world may be needed, as Marshall McLuhan has suggested. He notes that:

> . . . amateurism seeks the development of the total awareness of the individual and the critical awareness of the ground rules of society. The

amateur can afford to lose. The professional tends to classify and to specialize, to accept uncritically the ground rules of the environment. The ground rules provided by the mass response of his colleagues serve as a pervasive environment of which he is contentedly unaware. The "expert" is the man who stays put.

Planning is among the broadest, most divergent, fields of human endeavour, and we cannot expect to tackle it as specialists on blinkered sequences through time. Since it is all-embracing and since we may never hope to know the universe, past, present and to come, we are left with an approach to planning that is necessarily adaptive and creative.

At the same time, responsibility for taking decisions should be placed, as far as possible, at the point or level where most relevant information is available, where the necessary action can be initiated, and where the consequences are most likely to be felt. A well-managed company or country is one in which these three conditions tend to coincide.

Planning without decisions is not planning at all, since action cannot follow. Planning is active, not passive, and therefore disturbs us, so on a national scale we tend to compromise by what is known misleadingly as indicative planning. It is essentially passive in that a table of interrelated targets is prepared, but no steps are taken to see that they are met.

Since indicative planning is not enough and centrally directed planning either unpalatable, unworkable or both, I believe that catalytic planning may provide the answer in which the motor elements to action are well distributed. It is not just another name for the price mechanism, which is only one example, but a framework within which a representative government can introduce and withdraw active agents, promoting action, making possible a prompt response to change.

In the same way, a company equips itself for optimum (not maximum) adaptability through dynamic planning, and so its plans do not become a straitjacket. Both dynamic and catalytic planning are adequately flexible, assuming an organic world, in which currents, tides and winds are used to our advantage.

National Economy

We have become aware how enormous is the problem of planning our whole national economy. As noted in an earlier chapter, a limiting factor in processing and transmitting the necessary data may be the speed of light itself. We must therefore set ourselves only manageable tasks. If the problem or the information presented to us is so complex and diverse that we cannot handle it, we may suffer a figurative nervous breakdown. Professor W. Ross Ashby has suggested that the limit to the understanding of data occurs when the complexity of the data exceeds the complexity of the observing channel, notably ourselves.

If, on the other hand, we can define specific purposes, or at least temporary aims, and insert into the economy self-contained activating elements that, of their own accord, would tend to generate the desired results, the problem is adequately broken down and simplified. We do not need to understand the whole process to achieve some measure of control. If these elements can also be withdrawn when they have achieved their purpose or when the purpose is no longer thought desirable, then we have a practical tool of national management.

As I have emphasized, in conditions of uncertainty, particularly where the uncertainty varies in degree and over time, progressive adjustment is essential. Nature itself deals with such a situation by organic principles of change. In Chapter 2, I presented the equation

$$\text{Planning} = \text{Purpose} + \text{Anticipation}.$$

For dynamic planning, concerned with a company and its environment, I defined Purpose as Identity plus Motivation. In catalytic planning

$$\text{Purpose} = \sum \text{Interacting Purposes}.$$

Such aims can be in conflict and sometimes the interaction may be marginal, but as with the psychosomatic effect of worry on the stomach, no sector of the universe is truly independent of another, and "no man is an island", as John Donne reflected some centuries ago.

Dynamic planning, by individuals and institutions, and catalytic planning, for the context in which they live or operate, together form a basis for organic progress, resolving conflicts by interaction instead of legislation, embracing people, companies, nations and the world.

In other words, we require a widespread distribution of the motor elements, but, hopefully, driving in the same direction, like the four-hub motors in an electric or hydraulic motor-vehicle.

Catalysis

I have called the tool "catalytic planning", aware that the metaphor is not chemically precise but believing that it clearly conveys the principle. As defined above, it is the introduction of self-contained and self-sustaining agents into a country's economy that of their own volition will generate nationally desirable results. In other words, it combines the advantages of planning with the energy of enterprise.

National planning in general is the attempt by government to influence the economy towards objectives believed to be in the short- or long-term common interest. Perhaps the two most familiar forms of planning on a national scale are: indicative planning, which as I have suggested is a combination of forecasting and the formulation of interrelated targets for industrial expansion; and second, the application, often *ad hoc*, of economic pressures, normally through fiscal devices, in order to make short-term and sometimes longer-term adjustments to the economy.

Indicative planning provides a context in which desirable aims can be pursued, but is insufficient in itself unless supplemented by direct or indirect sanctions. In the present state of data processing, planning through the application of economic pressures is a cybernetic nightmare, with side effects, residual trends, hysteresis, cumulative feedback, instability, oscillation, hunting, noise and sometimes completely unforeseen results, where the desirable is heavily outweighed by the undesirable.

On the other hand, by creating or identifying motive elements in the economy and giving them qualified power, desirable results can be achieved by a sort of fermentation. This fermentation can be controlled by activating or inhibiting the "yeast".

One approach is by tapping or directing vested interests through some such investment body as the Industrial Reorganization Corporation, which was set up in the belief that rationalization in certain industries, probably with the formation of larger units through mergers, was nationally desirable. The anti-trust laws in the United States presumably had a similar catalytic purpose, though many would now consider that the unfavourable consequences are beginning to exceed the favourable. The danger arises when the catalyst has existed for so long that its original purpose is forgotten. Size is not a virtue in itself, nor monopoly necessarily an evil. Likewise, we sometimes think of innovation as an ultimate good, but its real value will depend on what we consider to be our purpose. Withdrawal of a catalyst is as important as its introduction.

Other catalytic elements have been the patent laws, the National Research Development Corporation (NRDC) and Technical Development Capital (TDC), all of which have promoted the exploitation of inventions. Again, the formation of the Industrial and Commercial Finance Corporation (ICFC), at the instance of the Macmillan Committee, has helped in the creation and expansion of smaller businesses. It has also been self-sustaining, indeed exceptionally successful, in commercial terms, since investment in small companies provides more scope for growth than participation in large companies, which already dominate their markets.

Again, unlike several smaller countries, South Africa has no television. Currently, Afrikaans-speaking outnumber English-speaking South Africans in the ratio 60:40 and to maintain their influence are seeking to establish Afrikaans as the country's major language. The economics of television are such that a practical service can only be offered, particularly where the population is relatively small, by showing films; and films in Afrikaans must be relatively few. The introduction of television might therefore lead to the wider use of English (or American), a change in the balance of power and an overall reorientation of the society.

Effective catalytic planning involves two conditions, namely motivation to act and power to achieve. In other words it depends on active agents, with motivation and power, that will work towards defined objectives and will continue to operate until withdrawn. The following are six examples:

(1) For an industry believed to have fallen behind its overseas competitors, the formation of a development, manufacturing and marketing agency, free to award development contracts to commercial companies within the industry, but also to compete with them. It should be financially accountable, but over a longer than normal cycle (say 5 years).

(2) Savings as a substitute for freezing wages (or taxation). It may be that, in times of inflation, saving could be offered as an option to a wage freeze. The resulting fund could be administered by, say, a consortium of finance houses. Spending power would be limited, as necessary; the nation would have access to funds; and the labourer would feel less cheated of his hire—though it would be essential to use the breathing space to create a healthy economy, or there is likely to be trouble later.

(3) The creation of product-planning and capacity-exchange centres in the regions. Such centres could provide new product and market information, plus subcontracting work, on a commercial basis, and help to generate spontaneous revival of declining industries.

(4) A study of amenity patterns, as proposed by my former colleague, Robert Staton, whereby local authorities could be provided with data that would enable them to attract suitable self-sustaining commercial and industrial business to their areas. Amenity indices have been investigated with this in view.

(5) Equipping a consulting company through a sponsored study to advise general managements on the planning of research. Once the consultants have gathered experience through this initial project, they will be at pains to offer their knowledge to other companies. Formal studies or commissions of inquiry tend to be ineffective, since their reports often remain unread, whereas consultants have a vested interest in selling their services and hence would provide an impetus towards research effectiveness throughout the country.

(6) The identification and development of one or more key assets that will trigger off sustained growth in a backward region. Thus, given certain other, perhaps marginal, resources, such as harbourage or minerals, cheap power in the Scottish Highlands might promote the formation of several interrelated industries. Such power could be provided by local power plants independent of the grid and once take-off had occurred, development would be economically self-generating.

The last of these examples leads me to consider regional development and the possible contribution of catalytic planning.

Regional Development

Not only individual companies, but whole industrial areas, may face a changing market environment. The development of Tees-Side, for example, was based on river access to the sea and local coal. Now the coal is too expensive and the river is in many places not deep enough for modern shipping. Clydeside's dependence on one major industry has made south-west Scotland similarly vulnerable.

With the contraction of their traditional activities, these regions have to devise new product policies. But only within the regions themselves can this be done effectively.

Firstly, if each manufacturer and entrepreneur were alive to his opportunities, the problem might well resolve itself. Where every company has a dynamic product policy and a procedure to identify emerging market needs, growth will be organic. Companies have only to look at every changing situation in the outside world and ask themselves how they can gain advantage from it.

But assets are often considered in such narrow terms that the most promising are overlooked. Any company, by careful study, can identify those special assets (skills, resources, experience, location and market outlets, for example) which in combination suggest unique lines of diversification or development. The same is true of regions.

So many plans for regional development depend on outside leadership—special encouragements to attract industry from elsewhere, capital injection, investment allowances, tax and rating concessions, grants, government contracts and exhortation, few of which lead to economic take-off. Valuable though many of these measures may be, real vitality can only spring from within an organism. Growth must be self-generating, occurring spontaneously at every point. Some device is necessary to release this energy.

In catalytic planning we are concerned with the interaction of human and material resources and, if we can identify and analyse the combination of differentiated assets that gives a region its key competitive advantages, we may be able to determine a pattern of industry that could be economically established there. If in addition we can isolate a missing asset that, when introduced, would enable the region to take off into sustained growth, together with an entrepreneur committed to that region, the basic elements are there.

As illustration, reference is made to a proposed development on the Moray Firth, where cheap electric power might be the missing asset.

An exploratory study was put in hand several years ago in order to identify the exploitable assets of the region. There did not seem very much—some barytes, rather poor coal, sea and scenery. But there was a deep-water anchorage in the Cromarty

Firth, perhaps the best in Britain and at the same time facing Europe. There were also whisky distilleries.

One suggestion was that waste carbon dioxide gas, discharged by distilleries in quantity, might be used for fire extinguishers, for ice cream plants, or as a chemical feedstock. Urea fertilizer was considered as a product, but it was soon discovered that major plants were already being built and chemical instability created certain problems.

But from this tentative beginning, Jonathan Jenkins, in dialogue with colleagues trained in many disciplines, gradually conceived a chemical complex based on groups of largely dissimilar materials which, if produced together in a single integrated scheme, could be made more economically than by any conventional approach. After some false starts and diversions, the process flow sheet was completed—though the final version of the complex was found to discharge many times as much carbon dioxide as had first prompted the inquiry. (I have just seen in the Press that soil and aerial surveys are to start next week.)

Beginning from scratch, on a grass-roots site, made it possible to build a complex more advanced (compare Japan's recent development) than any yet constructed in the British Isles. The success of the complex might depend on the provision of electric power at 4 or 5 mills per kilowatt-hour. A high tariff for electric power is partly a function of distribution costs. But if a power-generating plant were built on site and power charges did not include the cost of distribution, the target could be readily achieved.

But such a step would break the rules: it is important to be fair and electricity boards are obliged to charge all users at a common price. Would it be sensible to do so in the present case?

According to W. Arthur Lewis there is in the location of industry a tendency to neutralize the price mechanism and maintain or augment the differential pressures that promote the ever-increasing development of conurbations, already over-large. A separate power plant might therefore adjust the differential forces and benefit not only the Moray Firth but also Edinburgh and

Glasgow. And it would not constitute a subsidy but simply a trigger to spark off an industrial programme of advantage to Britain as a whole.

Another example, based on a simple market study, relates to South-east Asia. Large schemes for generating power or producing iron and steel are sometimes considered the only ways in which industrial countries can assist emerging nations. But, as Gunnar Myrdal has emphasized, the take-off into sustained growth requires such nations to lift themselves by their own bootstraps.

South-east Asia is a region of the world with water, sewage and irrigation problems, suggesting needs for such products as vessels, pumps and pipes. Vessels are in general tailor-made and the added value is relatively small. Pumps are often sophisticated engineering products, which at this stage are best imported. To produce seamless pipe and tube requires expensive machinery and very special skills.

If, however, a comparatively simple machine could be purchased, designed to make tube automatically from metal strip, then a project might be worth considering. Such machines do in fact exist and can be bought from Britain, the Continent, Japan and the United States. A commercial proposition of this kind could help to catalyse self-sustaining industrial development.

In Britain, we should seek to identify and reinforce our national differentiated assets. Of the ten countries in the world with the largest populations, Britain is the most densely populated. Intercommunication among so many people in so small an area should be relatively easy, suggesting that to strengthen this advantage we should devote a considerable proportion of our national resources to transport and to education.

Focusing the Future

The danger of taking the future for granted is particularly apparent on the national scale. During the American business recession in 1958, James Hagerty was press secretary in the White House. I remember seeing on his desk a card with the following inscription:

One day, as I sat thinking, almost in despair, a hand fell on my shoulder and a voice said reassuringly: "Cheer up, things could be worse."

So I cheered up and, sure enough, things got worse.

Cheering up alone is not enough. We have to make the most of our resources—systematically and unremittingly.

Dynamic and catalytic planning are only phrases that in some modest way may focus thinking in practical directions. What I have called catalytic planning, for example, has always existed, but in giving it a name we may be better able to direct its application. The impact of innovation or a new material, for example, may be studied on these lines.

I believe I said earlier that just before a projectionist at the cinema changes a reel in the middle of a film, a black or coloured spot appears in the top right-hand corner of the screen. I had never noticed it until some years ago when a friend drew it to my attention. Now it is difficult to miss. Dynamic and catalytic planning are intended to increase the strike rate of relevant ideas, the shock of recognition; to focus forward thinking; and to open human consciousness to opportunity.

PLANNING BIBLIOGRAPHY

The following books, articles and papers bear on the subject of this book, but the list is by no means comprehensive.

1969

The Management of Technological Innovation, Proceedings of a National Conference, sponsored by the Ministry of Technology, *Management Today* and the University of Bradford (12 and 13 March).

Matching Technological Capability with Needs: The Consultant's View, E. P. WARD, National Conference on the Management of Technological Innovation. (12 March.)

Top Management Planning, GEORGE A. STEINER, Collier–Macmillan.

Marketing Research and Information Systems, R. D. BUZZELL, D. F. COX and R. V. BROWN, McGraw Hill (June).

Management of Research, Development and Design in Industry, T. S. McLEOD, Gower Press.

1968

Status Survey on Technological Forecasting, W. D. CONN, Worcester College, Oxford, and Scientific Control Systems Ltd.

The Year 2000, HERMAN KAHN, Macmillan.

2001: A Space Odyssey, ARTHUR C. CLARKE (and STANLEY KUBRICK) Hutchinson.

The Assessment of Industrial Markets, AUBREY WILSON, Hutchinson.

Corporate Planning in Industry, ARIS PRESANIS, Business Publications Ltd.

Marketing for the plastics age, G. ADER, *Symposium on Plastics Towards 2000*, Borough Polytechnic. (24 Oct.)

Invention and innovation in retrospect and prospect, V. E. YARSLEY, *Symposium on Plastics Towards 2000*, Borough Polytechnic. (24 Oct.)

Training tomorrow's children in plastics technology, J. E. PROCTOR, *Symposium on Plastics Towards 2000*, Borough Polytechnic. (24 Oct.)

Dynamic and catalytic planning, E. P. WARD, *Symposium on Plastics Towards 2000*, Borough Polytechnic (24 Oct.)

Courtaulds plan for its research, E. W. OSMOND, *Financial Times*. (2 Oct.)

A Structure in Favour of the Future, E. P. WARD, ESOMAR Congress. (11 Sept.)

Financial Planning, C. D. CECIL, Interplan Research Ltd. (July.)

The marketing concept, B. G. ALLISON, *Journal and Proceedings of the Industrial Marketing Research Association*, 4 (2) (July.)

National Conference on Technological Forecasting, Management Centre, University of Bradford. (4–5 July.)

Planning in conditions of uncertainty, E. P. WARD and B. G. BODROGHY, *European Conference on Technological Forecasting*, University of Strathclyde. (24–26 June.)

Research appraisal in confusion—where can the user turn? R. V. BROWN, *AMA Summer Conference*. (18 June.)

Practical Industrial Marketing, D. W. FOSTER, British Institute of Management: Seminar. (2 May.)

Efficiency in industrial research and development, T. S. MCLEOD, *Electronics and Power*, Journal of the Institution of Electrical Engineers. (May, pp. 202–5.)

Management—a control system, F. L. PITT, Third Control Convention, *Advances in Control Systems*, University of Leicester. (April.)

Why business always loses, T. LEVITT, *Harvard Business Review*. (March–April.)

The importance of marketing education in developing countries, J. A. ALOFE, *Marketing Forum*, Journal of the College of Marketing. (March–April.)

The Age of Discontinuity, PETER F. DRUCKER, Heinemann.

Technical forecasting: the art and its management, G. WILLS, *Commentary*. 10 (2), 87–101, Journal of the Market Research Society.

Corporate Planning, JOHN ARGENTI, George Allen & Unwin. (Jan.)

1967

Manufacturing under Licence, D. EDMUNDS BRAZELL, Kenneth Mason Publications.

Management of Industrial Research, E. D. REEVES, Reinhold.

Industrial Marketing Management and Controls, L. A. WILLIAMS, Longmans, Green & Co.

The dynamics of business planning, E. P. WARD, *Marketing Forum*, Nov.–Dec., pp. 3–33, Journal of the College of Marketing.

Strategies for technology based industries, H. I. ANSOFF and J. M. STEWART, *Harvard Business Review*. (Nov.–Dec.)

La Dynamique de la politique de produits, E. P. WARD, *Revue Française du Marketing*, No. 24, part 3, pp. 3–24.

The selection of industrial research projects, D. H. ALLEN, *Anglo-Polish Symposium*. (9–12 Oct.)

Technological forecasting, J. E. QUINN, *Harvard Business Review*.

Planning tomorrow today through successive focusing. E. P. WARD, *Journal of Marketing* (*USA*) 31 (3), 23–27 (July.)

The Innovators, MICHAEL SHANKS, Pelican.

Human Use of Human Being, NORBERT WIENER, Avon.

Two new tools for project evaluation, D. H. ALLEN, *Chemical Engineering*, (3 July.)

Technical Sales Training, O. TURNER, National Development and Management Foundation of South Africa. (June.)

New markets for new products, B. G. BODROGY, *Product Licensing Index*, No. 36. (April.)

World markets and new products, B. G. BODROGHY, *Product Licensing Index*, No. 37. (May.)

Catalytic planning, E. P. WARD, Paper presented at a private meeting for the Minister of Technology, attended also by the Secretary of State for Education and Science. (4 March.)

Long Term Planning Manual, B. RUTTER, Management Sciences (Australia). (March.)

What business are you really in?, T. LEVITT, *Business Week*. (11 March.)

Special report: technological forecasting—half science, half mumbo-jumbo, DORA K. MERRIS, *Product Engineering*. (16 Jan, pp. 80–89.)

The development of industrial market research and marketing, E. SHANKLE-MAN, and America and the rest—some comparisons, A. S. C. EHRENBERG, *Commentary*, **9** (1), (Jan.), Journal of the Market Research Society.

Shepherding a new product from brainwave to hardware, JOHN KOLB, *Product Engineering*. (16 Jan., pp. 38–41.)

The New Industrial State, J. K. GALBRAITH, Hamish Hamilton.

Management Science: The Business Use of Operations Research, STAFFORD BEER, *Aldus Books*.

The Medium is the Massage, MARSHALL MCLUHAN and QUENTIN FIORE, Bantam Books.

Economics of Research and Development Seminar, Polytechnic School of Management Studies. (Jan.)

How marketing men can eliminate roadblocks to new product success, W. S. WESSON. *Paper Trade Journal*, **150** (7 Nov.), 49–50.

The Effective Executive, PETER F. DRUCKER, Heinemann.

Technological Forecasting in Perspective, E. JANTSCH, OECD, Paris.

Bradford Exercises in Management, PROF. T. KEMPNER, Thomas Nelson & Sons Ltd. (Nos. 1–12.)

1966

Decision and Control, STAFFORD BEER, John Wiley (London).

How line executives can eliminate roadblocks to new product success, W. M. RIEGEL, *Paper Trade Journal*, **150** (7 Nov.), 51–52.

Discarding plans for a new product?—management takes a second look, E. B. WEISS, *Advanced Age*. (7 Nov., pp. 94–00.)

Research effectiveness in a commercial context, E. P. WARD, *Proplan: Draft Outline for Multicompany Study*. (Nov.)

Identifying and evaluating new product opportunities, E. P. WARD, *IMRA Journal*, **2** (3) (Nov.), 114–29.

Choix et controle de projets de recherche et de developpement, T. S. MCLEOD, *Synopsis*. (Nov.)

Five ways to go about developing a new product, R. D. CRISP, *Advanced Age*, **37** (31 Oct.), 115–16.

Implementing the Marketing Concept, A. CORBIN, British Institute of Management publication.

Product development speeds up, *Business Week*. (15 Oct., p. 130.)

Sales management asks marketing executives, how do you test market a new product?, *Sales Management*, **97** (1 Oct.), 81–83.

Purchasing know-how aids product development, T. F. DILLON, *Purchasing*, **61** (8 Sept.), 48–50.

Innovative imitation, T. LEVITT, *Harvard Business Review*, **44** (Sept.), 63–70.

Product diversification and living costs, a further comment, *American State Association Journal* (Sept., p. 788.)

Organization for New Product Development, a Symposium, National Industrial Conference Board, Inc. (USA).

A framework for thinking about a company's future, E. P. WARD, *Achievement.* (Aug.–Sept., pp. 13–16.)

New products: how to avoid joining the failures, M. J. MILLS, *The Director.* (Aug.)

Industrial market research, B. W. WEEDON, *Engineering.* (5 Aug.)

Convenience oriented patron demands more new products, W. H. SAHLOFF, *American Druggist*, **154** (1 Aug.), 64.

Mergers in Modern Business, N. A. H. STACEY, Hutchinson & Co.

Dune, FRANK HERBERT, Victor Gollancz.

Risk, return and DCF, B. G. BODROGHY, *The Director.* (July.)

Long-range planning for a consumer industry, W. S. MARTIN, *Research Management*, **9** (July), 221–8.

Demon: decision mapping via optimum go-no networks; a model for marketing new products, *Management Science*, **21** (July), 865–7.

How to avoid costly mistakes when introducing a new product, R. J. MOCKLER, *Advanced Management Journal*, **31** (July), 45–52.

R and D's role in product development, R. F. SHERMAN, *Industrial Research*, **8** (July), 32–34.

Keys to successful product planning, B. C. AMES, *Business Horizons*, **9** (Summer), 49–58.

Tomorrow's management: a more adventurous life in a Free-form Corporation, M. WAYS, *Fortune* (1 July.)

Some Problems of the Growing Firm, Proceedings of Series of Conferences given by Industrial and Commercial Finance Corporation Ltd. (Jan.–June.)

Marketing Research, J. Tyzack and Partners (Training) Ltd., Occasional Paper. (June.)

Modern Marketing, J. Tyzack and Partners (Training) Ltd., Occasional Paper. (June.)

Advertising and Sales Promotion, J. Tyzack and Partners (Training) Ltd., Occasional Paper. (June.)

Diversification paying off, *Financial World*, **125** (8 June), 17.

Pruning of sick products, H. L. CLAYTON, *Management Accounting*, **47** (June), 17–18.

MacManus forms product planning, development unit, E. A. JONES, *Advanced Age*, **37** (30 May), 2.

New products get boost: commercial newsletters tell their story to 50,000 businessmen in over 150 cities abroad, W. F. CLARK, *International Commerce*, **72** (9 May), 2–3.

Wall Paper, *Management Today.* (April.)

Keeping ahead of tomorrow (sales management round-table on product planning, market testing and broad scope innovation), *Sales Management*, **96** (15 April), 54.

American Marketing Association, New York Chapter, Annual New Products Conference, *Advanced Age*, **37** (4 April), 6.

The pains and prizes of business growth, W. G. NORRIS, *The Director*. (April.)

New Product Development, Proceedings of a Conference held in September 1965, University of Strathclyde. (March.)

Product Screening Procedures and *Marketing Considerations in New Product Planning*, E. P. WARD, Conference on New Product Development, University of Strathclyde (proceedings published March).

Product planning and packaging, *Sales Management*, **96** (7 Jan.), 82.

Product planning—past, present and future (in automotive industry), G. W. GIBSON, *Automotive Industry*, **134** (1 Jan.), 53–60.

Product mix analysis by linear programming, O. L. RAUN, *Management Accounting*, **47** (Jan.), 3–19.

Market Research in the USA, H. P. HODGE, Industrial Marketing Research Association. (27 Jan.)

Time Lag in New Product Development, LEE ADLER, *Journal of Marketing*, **30** (Jan.), 17–21.

Product planning makes an ally of change, E. P. WARD, *Taylor Review*. (Jan.)

New Product Decisions: An Analytical Approach, E. A. PESSEMIER, McGraw-Hill.

Corporate Research and Profitability, Proceedings of First National Conference on Industrial Research, Industrial Research Inc.

Selection of Materials, A. L. DAVIES, reprinted from *The Design Method* (edited by S. A. Gregory on behalf of Design and Innovation Group, University of Aston in Birmingham), Butterworths.

New Product Development, Booz Allen & Hamilton.

The Changing Pattern of Distribution (2nd edn.), AUBREY WILSON and N. A. H. STACEY, Pergamon Press.

Marketing Concepts and Strategy, MARTIN L. BELL, Macmillan.

The Will to Manage: corporate success through programmed management, MARVIN BOWER, McGraw-Hill.

1965

Improving the Effectiveness of Research and Development, R. E. SEILER, McGraw-Hill.

Research Management: Principles and Practice, J. E. WALTERS, MacMillan.

Assessing industrial research projects, D. H. ALLEN, *Science Journal* (Dec., pp. 79–83.)

The dynamics of product planning, E. P. WARD, *Metra*, **4** (4) (Dec.)

New products get more attention, do better, BOOZ ALLEN, *Advanced Age*, **36** (13 Dec.), 19.

Exploit the product life cycle, T. LEVITT, *Harvard Business Review*, **43** (Nov.–Dec.), 84–91.

Galloping trend towards diversification that calls for sound management first and foremost, R. E. KELLY, *Magazine Wall Street*, **117** (27 Nov.), 248–51.

Marketing in a Competitive Economy, LESLIE W. RODGER, Hutchinson.

The Marketing of Industrial Products, AUBREY WILSON, Hutchinson.

Finding the key to success in new product failures, H. LAZO, *Industrial Marketing*, **50** (Nov.), 74–77.

Licences and product strategy for the smaller company, B. W. WEEDON, *Product Licensing Index*, No. 17. (Sept.)

New product evaluation, B. G. BODROGHY, *Product Licensing Index*. (Oct.)

Making project management work, J. M. STEWART, *Business Horizons*.

The firm of the future, H. IGOR ANSOFF, *Harvard Business Review*. (Sept.– Oct.)

Dilemma: People in Motion, United States Steel Corporation.

New products: beware of outside ideas: abstract, R. P. AUBER, *Management Review*, **54** (Aug.), 22–26.

How much profit should a new product make?, T. J. MOULSON, *Printers Ink*, **291** (23 July), 13–14.

Corporate strategy, H. IGOR ANSOFF, McGraw-Hill.

Getting higher dividends from research, J. T. KENDALL, *The Director*. (July.)

Success begins with the customer (create products to fill his needs), D. C. BURNHAM, *Iron Age*, **196** (1 July), 39.

Product management, T. M. FULMER, *California Management Review*.

New product search and acquisition, D. F. JAMIESON, Beckingsale & Company (Melbourne, Australia). (June.)

Can you do it by numbers, *Printers Ink*, **290** (25 June), 55.

How to use market research as a diversification tool, P. E. MCLEAN, *Pulp and Paper*, **39** (21 June), 51–52.

Managing the product life cycle (abstract), D. K. CLIFFORD, *Management Review*, **54** (June), 34–38.

How to doom new product planning, A. C. WEST, *Iron Age*, **195** (6 May), 69.

Leverage in the product life cycle, D. K. CLIFFORD, *Dun's Review and Modern Industry*, **85** (May), 62–64.

Case of diversification dilemma, C. H. CLINE, *Harvard Business Review*, **43** (May), 12–14.

Taking the chances out of product introductions (using the PERT technique), P. GLISSER, *Industrial Marketing*, **50** (May), 86–91.

Marketing knowledge: key to diversifying, W. F. HAFSTROM, *Iron Age*, **195** (May), 82.

New products under closer scrutiny (gauging prospects of new products), *Printers Ink*, **240** (9 April), 49.

New game: find your way through this hazardous maze: pitfalls for new products, *Advanced Age*, **36** (5 April), 134.

Phasing out weak products, P. KOTLER, *Harvard Business Review*, **43** (March– April), 107–18.

Financial concepts in new product development, W. H. LAWSON, *Financial Executive*, **33** (March), 38–40.

New direction for new product R & D, K. H. TIETJEN, *Printers Ink*, **290** (12 Feb.), 14–16.

Market research can aid in new product development, J. B. BELL, *Steel*, **156** (1 Feb.), 26.

Organizing for product innovation, J. W. LORSCH and P. R. LAWRENCE, *Harvard Business Review*, **43** (Jan.), 109–18.

Prepare the company for the product, J. S. RANDALL, *Iron Age*, **195** (7 Jan.), 153–6.

Take a fresh look at your old products, R. FREAS, *Sales Management*, **94** (1 Jan.), 21–23.

The dynamics of product planning, E. P. WARD, *The Chartered Mechanical Engineer*, **12** (1) (Jan.), 29–34.

Behavioral science offers fresh insights on new product acceptance, S. J. SHOW, *Journal of Marketing*, **29** (Jan.), 9–13.

How long does it take to introduce new products?, D. W. TWEDT, *Journal of Marketing*, **29** (Jan.), 71–72.

New products will be key to growth of economy, inter-public study finds (excerpts from Decade of incentive), *Printers Ink*, **289** (1/8 Jan.), 49–50.

The Profitable Product, its Planning, Launching and Management, Prentice-Hall.

Business policy: text and cases, EDMUND P. LEARNED, Richard D. Irwin.

Long-range planning in American industry, BRIAN W. SCOTT, American Management Association.

1964

Insight, JACOB BRONOWSKI, Macdonald.

The Act of Creation, ARTHUR KOESTLER, Hutchinson.

Critical path analysis for new product planning, Y. WONG, *Journal of Marketing*, **28** (Oct.), 53–59.

Practical planning for small business, R. A. GOLDE, *Harvard Business Review*. (Sept–Oct.)

Dynamics of new product campaigns, H. D. MILLS, *Journal of Marketing*, **23** (Oct.), 60–63.

Case of the unproductive products (appraising a hypothetical company's new product development, cross-section of executive thinking), S. A. GREYSER, *Harvard Business Review*, **42** (July), 20–21.

Space age technique to launch new products (PERT programme), J. F. STOLLE and J. C. PAGE, *Sales Management*, **93** (3 July), 23–27.

Why and how to diversify (ten principles of diversification planning), G. A. STEINER, *Californian Management Review*, **6**, 11–18.

How do you pick the next winner? Product Engineering magazine's blue-ribbon panel selects previous year's outstanding new products, *Business Week*. (16 May), 81–82.

Pet diversifies as evaporated users fade (new product outpouring), R. CRAIN, *Advanced Age*, **35** (11 May), 41.

American Marketing Association, New York Chapter, Annual New Products Conference, *Advanced Age*, **35** (11 May), 74.

New products marketing; special issue, *Printers Ink*, **287** (May), 3–296.

Beyond Automation: Material Problems of an Exploding Technology, JOHN DIEBOLD, McGraw-Hill.

Post-audits and qualitative factors, A. J. WEINBERGER, *Chemical Engineering*. (27 April.)

Death and burial of "sick" products, *Journal of Marketing*.

Master plan guides new products to money-making maturity (how Carborundum Co. does it), J. E. SANDFORD, *Iron Age*, **193** (2 April), 51–53.

Profit measurement by product group, H. W. HORNIK, *Financial Executive*, **32** (March), 45–48.

The strategy of nylon's growth creates new markets, J. P. YALE, *Modern Textile Magazine*. (Feb.)

New product planning in medium sized technically oriented industrial firms, R. DARLEY, *Business Inquiry*, **3** (1), 7–17.

New product development and commercialization (annotated bibliography of materials concerned with planning and marketing new products), J. A. DONALDSON, *Business Literature*, **36** (Jan.–Feb.), 9–12.

How to lengthen the life of a profitable product, *Business Management*, **25** (Jan.), 30–33, and continued in *Management Review*, **53** (March), 56–59.

Risk analysis for capital investment, DAVID HERTZ, *Harvard Business Review*

Organizing for product planning, J. E. STAFFORD and J. U. MCNEAL, *Advanced Management Journal*, **29** (Jan.), 28–33.

Estimating sales and markets, A. J. WEINBERGER, *Chemical Engineering*. (20 Jan.)

Marketing Organization in: Marketing—An Introductory Analysis, J. B. MATTHEWS, McGraw-Hill.

Product Analysis Pricing, WILFRED BROWN and ELLIOTT JAQUES, Heinemann.

Multiproducts Ltd., LISL KLEIN, Department of Scientific and Industrial Research, H.M.S.O.

Inventing the Future, D. GABOR, Penguin Books.

Managing for results: economic tasks and risk-taking decisions, PETER F. DRUCKER, Heinemann.

1963

United States. Small Business Administration. New Product Development and Sale, G. A. SIMON and F. V. FORTMILLER (Small Business Bibliography No. 4).

Productivity in Research, Symposium, Institution of Chemical Engineers. (11–12 Dec.)

New Products: Are we organized for them?, H. LAZO, *Industrial Marketing*, **48** (Dec.), 82–87.

Is newness the key success factor?, W. CAPITMAN and G. J. ABRAMS, *Printers Ink*, **285** (15 Nov.), 141.

How we appraise new-product proposals, J. L. FORRESTER, *NAA Bulletin* **45** (Nov.), 23–28.

Improving R & D's batting average, A. J. WEINBERGER, *Chemical Engineering*. (28 Oct.)

Unexplored assets for diversification, G. CONRAD, *Harvard Business Review*. (Sept.)

The Management Problems of Diversification; A Pilot Study of the Corporation Diversifying from an Established Base, STANLEY S. MILLER, Wiley. (13 Sept.)

Decisions for top management in product-line planning, M. E. MENGEL; Getting a new product launched on schedule, R. L. MARTINO; Direction and control of productive research and development, L. A. HATCH; all in CIOS XIII Symposium B13.

Transferring research results to operations, J. B. QUINN, *Harvard Business Review.*

Creativity is not enough, T. LEVITT, *Harvard Business Review.* (May–June.)

Mergers and Acquisitions: Planning and Action, Financial Executives Research Foundation Inc.

London 2000, PETER HALL, Faber and Faber.

The Expert Dreamers: Science Fiction Stories by Scientists, Edited by FREDERIK POHL, Victor Gollancz.

Product Strategy and Management, Edited by T. L. BERG and A. SHUCHMAN, Holt, Rinehart & Winston, Inc.

Research in the United States, S. E. SEASHORE and A. S. TANNENBAUM, CIOS XIII Symposium A9, Paper No. A9b.

Basic guide to planning new products, R. G. MURDICH, *Industrial Marketing,* **48** (Aug.), 91–95.

My years with General Motors, ALFRED P. SLOAN, Doubleday.

Organizing the product planning function, K. H. TIETJEN, American Management Association.

Pruning the product line, C. BERENSON, *Business Horizons,* Summer, pp. 63–70.

Is product research much too haphazard?, D. B. LEARNER, *Printers Ink,* **283** (28 June), 12.

American machine and foundry's new product battle plan, C. J. SIREY Jnr., *Sales Management,* **90** (21 June), 29–41.

Reporting for more profitable product management, M. SCHIFF, *Journal of Accountancy,* **115** (May), 65–70.

New product success built on old know-how (at Thompson Ramo Wooldridge Corp), T. M. ROHAN, *Iron Age,* **191** (9 May), 120–2.

3M's formula for new products, T. R. BROOKS, *Dun's Review and Modern Industry,* **82** (April), 32–41.

Industrial Marketing Research, N. A. H. STACY and AUBREY WILSON, Hutchinson (London). (March.)

New products need new techniques, W. I. THOMPSON, *Office Appliances,* **117** (Jan.), 86–88.

Marketing Management Analysis and Planning, JOHN A. HOWARD, Irwin Homewood, Ill.

Isolate the scientists, M. RALSTON, *Product Engineering.* (3 Sept.)

1962

Need to stimulate new product development, S. N. ROSENTHAL, *Office Appliances,* **116** (Sept.), 98–99.

New product boom, *Sales Management,* **89** (3 Aug.), 44–61.

How extensive the planning and development programme?, R. E. WEIGAND, *Journal of Marketing,* **26** (July), 55–57.

Marketing oriented technical product development programme, J. G. CROCKETT, *Journal of Marketing*, **26** (July), 42–46.

The Management of Capital Projects, R. J. S. BAKER, Richard Clay & Co.

A Methodology of Systems Engineering, ARTHUR D. HALL, D. van Nostrand.

Problems of marketing development, J. MARTIN RITCHIE, Dir. Bowater Corp., BIM Scottish Management Conference.

How Companies Plan, STEWART THOMPSON, American Management Association.

1961

The effect of national character on production methods, E. P. WARD, *The Production Engineer*, **40** (8) (Aug.)

Diversification or concentration, J. E. WALL, *The Manager*. (Aug.)

Product development, H. J. NOVY, Paper presented at a meeting on Market Advisory Services provided by Industrial Associations organized by the European Productivity Agency (OEEC) at St. Gallen, Switzerland.

The Stagnant Society, MICHAEL SHANKS, Penguin.

Cybernetics (2nd edn.), NORBERT WIENER, Massachusetts Institute of Technology.

The Management of Innovation, T. BURNS and G. M. STALKER, Tavistock Publications.

Selecting profitable products, J. T. O'NEARA, *Harvard Business Review*. (Jan.)

New product profile chart, J. S. HARRIS, *Chemical and Engineering News*. (17 April.)

Product strategy and future profits, C. F. RASSWEILER, *Research Review*. (April.)

1960

New sources of product ideas, H. HERMAN, *The Management Review*. (Oct.)

New Directions in Metalworking Practice, reprinted from *Engineering*. (June–July.)

Essentials of corporate planning, *The Controller*. (May.)

The New Product, D. W. KARGER, The Industrial Press.

Functional features in product strategy, JOHN B. STEWART, *Harvard Business Review*.

Marketing myopia, T. LEVITT, *Harvard Business Review*. (July–Aug.)

Top Management Handbook, H. B. MAYNARD, McGraw-Hill.

The Foreseeable Future, GEORGE THOMPSON, Cambridge University Press.

How to evaluate research output, J. B. QUINN, *Harvard Business Review*. (March–April.)

Industrial Development—A Guide for Accelerating Economic Growth, M. D. BRYCE, McGraw-Hill.

1959

Organizing for Product Development, American Management Association.

Cybernetics and Management, STAFFORD BEER, Universities Press.

The Sleepwalkers, ARTHUR KOESTLER, Hutchinson.

Executive Committee Control Charts, E. I. Du Pont de Nemours & Co.

Auditing product programmes, P. MARVIN, *Machine Design*, Penton Publishing Co. Cleveland, Ohio, pp. 107–11.

Criteria for Evaluating Existing Products and Product Lines, AMA Management Report No. 32, pp. 91–101.

Profit planning and control at Heinz, *American Business*. (Sept.)

A practical approach to management planning and control, E. G. KOCH, *Advanced Management*. (July.)

Industrial technical intelligence: tool for long term planning and prevention of technological surprise, RALPH SIMS, Jnr., *Advanced Management*. (July.)

What do we know about using long-range plans?, GEORGE A. STEINER, *California Management Review*. (Fall.)

New dimensions in creative planning, S. THOMPSON, *The Business Quarterly*. (Summer.)

The common sense of long range planning, E. J. BENGE, *Advanced Management*. (June.)

1958

Long range planning: challenge to management science, P. F. DRUCKER, *Management Science*. (April.)

The 1960's Now; Planning New Products and Improved Designs, reprinted from *Engineering*. (17 April.)

Developing a Product Strategy, American Management Association, Management Report No. 30.

Report of Engineering *Inquiry into the British Aircraft Industry*, reprinted from *Engineering*. (May.)

Talking to Americans, E. P. WARD, reprinted from *Engineering*. (June–July.)

New product revolution: is management organized for it, Special report, *Printers Ink*. (Oct.)

Research as a tool in long-range company planning, WILLIAM S. ROYCE, *The Controller*. (Nov.)

Organization of the planning process, RICHARD C. ANERSON, *Advanced Management*. (May.)

Eight ways to doom a new product: eleven ways to help it, ARTHUR C. NEILSON Jnr., *American Business*. (March.)

Plan tomorrow's profits, *Nation's Business*. (Aug.)

Product planning for future profits, R. D. CRISP, *Dun's Review and Modern Industry*. (March.)

New profit planner: what he does, how paid, HERBERT HALBRACHT, *Sales Management*.

Computer and Brain, JOHN VON NEUMANN, Yale Towne.

Long-range planning for management, DAVID W. EWING, Harper & Bros., New York.

Sources of Invention, J. JEWKES, MacMillan.

The Affluent Society, J. K. GALBRAITH, Hamish Hamilton.

The Naked Sun, ISAAC ASIMOV, Michael Joseph.

Planning Ahead for Profits, American Management Association, Management Report No. 3.

How to initiate effective long-range planning, MASON SMITH, *The Dynamics of Management*, Management Report No. 14.

1957

The conservation of natural resources, HAROLD HARTLEY and others, *Conference Proceedings*, published by The Institution of Civil Engineers.

New insight, new progress for marketing, JOSEPH W. NEWMAN, *Harvard Business Review*. (Dec.)

How Good are Soviet Engineers?, E. P. WARD, reprinted from *Engineering*. (Sept.–Oct.)

Effective systems through long-range planning, G. P. GRANT and R. W. SELLERS, *Systems and Procedures*. (Jan.–Feb.)

Product search and evaluation, PAUL STILLSON and E. LEONARD ARNOFF, *The Journal of Marketing*. (July.)

Steps in long-range planning, BRUCE PAYNE, *Harvard Business Review*. (March–April.)

Organization for long-range planning, H. E. WRAPP, *Harvard Business Review*. (March–April.)

Marketing Research, RICHARD D. CRISP, McGraw-Hill.

The Black Cloud, FRED HOYLE, Heinemann.

1956

Three in one marketing, REAVIS COX, *Harvard Business Review*. (Dec.)

Long-range planning for company growth, WILLIAM E. HILL and CHARLES H. GRANGER, *Management Review*. (Dec.)

Executive find long-range planning pays off, *Business Record*, National Industrial Conference Board, New York. (Oct.)

Cash McCall, CAMERON HAWLEY.

Conditions of marketing leadership, ARTHUR P. FELTON, *Harvard Business Review*. (April.)

1955–56

Long-range Planning in an Expanding Economy, American Management Association General Management Series No. 179.

The Fabulous Future: America in 1980, DAVID SARNOFF, JOHN VON NEUMANN and others, with an introduction by the Editors of *Fortune*, E. P. Dutton & Co. Inc., New York.

1955

The Practice of Management, PETER F. DRUCKER, Heinemann.

Projecting the profitability of new products, T. T. MILLER, *The Controller*. (Oct.)

Long-range planning business raises the sights, *Management Review*. (Oct.)

How to plan profits five years ahead, *Nation's Business*. (Oct.)

The strategy of product policy, CHARLES H. KLINE, *Harvard Business Review*. (Aug.)

The product and the brand, BURLEIGH B. GARDNER and SIDNEY J. LEVY, *Harvard Business Review*. (April.)

Planning, Managing and Measuring the Business; A Case Study of Management Planning and Control at General Electric Co., Business Planning and Control Report Series II, No. 3, Controllership Foundation Inc., N.Y. (Jan.)

Launching a Company Expansion Programme. III: Long-range Planning Procedures and Organization, C. W. PRITCHARD, Financial Management Series No. 112, American Management Association.

Long-range Planning: New Dimensions and Established Principles, ROBERT C. TAIT, General Management Series No. 177.

The Theory of Economic Growth, W. ARTHUR LEWIS, Allen & Unwin.

The Great Crash, J. K. GALBRAITH, Hamish Hamilton.

1954

What it takes for a changeover, *Business Week*. (13 Nov.)

More Than Human, THEODORE STURGEON, Victor Gollancz.

The Caves of Steel, ISAAC ASIMOV, T. V. Boardman.

Planning to meet competition today and in ten years, CHARLES A. JURGENSEN, *Advanced Management*. (July.)

Mathematical programming: better information for better decision-making, *Harvard Business Review*. (May–June.)

Forecasting, *Journal of Business of the University of Chicago*. (Jan.)

Long-range economic projection studies in income and wealth, *The Conference on Research in Income and Wealth*. National Bureau of Economic Research, Princeton University Press, vol. 16.

Planning for Profit, The 3rd Conference on Controllership, sponsored by the School of Business, University of Chicago and Controllers Institute of America.

Expedition to Earth, ARTHUR C. CLARKE, Sidgwick & Jackson.

Charting the Company's Future, American Management Association, Financial Management Series No. 108.

Men, Markets, Machines and Money: Long-range Planning, Management Planning and Manpower Development, American Management Association, General Management Series No. 173.

Organizing for Growth and Change, WESLEY A. SONGER.

Tomorrow is Already Here, ROBERT JUNGK, Hart-Davis.

Management Takes a Long View, General Management Series No. 171.

1953

Planning for profit control when volume changes, HATWELL A. GREENE, *NACA Bulletin*. (Nov.)

Business Planning in a Changing World, American Management Association, General Management Series No. 167.

Operations Research and its Role in Business Decisions, R. W. CRAWFORD, American Management Association, Manufacturing Series No. 206.

Limbo '90, BERNARD WOLFE, Secker & Warburg.

Theory of Games and Economic Behaviour, JOHN VON NEUMANN and OSKAR MORGENSTERN, Oxford University Press.

Demand Analysis, H. WOLD and L. JUREEN, John Wiley & Sons.

How H. J. Heinz Manages its Financial Planning and Controls, American Management Association, Financial Management Series No. 106.

Long-range Business Policies: A Case Study, K. S. McHUGH, Progressive Policies for Business Leadership, American Management Association, General Management Series No. 156.

A programme of financial planning and controls—The Monsanto Chemical Co.,
American Management Association, Financial Management Series
No. 103.

1952

How to decide which products to junk, LYMAN HOUFLEK, *Printers Ink.*
(Aug., pp. 21–23.)

Thinking Ahead for Business, E. C. BURSK, Harvard University Press.

Design for a Brain, W. ROSS ASHBY, John Wiley & Sons.

Techniques of Long-range Company Planning, National Industrial Conference
Board, Round-Table Panel, New York. (15 May.)

1951

Management Planning for Corporate Taxes, Controllership Foundation Inc.,
New York.

Inventions and their Management, A. K. BERLE and L. S. DECAMP, International Textbook Co.

Administrative Action, WILLIAM H. NEWMAN, Prentice-Hall.

1950

Product line policy, JOEL DEAN, *Journal of Business.* (Oct., pp. 248–58.)

1949

Financial planning—long-term forecasting, H. H. SCAFF, *Corporate Treasurer's
and Controller's Handbook*, edited by Lillian Doris, Prentice-Hall.

Management Planning and Control, B. E. GOETZ, McGraw-Hill.

1948

The Management of Marketing Costs, JAMES W. CULLITON, Harvard University Press, chap. 7.

Planning the Product, D. M. PHELPS, Irwin Homewood, Illinois.

1947

Business Planning and Control, FLOYD H. ROWLAND, Harper & Bros., New
York.

1946

The Creative Mind, H. L. BERGSON, Philosophical Library.

1945

Mind at the End of its Tether, H. G. WELLS, Heinemann.

1938

Economics, FREDERIC BENHAM, Sir Isaac Pitman & Sons.

1930

The Shape of Things to Come, H. G. WELLS, Hutchinson.

1927

Selected Short Stories, H. G. WELLS, Ernest Benn.

1902

The Discovery of the Future, discourse to the Royal Institution, H. G. WELLS,
Unwin.

1901

Anticipation, H. G. WELLS, Chapman.

BIOGRAPHY: E. PETER WARD

E. P. WARD, M.A., C.Eng., F.I. Mech.E., is Managing Director of Peter Ward Associates (Interplan) Limited, forming this company after building up and managing a similar consulting business in the European Metra group. Mr. Ward is a member of the Market Research Society, the Industrial Marketing Research Asosociation and the European Society for Opinion and Marketing Research (ESOMAR).

He graduated with honours in mechanical sciences while resident at Trinity College, Cambridge, following 4 years' army service, during which time he was commissioned into an infantry regiment, qualified as a Russian interpreter and as a parachutist, and worked on technical investigations in Germany. Apart from Russian, he has a knowledge of the German language and is familiar with mechanical, civil, nuclear and process engineering.

From 1951 to 1952 he was a trainee with the APV Company Limited, gaining experience in food, chemical and allied technologies. Subsequently he worked on the Owen Falls Dam, Uganda, as a civil engineer, returning to the United Kingdom to take up a position with the technical journal *Engineering* where he became a deputy editor and director. In 1961 he joined Martech Consultants Limited and formed a product planning division, which expanded rapidly and, in 1964, was made a separate company. While with Martech and Proplan, he was concerned with product seeking and evaluation, market exploration and regional development.

Arising from this experience, he developed the concepts of dynamic and catalytic planning, which have been the subject of talks and seminars presented on behalf of many British, Continental and Commonwealth institutions concerned with management, marketing and technology.

In addition to *The Dynamics of Business Planning*, which has been widely reproduced and translated into French and Spanish, he has written a variety of articles and papers, including a study of diversification in the British aircraft industry in the light of reduced defence contracts, a diagnosis of power requirements in emerging countries, a report on the quality of Soviet engineers and an analysis of forward technical and economic thinking in the United States. In 1961 he was awarded the Institution of Production Engineers' Silver Medal for the best paper by a non-member, entitled "The impact of national institutions on production methods".

He formed Peter Ward Associates (Interplan) Limited in early 1967, applying to consultancy his own philosophy of dynamic planning, with particular reference to problems embracing both technology and marketing over a broad cross-section of Industry. Later he secured the backing of the Industrial and Commercial Finance Corporation, and other shareholders included the managing director of a large communications company, a professor of the Harvard Business School and the marketing adviser to a leading national organization. By the end of 1967 Interplan had already broken even, and during 1968, its first full year of operation, the company grew into a substantial business, yielding a comfortable return to shareholders.

INDEX